W9-AFS-377

MODERN FRENCH THEATRE

from Giraudoux to Beckett

MODERN FRENCH THEATRE

from Giraudoux to Beckett

JACQUES GUICHARNAUD
in collaboration with June Beckelman

New Haven: Yale University Press

To Louisa, Marc, and Willie

This book is not intended to be a systematic study of contemporary French theatre. All the facts and dates are not included, although the most important can be found in the Appendices. The following chapters deal primarily with those playwrights who have proved to be or show promise of becoming first rate and describe in general terms the dramatic universe of each. If neither Sacha Guitry, nor Madame Simone, nor Maurice Rostand, nor André Roussin are considered, the reasons for omitting them will soon become apparent; while if Supervielle, Georges Neveux, André Obey, and Marcel Achard are barely mentioned (or not mentioned at all), it is only because they unfortunately wrote at the same time as others greater than they.

From Jean Giraudoux to Ionesco and Beckett, French theatre has exploited a marked and powerful trend that began with the revolution of 1890 and other works outside the trend now seem insignificant. For the last thirty years it has been a theatre of exploration. Its objective has not been to offer ready-made solutions, either on the level of form or of substance; it does not give reassuring answers to everyday problems, nor does it flatter the public's esthetic lethargy with established forms. Each writer, rather than just tell a story in more or less dramatic form, has tried to express the human condition metaphorically. In comparing American and French theatre of the fifties Robert Brustein has remarked:

> While we are trying to come to terms with human conditioning, the French are trying to explore the boundaries of human limitation; while we are seeking security, ease, and happiness within the social unit, the French are seek-

ing metaphysical freedom outside of human institutions; while our key words are *adjustment* and *affirmation,* the key words in France are alienation and negation.*

Not all the playwrights treated in this book are necessarily nihilistic. But all have tried to define man in metaphysical terms and outside of human institutions. Giraudoux's universe or Claudel's is no easier to live in than Sartre's or Beckett's: man is defined in terms of his agony, and the universe itself is seen as being fundamentally in a state of conflict. Giraudoux's search for harmony is not situated "within the social unit," Claudel's religion is hardly concerned with accepted ethics. On the whole, the hero of modern French theatre is a character who refuses to play the game of "adjustment" but rather tries to find himself through a higher game, if only that of theatre itself. According to the playwright's degree of optimism or pessimism, souls are saved or man is brought back to man. Whichever, the basic conflict is a vertical one in which man is not limited to socio-psychological tensions easily resolved through what Brustein calls "pious pronouncements."

Nor is the anecdote ever separate from the form. Each vision of the world is not only dramatic but theatrical, whether it be the spectacle God has created for himself, as in Claudel, or Beckett's life-farce. The hero of such theatre is not only constantly torn apart and situated beyond himself, he is also an actor who struggles with his own masks. The universe presented on stage is not given as the real universe but rather as a metaphor of it. Everything is in fact unreal. The spectator is asked to put himself in the state of consciousness in which he both accepts and rejects the reality of what unfolds before his eyes. Everything on stage happens "as if . . . ," implying that in life, also, everything happens "as if. . . ." Reality is always elsewhere. Life and theatre are but approximations of it, images, reflections. And in the past few years, the reflections have

* "Nihilism on Broadway," *The New Republic,* February 29, 1960.

evolved more and more distinctly toward reflections of nothing.

Whether or not his humor is as "dark" as that of the French theatre today, Henri Peyre's lively encouragement and perceptive advice in the writing of this book were, as always, inspirational. We should also like to thank Edwin Stein for his sharply critical eye and Benjamin F. Houston for seeing the manuscript through to its final stages.

J.G.
J.B.

October 1960

CONTENTS

*. . . and if these powers and possibilities
are dark, it is the fault, not of the plague,
nor of the theatre, but of life.*

Antonin Artaud, *le Théâtre et la Peste*

THEATRE RESURGENT

The representational arts are most particularly open to prostitution. Poets and novelists can always dream about the love or recognition that their works provoke in their readers—even in one single reader. They rarely witness it. The playwright or the author of a film script hides in the theatre and takes part in a mass phenomenon. One reader's letter overjoys a poet; one satisfied spectator in a hostile audience does little more than emphasize the failure of a play or film. Outbursts of enthusiasm, laughter, tears, and applause are collective. They are addressed, beyond the performed work, to the author and have meaning only in terms of quantity. Success in the theatre is concrete, sensual. It is communicated through calls for the author, facial expressions that penetrate beyond the footlights, the roar of bravos. At that level, it is often difficult to evaluate the quality of the emotion provoked.

"The great art is to please," said Molière—an ambiguous statement of principle which leaves the door open to all interpretations. The question is: what, in the spectator, does one aim to please? "They like it," says the complacent writer or director who has been reproached with turning out degrading theatre. Obviously "they like it!" The audience is almost always ready to be satisfied with little. But the audience is almost always open to quality as well. The charms of quality may work slowly and sometimes require subtle strategy, where the audience, long accustomed to mediocrity, has ended by being corrupted. The public can easily allow itself to be dragged down because of a quite natural human penchant for what is facile. How relatively little it takes to entertain! And, as enter-

3

tainment is an important dimension of art, art and entertainment are easily confused. We are indulgent; we succumb to flattery and, in utter bad faith, we give purely entertaining works an esthetic value.

An audience is made up of people who are perpetually concerned with the problems of their everyday lives and therefore infinitely more amused by what reassures and upholds them in their own realms than by any offer of an opening onto something else. Their realms consist of the ready-made vision each one has of himself and of life, as well as the conception, also ready-made, of the art forms which express that vision.

Asking the playwright to present the bourgeoisie with a show representing the bourgeoisie, as did Diderot, was not only to go from classical realism (which aimed at the reality of universal man) to post-revolutionary realism (which aimed at man in relation to his milieu), but also to lay the first stone in the foundation of a theatre of complacency. The tradesman who spent his time developing commerce or avoiding bankruptcy or quite simply in arranging a good marriage for his daughter, did not like the fact that the contrast of Phèdre's passion or Polyeucte's martyrdom relegated his particular values to the background. The merchant who attended a performance of *Phèdre* was in great danger of wondering whether his trading was worthy of quite so much effort and of questioning the meaning of his life—in short, of suffering.

Diderot and Beaumarchais were the originators—at least in their theoretical works—of a theatre of reassurance. In the second half of the nineteenth century, when their conceptions were picked up and extended by writers in the service of triumphant merchants, there resulted a whole doctrine of systematic indolence in the theatre. *Vaudeville,* comedy, and bourgeois drama seemed to join forces in order to give the maximum of good conscience to the ruling bourgeoisie, both in their virtues and their vices. Each performance persuaded the audience that man, life, and the real were no more than what they believed them to be. The public and its art closed in upon each other. Their agreement was so perfect that the theatre did not present the audience with an image of what it was, but of what it wished to be—hence the innumerable basic conventions which had almost become an institution. Everything took place as if the self-satisfied performance of mediocrity ennobled that mediocrity, and as if the closed doors of the bourgeois drawing room, on which the curtain usually went up, symbolized the sanctification by art of the limitations of the bourgeois' intellectual, spiritual, and moral horizons.

Familiar form is meant to spare the public any surprising inventiveness and as such is perfectly in keeping with reliable content. Faced with an art of skillful imitation—rather than disturbing revelation—the spectator knows straight away that he is in the theatre. What he sees can be nothing other than theatre, since theatre is nothing other than what he sees. Such recognition is quite the contrary of the higher reminiscence through which the spectator recognizes what has not yet been said or done, what has been a dormant possibility until then and is suddenly realized both in art and in life.

An image of what the public believed itself to be was presented in forms that were thought to be the only forms possible. Derived from the "well-made" play, late nineteenth-century theatre reduced the Aristotelian notion of action to its most superficial level. Made up of proven stage tricks and conventions of dialogue and staging, the plays never questioned the idea of theatre itself, nor did they ever suggest a universal Drama. They always recalled something which already existed, both in the technique of detail and in their basic conception.

As soon as the rules of an art cease being thought and felt, they are simply applied and imitation sets in. The French theatre of 1840–1880 is not a unique example; eighteenth-century pseudo-classical tragedy, the French Boulevard theatre of today (often spoken of as "Boulevard recipes"), and a great part of the American naturalistic theatre of the last few years are cases in point. The result in the late nineteenth century was a progressive disbelief in dramatic art. Those who studied the theatre in the light of their own philosophies signed its death warrant. Auguste Comte went so far as to say that the very institution of theatre had no meaning in modern society. Barbey d'Aurevilly spoke of the "fundamental inferiority" of theatre as a genre. Mallarmé dreamt of a theatre-Mass, but one assimilated to his universal "Book," and emphasized the absolute degradation of the theatre of his time. (Jacques Copeau used the following lines of Mallarmé as an epigraph for the programs of the Vieux Colombier: "Do you go to theatre? —No, almost never. —Well! neither do I.")

The last years of the century brought about a dual awakening: that of the theatrical world in general and that of the playwright. Almost simultaneously, the attempted reform took two divergent directions: Antoine's *Théâtre Libre,* founded in 1887, became the champion of realism and naturalism, and Paul Fort's *Théâtre d'Art,* 1891, champion of the so-called poetic theatre. In fact this was but the prelude to a revolution. The *Théâtre d'Art* was held up to ridicule; the *Théâtre Libre* failed with the decline of the naturalist vogue. Yet both experiments were carried on in other forms. They were but the first manifestations of a reform which sought to formulate its program and its doctrine. There was a general reaction against clichés, conventionalism, and tricks which corresponded to no reality, outer or inner, and were neither the fruit nor the seed of any truly esthetic experience. Not that conventionally mediocre and vulgar plays were eliminated—even today they continue to fill Parisian theatres—but by about 1890 true theatre began to take back its rights.

Although they agreed on a negative program, the two camps were radically opposed when it came to defining positively the art of theatre, one claiming that theatre should be an imitation of the real, the other defining it as a poetic interpretation of that same reality, as the creation of an independent universe, or even as an almost mystical experience.

A detailed analysis of the origins of the two tendencies would be more involved than this study will allow.[1] The various forms of bourgeois theatre originated in Romantic theatre, but the Romantic theatre and its manifestoes were also at the root of the principles of both realism and symbolic theatre. Behind the dual orientation there lies the example of Shakespeare, Aeschylus, and, in some ways, the ambiguity of Aristotle's formula, according to which a dramatic work is "the imitation of an action." It would be necessary to go back to Aristotle and show how different styles, schools, and cultures have interpreted the formula, both analytically (what is imitation? what is action?) and synthetically. Would one be faithful to Nature (what Nature?), cultivate the natural, paint a tableau of Life, reveal the essence of man, represent the Idea or the Spirit which *is* Reality, reconstruct the true definition of man? Were the human drama to be restricted to the phenomena of psychological and social behavior that we perceive directly in daily life, the imitation of that drama would consist in reconstructing on stage the very behavior we observe around us, with the fidelity of a documentary film. Here the definition of action necessarily involves that of imitation, that is, a way of writing, directing, and acting the play. It would seem today that certain American writers and directors have become masters of this style. If one puts aside the meaning of the play and the juggling tricks involved in the denouement, the verism of the slices of life is almost too convincing. On the other hand, if we situate truth as above, below, or beside the daily perceptible phenomena, the arts of theatre have in fact nothing to imitate. They interpret or they reveal or they invent. Or, if they imitate, it is no longer the real such as we perceive

1. See John Gassner, *Form and Idea in Modern Theatre.* (*Note:* Full bibliographical data for works referred to in the footnotes may be found in the Selected Bibliography, pp. 285–95.)

it, but rather the alleged image of a reality situated beyond the perceived universe.

Since 1890 it has become more and more fashionable to disparage realistic theatre: the style never leaves the ground, it lacks grandeur. The slice of life is "dull," to use Diderot's adjective describing a valet played "naturally." [2] And it is dull for two reasons. First, as a reaction against artificial gaiety or moral optimism, realism has been directed toward a portrayal of the commonplace, the mediocre, the boring; secondly, by its very definition, total realism is unable to break away from psychology and sociology. By excluding any transcendency (religious, mythical, ontological) and explaining directly in psychological or sociological terms, realism and its offshoot, naturalism, do not transfigure our participation in human misery or human happiness; they merely repeat it. If a vague transfiguration does take place, it is because the work has departed from its principles. Irony of the *comédie rosse,* "miserabilism," or elements of satire are actually distortions of reality. As for *epic* realism (Brecht), the term itself implies a synthesis.

However, realism in the theatre—that "renaissance in reverse," as it was called by Jean Hort [3]—in addition to giving a welcome and thorough cleaning to the French stage, restored a human quality to the art of theatre. "Realism," according to John Gassner, "gave [man] the recognizable features of a functioning human being." [4] And the *Théâtre Libre* reaffirmed a professional conscience, the notion of the production as a co-ordinated and unified whole, the idea of harmony between the character and his surroundings (just as valid for fantastic or

2. "If a valet speaks on stage as he would in society, he is dull; if he speaks in any other way, he is false" was the way Diderot formulized the main dangers of realism and anti-realism. (Diderot, "Entretiens sur *le Fils naturel*," *Oeuvres,* Paris, Gallimard, Pléiade, 1946, p. 1276).

3. Jean Hort, *les Théâtres du Cartel.*

4. *Form and Idea,* p. 93.

abstract surroundings as for the piece by piece reconstruction of a shoddy hotel room). Since the *Théâtre Libre*, the famous actor's number has been replaced by an attempt to convince the spectator of the real, sensual presence of the character and the play's universe.

To that extent at least, all great theatre profited from the demands of the *Théâtre Libre*. Although the anti-naturalists' reaction was to go beyond its limitations, they had every intention of keeping the basic tenets. But extremes provoke extremes and an absolute estheticism took the place of the sordid boredom of certain slices of life. As a result, theatre was in danger of being completely dehumanized, and even negated. Obviously neither the German set-designers nor Gordon Craig went quite so far. But in 1891, the *Théâtre d'Art* planned to end its production "by putting an unknown painting on stage," with musical accompaniment and wafts of perfume sprayed throughout the theatre.[5] A fear of superficial anecdotes led to the suppression of all action; a fear of psychologism transformed the character into an entity: the danger of symbolist theatre was that of becoming a play of static shadows. An intense search for hidden meanings of the "modern" world often resulted in a mechanical stylization, beautiful perhaps, but cold and inhuman. The esthetic value of these attempts is undeniable, but are they truly theatre? Drama does not consist in the ghosts of man, but in the relations between man and his ghosts; it does not consist in mechanized man, but in the search for the man within the mechanized man. In short, anti-realism can be just as limited as realism: the highest plane, if only a plane, is as desperately flat as any other. The realistic and naturalistic universe is often suffocating; but it is just as easy to die of asphyxiation at heights where the air is unbreathable.

Despite its dangers, anti-naturalism did restore theatre to its

5. See Jacques Robichez, *le Symbolisme au théâtre: Lugné-Poe et les débuts de l'Oeuvre*, p. 112.

real possibilities. It affirmed that man is not defined solely by psychology and his material and social environment. Man is also a metaphysical and poetic being. By the same token, anti-naturalism made it possible for theatre once again to become a fund of ideas and realized images. It gave the word "action" its full meaning by reestablishing various forms of the transcendency without which there is no tragic dimension, only laws and chance.

Today realism has been conquered; it has only to be perfected. A good naturalistic drama, with real wine in a real bottle, no longer surprises anyone. Add a bit of psychoanalysis, a few moral and current political ideas, or the savor of a detective story and the spectator feels that he is in the presence of an honest and solid work. Any true effort at inventiveness and discovery consists in going beyond the solid foundation. Since 1890, theatre in general, and French theatre in particular, has been searching for its own special poetry. The definitive step forward came a little before 1930: four great directors joined together in 1927 to form a group called *le Cartel des quatre* [6]; Jean Giraudoux had his first play produced in 1928. Behind the new spirit was a solid organization and a really great writer.

From 1890 to 1930 the most active agents of the reform were directors and theorists, whose most important conceptions can be found in Appendix I. After the somewhat chaotic experiences early in the century, Jacques Copeau—the revolution's master hand—finally established the idea of total renovation by demanding "a bare stage" to start with. That accomplished, new staging—both simplified and imaginative—gave back dramatic energy, poetry, and meaning to great works of the past, with the result that the Greeks, Shakespeare, Racine, Molière, and others were successfully reinterpreted.

6. See Appendix I, p. 251.

But the program had another point: that of creating a truly modern theatre with the help of living playwrights. There the work was slower. The reform of the written text was hardly comparable to the activity of theorists and directors. Directors were the first to complain. Where were they to find good modern plays, corresponding to the new principles of theatre? The realist revolution did eliminate a good many absurd conventions even from commercial theatre. But although certain playwrights gave up being entertainers to become authentic dramatic writers, the form of the written play was not as completely revolutionized—at least not until the last few years—as were the forms of staging; and, quantitatively, there were more modern or revolutionary stagings than truly new texts.

The idle indulgence, even the admiration of many critics for the Boulevard "masters," the official respect surrounding the "thinkers" and "psychologists" of the Third Republic, saved from oblivion by traditionalists and textbooks, can hardly be said to have clarified the situation. There is no need to take into account all the works, or even all the dramatic currents of those years. More than a hundred playwrights were relatively much talked about from 1900 to 1930. But how many really contributed to the development and modernization of theatre?

Certain names—even "great" names—would today seem like survivals of a dead past that is better forgotten. Porto-Riche, Maurice Donnay, François de Curel, Paul Hervieu, Eugène Brieux, even more contemporary names such as Bernstein and Bataille, had less to say and were of less value to the theatre than, for instance, Dumas Père. We no longer consider the creation in 1919 of François de Curel's *l'Ame en folie* as an important event, but we do remember that of Lenormand's *le Temps est un songe* in the same year. The opening of Henri Bataille's *le Scandale* (1909) had best be forgotten, but how can one forget the arrival of the Ballets Russes in Paris also in 1909? In other words, one *Ubu Roi* (1896) by Jarry is worth ten *Amants* (1895) by Maurice Donnay.

To borrow a word from André Gide, we judge "discourteously" everything that caused the theatre to mark time or set it on the wrong track. Of course many poets wrote for the theatre, hoping to save it from mediocrity. But whether ignored or praised by the public at large, they were most often behind the times: Edmond Rostand, Saint-Georges de Bouhélier, François Porché, and even Paul Fort, who began his dramatic writing far too late. When successful, their success only showed the public's appetite for what was missing from commercial theatre or limited realism; it was no gauge of poetic maturity. Often their success was no more than the sign of a prudish reaction to the immorality of the naturalists. The pure and simple rejection of realism's limitations had meaning only when the realms explored beyond its limitations were new. A return to superficial Romanticism or the conventional exploitation of certain symbolist tricks represented no more than false revolutions.

What then is worth remembering? In the tradition of naturalism, either foretelling or following the principles of the *Théâtre Libre*: Henri Becque's *les Corbeaux* (produced in 1882), Courteline's *Boubouroche* (1893), Jules Renard's *le Pain de ménage* (1898) and *Poil de Carotte* (1900), Octave Mirbeau's *les Affaires sont les affaires* (1903). Obviously there can be no absolutely realistic work; all of the above plays contain a commentary, even a judgment on life. In other fundamentally naturalistic works, the commentary takes the foreground and directs the play beyond an imitation of everyday reality toward a more or less poetic universe. Such is the case of Charles Vildrac's *Paquebot Tenacity* (1920) and Simon Gantillon's semi-expressionistic *Maya* (1924).

Such is also the case of the plays of Henri-René Lenormand,

the most important playwright of the years 1919–1930. Doubt-less, Lenormand took a strong position against the restrictions of dramatic realism by his very collaboration with Pitoëff, for whom the minutiae of realism consisted in "hiding souls under false beards"—even when the false beards were made of real hair. Yet Lenormand's works are constructed upon a solid naturalistic foundation. Although he rises above it, he does so through exoticism (*Simoun*, 1920) or through the use of Freudian mysteries (*le Mangeur de rêves*, 1922). On the whole, Lenormand's poetry consists more in the evocation of outer and inner "atmosphere" permeated with the unknown than in the actual inquiry into that unknown.

The historical genre—in the broadest sense of the word—inherited from the Romantics and dehydrated, asepticized, and carefully wrapped up by Scribe and Sardou, gave rise to innumerable pseudo-Romantic works. Only two writers of this genre are worth considering, and then with reservations: Edmond Fleg (*le Juif du Pape*, 1925) and Romain Rolland (certain scenes in *le Théâtre de la Révolution*, 1898–1938), although the feeling of collective belonging is more successfully created by other means in Jules Romains' *Cromedeyre-le-Vieil* (1920).

As for truly poetic theatre, the symbolists and their successors produced little that is still performable or even readable apart from Maeterlinck's *Pelléas et Mélisande* (1893). The systematic experiments with fantasy, "unrealism," or surrealism, as a result of contempt for traditional forms, offer a richer and more alive production. Despite the purely militant nature of their boldness, and often because of it, two plays count among the most significant acts in the theatrical revolution and remain living examples for theatre today: Jarry's *Ubu Roi* (1896) and Apollinaire's *les Mamelles de Tirésias* (1917). Roger Vitrac, with the help of Antonin Artaud, tried to replace somnolent theatre with a theatre of shock: *Victor ou les enfants au pouvoir* (1928). Jean-Victor Pellerin's *Intimité* (1922) and *Têtes de rechange* (1926) are two plays which, although now obsolete, represent still another interesting experiment in theatrical allegory. Claudel and Cocteau were the most important contributors, but their really mature works were written or extensively performed after 1930.

Comedy in modern form can be found in the works of Jarry and Vitrac; in more traditional form, in Crommelynck's grating farce *le Cocu magnifique* (1921). Representative also, in a facile and often low genre, is Georges Feydeau (*l'Hôtel du Libre-Echange,* 1894) who, in applying the rules of *vaudeville* with the intransigence of a mathematician, arrived at a kind of formal perfection, a theatricalism which places him far above his predecessors, his contemporaries, and particularly his successors. Among the more recent writers, Marcel Achard, although lax in form and mediocre in message, could be mentioned for his *Voulez-vous jouer avec moâ?* (1923).

A good anthology of the French theatre from 1880 to 1930 would be made up of such plays—a subjective choice in some ways, and as such, perhaps somewhat unfair. But it does not claim to be representative: except for Feydeau, the enormous production of the Boulevard is excluded. It is based, not on statistics but on considerations of value, inventiveness, and real dramatic intuition.

We know that directors continued to complain about the small number of good or great texts written by modern playwrights. Too many plays, not enough good plays, they said. Therefore, almost all produced reinterpretations of old masterpieces. Almost all experimented and compromised with their own principles. All went out in search of new writers and produced their works even when certain of courting failure with the public. And almost all accustomed France to great modern writers of other countries: Ibsen, Strindberg, Chekhov, Pirandello, Shaw. Although the theatrical reform was clearly turned toward the present and the future, it was not iconoclastic and proved to be even less chauvinistic.

One tendency seems to dominate the French theatre of today: a clear movement toward anti-realism and its growing acceptance by the public. During the last years, French critics have frequently found fault with the "naturalism" of American plays produced in Paris, the "return to Antoine and *le Théâtre Libre.*" Detailed photography of the perceived real or purely psycho-sociological visions are without doubt capable of getting an emotional response from the spectator, but not the dual experience of real identification and theatricalist ambiguity.

To believe in the reality of what unfolds on stage, in the case of a realistic production, is no longer enough. Not only is the spectator meant to sympathize with the hero, he is meant to identify with his very being in the universality of his metaphysical condition. The invention of an imaginary world, a stylized mask, a special language is meant to emphasize the hidden meanings by turning the attention away from the perceived universe.

The mask of non-realistic theatre is ambiguous: it presents true and false at the same time. With anti-realism, theatre stops being documentary; but it is only art when it provokes a dual state of consciousness in the spectator, who at once believes and disbelieves. When the suspension of disbelief is total, the esthetic experience is nil. When disbelief is not suspended, the play remains an outer object and estheticism is void of all human content. In the simultaneity of the two states of consciousness lies the state of grace which is precisely that of a complete dramatic experience.

Modern French theatre is more and more oriented toward a search for that simultaneity. Anti-realist, but also suspicious of pure estheticism, French playwrights and directors have tried to synthesize a concrete equivalence of their creation and the world in which we live *and* the constant reminder of theatre's unreality. Identification is meant to take place, not with the surface anecdote, itself a fiction, a masquerade, a poet's lie, but with the deep drama underlying it. Spectators and characters, each in his own way, wear masks which have no more reality one than the others. The characters' masks are simply more obviously illusory *and* more revealing.[7]

The play of masks leads to questions about life, theatre, and their reciprocal relations. It is not the creation of a new art but the return, with the help of new forms, to a simple and ancient conception, outside of which there is no theatre, only entertainment. Writers and directors have obviously gone back to the source, whether it be Greek or Shakespearian, and have directly or indirectly been influenced by foreign contemporary theatre, principally that of Pirandello. However the following chapters are less studies of sources and influences than portraits, descriptions of the principal masks presented to the French public, from Giraudoux to Beckett, each one seen in its fundamental ambiguity.

7. Theatricalist ambiguity is of course not the privilege of non-realistic theatre. John Gassner points out, in *Form and Idea in Modern Theatre,* that, in the presence of a realistic work, the spectator quickly becomes sensitive to its theatricality and that before an "imaginative" production, he ends by accepting the characters and décor as real. Yet theatrical disbelief, in the first case, often takes place in spite of the playwright's and director's intentions.

PART I

A THEATRE OF THE SUPERNATURAL

CHAPTER 1

THEATRE AS PROPOSITION:
JEAN GIRAUDOUX

When novelist Jean Giraudoux's first play, *Siegfried,* was produced by Louis Jouvet at the Comédie des Champs Elysées on May 2, 1928, the then fashionable playwrights suddenly seemed quite definitely second-rate. Giraudoux had created an original universe, corresponding to most of the demands for "true" theatre. Indeed, his was the first coherent and satisfying form of modern theatre presented to a general public. And his plays dominated the French stage all during the thirties and early forties, a time which might be called the Age of Giraudoux.

Although not one of his best plays, *Siegfried* does contain all the indications of what Giraudoux was to become and of the scenic universe he was to create and enrich from play to play. Clearly, he would use simple individual conflicts as metaphors of conflicts between great universal themes: the story of Siegfried, a German political hero who lost his memory during the first World War and discovers that he is in fact Jacques, a French soldier, is but the pretext for an allegorical dialogue between France and Germany, each country being considered in its atmosphere, its culture, its poetry. And clearly, by simplifying the terms of the conflict, Giraudoux would bring out the subtlety of their relations and play freely with the element of surprise in unexpected reversals: at the end of the play, Geneviève, having helped bring the French Jacques out from the depths of the German Siegfried, lets herself be charmed by Germany and at the very moment Siegfried has become Jacques, cries out "Siegfried, I love you."

But above all he would "write" his plays. And through the

writing itself, on every level of style and composition, both Giraudoux's universe and his true originality are revealed. One of his most apparent devices is the presentation of stylized debates in which the characters embody the great themes in question. One particular scene in *Siegfried* serves as a model or pattern of such precisely defined staging, structure, and composition, that it seems like a beautifully chiselled nail hammered right in the heart of the play, intended to hold down that delicately embroidered stuff, often so light that it would seem to fly off stage: the scene in Act III, in which Siegfried's anguished struggle is exteriorized, represented or acted almost allegorically by Geneviève and Eva, both throwing concrete and opposing arguments into the scale of a balance which is tipped in their favor, until finally the two women throw the conflict back within Siegfried.

Almost all of Giraudoux's works are organized around analogous debates: between war and peace in *la Guerre de Troie*, the love of a young man and the love of an old man in *Cantique des cantiques*, the human and the supernatural in *Ondine* and *Intermezzo*, English morality and natural amorality in *le Supplément au Voyage de Cook*, sensual love and saintliness in *Judith*, man and woman in *Sodome et Gomorrhe*. Each play leads the spectator toward a solution of the conflict by means of great contrasts and sudden reversals, as in *Siegfried*.

Within the debates themselves, Giraudoux would clearly use language to provide the most specific and unexpected images. Often the characters, in explaining themselves, make use of details that are comical in the contrast between their apparent insignificance and the importance of their function. In *Siegfried* Zelten explains that he was unable to bring about his counterrevolution for want of arms, but also and mostly for want of glue to stick up his manifestoes. In a similar way in *Electre*, Clytemnestra explains that much of her hate for Agamemnon stems from the way in which he always, in no matter what circumstances, held his little finger up in the air.

An elaborately wrought language, the reversal of situations, great stylized debates accompanied by the most whimsical and singular details are unchanging in Giraudoux's works, in the masterpieces as well as in his less successful plays. His universe is created more through the fixed elements of his theatrical vision than through the choice and evolution of certain themes and ideas, so often catalogued and analyzed.

Essentially a theatre of language, Giraudoux's works relate to a strong tradition which has characterized the French stage since the Renaissance. From Garnier to Montherlant, French playwrights have been garrulous. Doubtless the reasons for this recourse to language are varied: plays written more to be read than performed, material conditions of staging (in the classical period, for example) reducing physical action to a minimum, the pride of poets. But the fundamental reason would seem to be always the same: a belief in the magic and power of words and combinations of words.

Characters on Giraudoux's stage talk more than they move. The greater part of certain scenes, even of certain plays, can be performed sitting down, for the drama can best be expressed through conversation or verbal debate. The characters reveal their inner struggles through the shock of words and phrases, or, as bearers of contrary truths, they oppose one another like lawyers in court before judges (the gods) and a jury (the spectators). Language, the weapon of poets and diplomats, is the primary instrument of poet-diplomat Jean Giraudoux.

The use of language in Giraudoux's theatre is not merely the result of a particular temperament but also of a deliberate choice. In his article "le Metteur en scène," [1] where he compares German and French theatre, Giraudoux defines French theatre in terms of the sovereignty of language. When the German public, just before the advent of Hitler, was reveling

1. In Jean Giraudoux, *Littérature,* Grasset, Paris, 1941.

in Max Reinhardt's great spectacles or participating in Pis-cator's "fire-arms" theatre, the Frenchman remained faithful to his traditions.[2] According to Giraudoux, "the true dramatic effect for him is not the clamor of two hundred extras, but the ironic nuance given to a phrase of the hero or heroine," for the Frenchman believes that the "great debates of the heart" are settled "by conversation":

> He persists in considering dialogue as the supreme form of the duel for the creature gifted with words. What he likes to experience is the power of that dialogue, its effective-ness, its form, hence the purely literary merits of the text. For him, theatrical action consists, not in submitting to a frantic massage of almost physical vision and emotion, from which he leaves exhausted, as from a Turkish bath, but in hanging his worries and the conflicts of his life and personal imagination on a model dialogue which can eluci-date them.

A model dialogue: such would seem to be Giraudoux's definition of theatre. Every drama would be one of the specta-tor's conflicts—conflicts in his life and in his imagination—put into model language. The words that never come, the vital discussions that daily life does not allow, the clarification by category of the soul's and heart's confusion—that is what the spectator would hear on stage. Language would become a prism in which the whitish, monotonous, and imperfect light of life is decomposed into basic and dazzling colors.

It would of course be easy to hold the conception up to ridicule. Do you have a great inexpressible love for peace? Go and see your love take shape in Hector's long speeches in *la Guerre de Troie n'aura pas lieu*. If you can't explain why your husband irritates you and why and how you have been un-faithful to him or killed him, go and listen to Agathe and

2. During the same period in France, Antonin Artaud was fighting for quite a different conception. See Conclusion.

Clytemnestra in *Electre*. If you are a minor civil servant and are unsuccessful in persuading the romantic young girl you're in love with to marry you, go and hear the Supervisor in *Intermezzo*. Or if you happen to be the young girl, listen to Isabelle in the same play. Yet there is no doubt that the characters' model speeches do more than replace political editorials in the newspapers or the correspondence of Miss Lonelyhearts.

The principle, confirmed by Giraudoux's theoretical writings and immediately apparent as a presupposition of his entire theatre, is that no reality can withstand human language. Giraudoux was a humanist, and doubly so: He not only based his conception of theatre on his knowledge and interpretation of European culture, but he had complete confidence in the human logic of language as a means of accounting for the universe. Language is the spider's web, spun by intelligence, in which reality and sur-reality and the supernatural are caught. The end of *Sodome et Gomorrhe* is the end of the world. But despite God's wrath, the war of the sexes will continue *ad saecula saeculorum*. It was characteristic of Giraudoux to have chosen as an image the voices of man and woman, continuing their discussion all the same:

> The Archangel: Are they never going to be quiet! Are they never going to die!
>
> The Angel: They are dead.
>
> The Archangel: Who is speaking then?
>
> The Angel: They are. Death was not enough. The scene continues.

Language, even with no support, perseveres in its existence. It lives on independent of the men who use it, just as for a believer the soul survives the body.

Although it does not necessarily create its objects, language does confer a privileged existence upon them, next to which their *unspoken* existence seems less important. In Giraudoux, not only does it give a different reality to the spectator's life

Theatre as Proposition

("the style smoothes out wrinkled souls . . ." *l'Impromptu de Paris*), but each character plays with the reality of his own universe by means of words. Ondine makes Hans' love exist by telling it; while another language, that of the Undines, gives a reality to treason in love. In *Judith* the heroine, in her duel with Holophernes, counted not on poison but on words. And through an ironic contrast Lucile's silence in the first act of *Pour Lucrèce* is what brings about the horrible drama that follows. Language does have the power of ordering the universe, either by defining situations in an intelligible manner, or by imposing a direction on the course of events. The importance of its function justifies all the adornments—sentences wrapped in ceremonial robes, as it were—and all the rites. Whence the privileged situation of the long speech in Giraudoux's theatre.

Reintroducing the monologue and the *tirade* was not simply the coquetry of a man of letters who wanted to show his originality through a return to outdated techniques. It is a form of theatricalism, the modern spectator being conscious of the unreality of the *tirade* or monologue. What he hears is not a dialogue of everyday life, but a reorganization of it. Giraudoux insists on such theatricalism by emphasizing the artificiality of the process. Characters and spectators are warned so that they can create suitable attitudes—the spectators within themselves, the others through their positions on stage.

Giraudoux used the monologue time and again. Whether the gardener's *lamento* in *Electre* or Mercury's monologue in the second act of *Amphitryon 38,* the speech is situated somewhat outside the action as an interlude addressed to the spectator, establishing the bridge between the play's universe and his own. It thus creates a higher complicity with the play, making the spectator into a kind of god, while reassuring him as to the humanity of the drama.

The so-called *tirade* is just as literary and artificial. During

24

scenes in which the drama is in full swing, there is suddenly a stop, to give the protagonist of the moment an opportunity to clarify the terms of the conflict he represents. This is true not only of Hector's prayer for the war dead in *la Guerre de Troie,* which is a ceremony in any case, but of long speeches situated in the heart of a debate. And Giraudoux's construction is such that the director is compelled to clear the stage, to arrange the other characters in secondary positions just as the chorus in an opera is grouped around the tenor.

In Corneille the *tirade* is an explanation through reasoning or a justification a posteriori; in Racine it is generally a narrative which results in the actual situation and which, by its very sequence, emphasizes the situation's inevitability; for the Romantics it was a poetic or pseudo-philosophical digression around a situation. In Giraudoux it is neither a digression, nor a minor slackening off of the situation, nor a step ahead. In the flow of the drama, it is a snapshot taken of all the tensions of a particular moment, catching the scenic athlete in mid-air and making it possible for us to examine it with care. It actualizes Lamartine's wish: "O Time, suspend your flight."

The spectator is warned about every stop in the movement by a key word, which carries within itself one of the basic elements of a particular tension. "My language," "my violence!" says Judith at the beginnings of two speeches addressed to Suzanne. "Yes, I hated him!" shouts Clytemnestra in *Electre.* The word "control" is the basis for Armand's speech about the proofs of his wife's fidelity in *Pour Lucrèce.* Giraudoux organized his speeches around a key word, just as in Wallace Stevens' poem *Anecdote of the Jar,* Tennessee takes shape around the jar that was placed upon a hill. In other cases the spectator is warned by a character who catches his breath by saying something like "Understand me," or by beginning with an inadequate response to the preceding line. It is rare for a character, having "answered back," as it were, to give the impression of continuing to speak without having given advance warning as to the length of his inspiration. The characters carry within themselves, in advance, the completed structure of their remarks. And here we are at the antipodes of naturalistic theatre, where language is at the mercy of all stimuli, which determine its successive forms and abundance.

The *tirade* constructed in such a way would seem to imply a conception of reality in which form precedes content. Sartre's article on Giraudoux's Aristotelianism[3] and the discussion taken up by Claude-Edmonde Magny in *Précieux Giraudoux*[4] poses the problem of Giraudoux's philosophy: Is he Aristotelian? Is he Platonic? There is no need here to go into the debate in detail, but it is worth noting that Giraudoux, like the courtly poet or the *précieux,* played on both sides. The characters in the plays and the plays themselves offer a Platonic vision of the world, in which the Idea precedes life. There is an Idea of love, an Idea of Electra, an Idea of Isabelle, an Idea of peace, an Idea of treason, an Idea of the couple situated in the heavens of the drama. The heroes and situations are the closest possible concrete expression of perfection. But the universe itself is not that of the spectator or the poet. For them, Ideas of which they are the imperfect realization do not exist. The poet expresses the Forms toward which our reality would seem to tend through images. The Forms exist only through the extrapolation of intelligence or the imagination. They are posterior to reality and invented by man in order to make his universe intelligible.

Giraudoux's "model dialogue" is the proposition of a poet. It implies a twofold movement in literary creation: the reduction of the real to a diagram, in which the intelligence is capable of establishing the continuity of interrupted lines and introducing symmetries; and the act of bringing concrete content to the perfected diagram. Peacock, in *The Art of*

3. Jean-Paul Sartre, *Situations I,* Gallimard, Paris, 1947.
4. See bibliography.

Drama,[5] described it as a "myth-allegory" form; and the process is in fact very close to allegorization. Yet it avoids allegory in that there is no reduction to separate abstract qualities, but to essences, whose totality Giraudoux preserves. The scenes of debate are the most characteristic. Whether domestic quarrels or the disputes of diplomats, they are illusory reconstructions, dreams of the intelligence, a fictional universe in which there is no break between the perceived real and the almost mathematical structure the mind seems to have discovered in it.

A product of the intelligence, Giraudoux's fictional universe is satisfying to the mind because it is made up of all the relations that the mind establishes between the things of the world. Whence the network of so-called *précieux* metaphors which establish its coherence. One of the characteristics of the *précieux* metaphor is the intellectuality of the bond that unites the two terms. Claude-Edmonde Magny points out that it begins with forms very close to the pun and results in a whole complicated reasoning in which contraries are united. It has nothing to do with any analogy imposed by illuminations of the subconscious; it does not spring from an intuition of the real, but gives form to the real from the outside. In Giraudoux it is part of the process of reconstruction. It adds secondary structures to the basic diagram. It contributes to the creation of an imaginary world in which the mind is always satisfied. In *Cantique des cantiques* the President asks Florence, apropos of Jérome:

The President:	Where did you find him?
Florence:	We bumped straight into each other on the boulevard. He was running with all his might . . . He hurt me.
The President:	He was coming from far away. He was given a start twenty years ago . . .

5. Ronald Peacock, *The Art of Drama*, London, Routledge and Kegan Paul, 1957, p. 205.

> *Florence:* Twenty-one . . . He hurt me . . . I still can't make up my mind whether the exhaustion within me is love or stiffness.

The basic diagram here is formed by a belief in the fatality of a meeting. But Giraudoux also brought in the comic note of a small accident. A purely intellectual liaison establishes a link between the destiny of the lovers and the accident, between what is already an image (the race of life) and Jérome's real race. Then the metaphor is prolonged and the consequences remain an intellectual proposition. The link of the metaphor is expressed by the word "exhaustion," but the two parts remain separate, in the forms of "love" and "stiffness."

Helen of Troy rubbing men against her "like great cakes of soap" to purify herself, Lia reinventing the *carte du Tendre* in her dialogue with the Angel, the Beggar advising Electra to "start from dawn," offer so many suggestive metaphors of a world in which the slightest glance of the mind sees the possibility of creating a web of analogies and correspondences.

Through language, Giraudoux has tried to create a universe which is not that of just a dream but of a dream of the intelligence. Claudel's theological universe, Audiberti's poetic universe, Montherlant's ethical universe, Sartre's phenomenological and ideological universe, Genêt's dream-like universe also claim to give concrete metaphors of the essence of reality, the metaphor being situated very precisely in a certain beyond, in certain depths of consciousness, or at a certain level of being. In Giraudoux the essence is *proposed* by the intelligence. There is no question of discovering the meaning of God's work, but of actualizing, through art, what the man gifted with reason would have created had he been God. It means rejecting Leibnitz's postulate according to which this world is the only possible world, and showing that with the same materials, a more intelligible world might be conceived.

Germany and France, war and peace, phantom and Supervisor, man and woman, virtue and vice, the President and Jérome, England and the South Sea Islands: Giraudoux's drama is based on simple conflicts. The conflicts are all the more intense in that Giraudoux, in his creation of an intelligible universe, starts out with particularly clear and distinct ideas. Germany is everything that France is not; the President is everything that Jérome is not; Andromache is everything that Helen is not. The drama somehow springs naturally from the clarity with which the essences are defined. The major bond between them, the field of conflict, is the hero or heroine—and here Giraudoux goes back to a classical conception of drama. Hector participates in both peace and war; Ondine is caught between man and the supernatural; Outourou finds himself at the junction between all the mysteries of Polynesia and Anglo-Saxon ethics, just as Siegfried carried within himself the definitions of both France and Germany. In Giraudoux's theatre the hero or protagonist is he who straddles two essences, he who believes he can participate in two essences at the same time or who is forced to participate or who is asked to participate.

Giraudoux's hero is also unique in that he carries his universe about with him. In Greek tragedy the plague was rampant in Thebes *because* of Oedipus' crimes; the series of contaminations, like the series of murders in Atreus' family, was causal. Giraudoux's hero walks about with a world that copies his definition or corresponds to it, just as at the end of *Electre* Aegisthus walks about with an eagle over his head. The Greek hero provokes events by his acts; Giraudoux's protagonist, like Wallace Stevens' jar, makes the surrounding world take part in his own being. Giraudoux has been reproached for his color-print landscapes, comparable to the illustrations in primary school textbooks. The France of *Siegfried,* the Bethulia of *Judith,* the Greece of *Amphitryon* or *Electre* are as naïve as pictures in a geography book and at the same time like a modern primitive dream à la Grandma Moses. What is important is the stylization, the structure brought to the landscape by the character's language and its transformation by his very presence. Indeed, the entire universe of the play is transformed: the elements of the landscape change from masculine to feminine, valets begin to speak in verse, villages are seized with poetic delirium, adulterers start to tremble.

The hero or heroine is the agent of a metamorphosis of the world, or an attempted metamorphosis, for the world sometimes resists and may win out. In *Judith* Giraudoux painted a stylized portrait of the Biblical world, with its mythology, its own necessity, and a structure whose evolution is known in advance; in other words, the essence of the Old Testament world as corrected and simplified by Giraudoux. According to its laws, Judith is destined to be the saintly heroine who saves her people by sacrificing herself. But Giraudoux's Judith embodies less the idea of sacrifice than an idea of the young girl. A virgin, she gives herself to Holophernes and then kills him. But she does not kill him to save her people. She kills him because she loves him and wants, through his death, to preserve the perfection of the night she had just spent with him. For Judith's world is not the same as that of the other characters, even in the most concrete details brought out by the dialogue. Her description of the battlefield is quite the contrary of her guardian angel's. Her description of her night with Holophernes is also quite the contrary of her guardian angel's. Were the soldiers on the ground dead or asleep? Did Judith caress Holophernes's body because she loved him or was she disgustedly locating the spot she would strike? Which is the truth? In fact, through language the play presents a kind of double truth: two worlds, or two essences of the world, coexist at the same moment, in the same place—Judith's and that of the angels and the God of the Old Testament. "A question of lighting," says the angel; and what we are asked to accept at the end of the play is the simultaneity of both lightings. The subject of the play is more the hesitation between two truths than the discussion of a problem of religious metaphysics, as André Gide thought.[6]

For Giraudoux's theatre is not a theatre of ideas in Gide's sense of the term. His plays are in the form of debates, but the debates are not really discussions. They are an esthetic equilibrium between contrary definitions. There are no problems concerning political ideas in *la Guerre de Troie;* there is a conflict between a definition of peace and a definition of war. Giraudoux's characters do not reason, they describe. In *Sodome et Gomorrhe* when Jean says that the weather is fine in Sodom, Lia answers that the weather is frightful. What directs the drama toward the victory of one essence or another is the weight of such or such description, of such or such definition. Often a definition or description grows richer by stealing, so to speak, from another, and finishes by conquering it through absorption. In *Intermezzo* Isabelle gives up her phantom, but only because the Supervisor managed to constitute the universe of civil servants as an equivalent of the specter's romantic world.

There are of course irreconcilable definitions, and then the "strongest" wins: war in *la Guerre de Troie,* the young man's love in *Cantique des cantiques.* But it would be vain to separate Giraudoux's plays into those in which contrary definitions are reconciled through facile satire, a feat of God, or a complicity between gods and men intended to satisfy them both, and those in which the reconciliation never takes place. It would mean putting too great an emphasis on the message or lesson contained in each play (we love peace but war is inevitable; shame on the mean capitalists who destroy the poetry of the French landscape; etc.) and reducing works whose subject is hesitation to some positive thesis. The subject of *la Guerre de Troie* is not the arrival of war, but the hesitation of the world between war and peace; the subject of

6. André Gide, *Journal,* November 12, 1931.

Judith is not the secret formula for making saints (what Gide perhaps wanted to find in it), but the oscillation between the lover and the saint; and it is hardly important, at the end of *Cantique des cantiques,* that Florence chooses Jérome: the subject is the simultaneous presence of two faces of love. What is important in *Sodome et Gomorrhe* is not the weather, and not even knowing whether Jean or Lia is right; nor is it to have the right one win: it is their disagreement; it is the fact that two incompatible universes occupy the same space, that the weather is fine and bad at the same time at the same point in the sky, that there is an essence of man and an essence of woman. Here Giraudoux's desire coincides with that of God: there should be an essence of the couple. Lia and Jean are opposed, and that duality is opposed to a desire for unity. Such is the play of perpendicular tensions underlying the drama.

The drama's intensity is in direct proportion to the range of difference between conflicting definitions. Through his choice of details and images, Giraudoux often increases the intensity to such a point that the spectator has the impression of an absolute impasse. Yet his plays present satisfying solutions. When the curtain goes down, the world is in order.

The denouement is partly determined by Giraudoux's *précieux* attitude. A work characterized as *précieux* generally ends with a usual or well-known solution, or one related to a familiar genre, the final conceit of an intellectual reconstruction of the world. For example, a sonnet of Voiture is resolved by a final conceit of an already known genre (the *concetto* or Petrarchian antithesis), and its value lies in the ingenuity of its twists. In the same way, the denouement of a Giraudoux play is one familiar to the spectator, after he has been led to expect almost anything else. Such acrobatics of intelligence and imagination are not a simple game. They represent a challenge. By means of perspective, the writer puts himself on a level with God, thus becoming His rival. He shows that one can arrive at the same result with more clarity, that in accentuating the contrasts and in multiplying the relations of things even the horrors of the universe can satisfy the mind.

The denouements are also determined by the play's genre, somewhat in the manner of the seventeenth century, when every play with more or less ridiculous bourgeois characters had to have a happy ending, every play with noble heroes had to end in a catastrophe or with spectacular acts of high generosity. Giraudoux's genres are personal and varied, but they always evoke a familiar literary horizon. In the historical plays, despite liberties taken with the story itself, the denouement comes from history. In spite of all the contortions, the Trojan War does take place, Hercules will be born, Judith does become a holy figure, Sodom is destroyed. Despite German influences, Giraudoux would have had Joan of Arc die on the stake in Rouen, and not, like Schiller's, on a battlefield. The play's finality comes from the already known denouement. And yet during the plays themselves, we realize that the Trojan War might have been avoided; Judith could have sent Suzanne in her place, her night of love with Holophernes is perhaps just a virgin's first night of love, and although Jupiter did sleep with Alcmene, it doesn't count. The denouement is faithful to history less because the plot leads to it than because the work must conform to an idea of the legend.

In the plays with invented subjects, it is the tone of the whole, their background of popular anecdote, which leads to suicide, separation, or a victory for the young man. In *Cantique des cantiques* Giraudoux applied his method no longer to Greek myth or to a Biblical or Germanic legend, but to an edifying popular romantic story. Therefore the young man had to win over the old. In *le Supplément au Voyage de Cook* Outourou's last speech is not determined by the play itself, but by anti-Christian eighteenth-century irony, which had originally furnished the idea for the situation. The Ubuesque character of the solution in *la Folle de Chaillot* is a final exaggeration of a secondary aspect of the play, revealing the cultural background of the play's universe: the melodramatic, romantic, and movie world of the mysteries of great cities. The underground chasm into which the pimps disappear is an exaggeration of the sewers in *les Misérables* or the dens of Eugène Sue's characters, just as in the rest of the play, the young lovers, the ragman, and the madwomen are very masked reminders of the fauna in that kind of literature.

In short, Giraudoux did not invent the denouements of the perfect dramas he proposed. Reality and myth or tradition took back their rights. Surprises comparable to the final pistol shots of Salacrou's *Histoire de rire* or of Montherlant's *Brocéliande* are unimaginable in his works. A higher form is superimposed on the drama, a form forged from an idea of tragedy, comedy, melodrama, fairy tale, history, sentimental anecdote, etc. The end of a Giraudoux play is not only the resolution of a conflict proposed during the play by the subject itself; it is also, and sometimes principally, the esthetic resolution of the distance between the subject and the genre to which it belongs.

The characters Giraudoux has put on stage are in full possession of their natures. Their degree of humanity depends largely on just how complex that nature is, and also on their rank in the drama. If the pattern is simple, they seem like puppets or personified entities. When they are neither heroes nor protagonists they are too exceptional for their dramatic situations and seem to be ornaments more than characters. But they all contribute to giving the play's universe its style and specifying its definition. On the whole, we must accept the fact that the world proposed to us by Giraudoux is peopled only by rare creatures. Little girls too intelligent for their ages, café waiter-poets, *précieux* soldiers are exceptional only in relation to the spectator. They are quite naturally in their places within the play's universe. Its form requires such fauna. Yet the play demands that we consider them as metaphors of ordinary humanity, caught of course in a drama played out by heroes.

The unreality of the secondary characters predominates, and the spectator's pleasure lies in his recognition of the writer's fantasy, not in the kind of participation or complicity provoked by Greek choruses, the confidants of French classical tragedy, or the sensible characters in Molière's comedy.

We must also accept the very *idea* of Giraudoux's theatre: a play of the reincarnation of perfected essences. Each character is therefore complete in himself and is nothing more than what he says and what Giraudoux tells us. When he expresses himself in clichés and hasty generalizations, he himself is a cliché or a generalization. In more naturalistic theatre, a character can be represented by traits which suggest a whole psychology and behavior, the postulate of such theatre being that each trait is a product, an effect within a whole determined system. For example, a sketchy character is comparable to those studies of certain great painters in which a detailed nose is enough to suggest the rest of the face and reveal a soul. When Giraudoux draws only a nose, it means that the character is nothing more than a nose. Or rather, the sketch of a face by Giraudoux would not consist in the suggestion of it by a study of one of its parts; he would draw a complete circle. Even when individualized to the extreme, Giraudoux's sketchy character will always give the impression of being an archetype—if only of himself— because in fact he is always complete. The same lighting falls on the hero as on the gardener or soldier; the structure of the main character is just more complex. And that is the basis for his hierarchy of characters.

Giraudoux's theatre gives rise therefore to a very special impression, quite the contrary of that ordinarily provoked by ambitious plays: the hero, he who rises above the common mortals, seems more human than the minor characters, who as a rule represent a world nearer to that of the spectator. In the same way that Siegfried, Eva, and Geneviève are more real than the German officers or the custom officials, Judith is more real than the rabbis or Holophernes' officers, Ondine more real than the members of the court, the Madwoman of Chaillot more real than the little people around her. What happens is that we accept the hero as exceptional and find it more normal to hear a hero accumulate metaphors than a soldier or café waiter. Given Giraudoux's method, only through actual excess can life be recreated, or at least an equivalent of the richness, complexity, and struggle of life. While the secondary characters are often prisoners of simple attitudes which completely define them, the hero, through an accumulation of details and retouching, assumes flesh, a personal history, and an illusion of humanity, distinctive of the dramatic character. Everything happens as if the process of adding details and colors to an anatomical diagram of the human body were to give it the quivering equivalent of a particular living human body.

Much of the severe criticism directed at Giraudoux's theatre is based on a judgment of his method, not on the works themselves. For the critic, the method is easily discernible. It implies an essentialist position; and it has been decreed in advance that a work which begins from abstractions (ideas, essences, forms) must necessarily be abstract or, at the very least, will always remain on this side of the illusion of reality. It is *"précieux"* or "formal."

Of course Giraudoux's works *are* those of a man of letters, works in which the writer seems to be both present and outside, in that he always gives the impression of knowing more than his characters. His tragedy, comedy, and criticism were all conceived in the same manner. He knew in advance that after *Phèdre* Racine would not write again; he knew in advance that the Trojan War would take place, that Judith would be a sanctified heroine, that Sodom and Gomorrha would be destroyed, with the result that the spectator may feel like both a god and Micromegas. The mathematical patterns of life, grasped directly in all their complexity, in time and in space, make life seem like a piece of ingenious machinery in which the observer knows everything but "lives" nothing. Yet beyond all the intellectualized movements directing the characters and the plays themselves, there is an *élan* which dominates the whole, creating a movement not only from one form to another or from one level of form to another, but from form to matter.

"Theatre," says little Véra in *l'Impromptu de Paris,* "is being real in the unreal." Giraudoux's ambition is just that elementary and just that unbounded. His universe is deliberately unreal. At the same time what upholds it and makes it vibrate is an intense effort toward reality. Starting from form at its most extreme (an almost medieval conception of the essence), he tried to arrive at the closest approximation of reality: the flesh and blood individual on a dramatic stage. Instead of just remaining the respectful transcriber or explorer of the Creature, Giraudoux tried to repeat the process of Creation, the passage from the plan to the act, and become the rival of that Architect, whose image, as Albérès has shown, constantly recurs in his works.[7]

Yet he always refused to give the illusion of reality by means of trickery which, in his case as in that of any anti-naturalistic playwright, would have consisted in introducing, at a given point, certain traits or remarks "taken from life"—what Anouilh did not hesitate to do, for example, in his *Antigone.* In Giraudoux the Greek hero speaking about his carriage or Judith talking like a fashionable young girl of the thirties is pure burlesque—that is, naturalistic or realistic details are introduced not for themselves or to give everyday reality to the play's universe, but for a pleasant effect of pure literary virtuosity.

An explanation of the life of Giraudoux's universe does not lie in the comic absurdities of its anachronisms. It lies rather in the synthesis, made by the spectator, of all the concrete elements accumulated by the writer. Just as Giraudoux asks the actress in *l'Impromptu de Paris* to recall her own emotions of the day in order to give life to Agnès' line in Molière's *l'Ecole des*

7. R-M. Albérès, *Esthétique et morale chez Giraudoux.*

femmes, "the little cat is dead," so the spectator feels Giraudoux's characters live through the presence within himself of his own life. His theatre is a theatre of collaboration—a rather different notion from the more fashionable one of participation, but not foreign to it, simply more active. Like reformers such as Jouvet and the Cartel, Giraudoux wanted his audience to be ready for action. He could be accused of illusions or of living in the dream of a world where ideal plays would be applauded by an ideal audience, had he not shown that he was perfectly aware of the sluggishness of his times (*l'Impromptu de Paris*). Like the reformers, he wrote neither for the real public nor for an ideal public but for the potential in the real public.

In the American "living newspaper" of the twenties, actors were mixed in with the audience so that the shouts on either side of a spectator would lead him to recognize the political entities on stage as living symbols of man's destiny on earth. Giraudoux waited for the shout to come spontaneously from within the spectator and assumed that his emotion would give the play its finishing touch: life. At that point, the spectator is truly a god, for he is observer and creator at the same time. There is no great theatre without the spectator's recognition, that last spark in the creation of a play.

At a time when theatre demands no more than immobility from a spectator so that it can painlessly graze him, Giraudoux demands cooperation, the presence of heart and imagination. Hence the "difficulty" of his theatre. His importance in the history of modern French theatre is both to have demanded a very active collaboration on the part of the spectator and to have given back the theatre its function of elucidating the world in fundamental terms. Certain types of theatre may force the spectator to use his mind so as to understand a particularly rare and complex problem. Others may pick up the notions of destiny, death, or love, and feed them to the passive spectator. Giraudoux's theatre is made neither for those in search of intellectual rarities, nor for the passive; it is made for a "normal" audience—the norm being defined as the audience of Greek tragedy, of the Spanish theatre of the *Siglo de Oro,* of Shakespeare, of French Classicism.

> Those who want to understand in the theatre do not understand theatre . . . The theatre is not a theorem, but a spectacle, not a lesson, but a philter. It should enter your imagination and your senses more than your mind . . .

say the actors in *l'Impromptu de Paris.* Moreover in *Visitations,* Giraudoux wrote that theatre must reveal to the spectator

> . . . these surprising truths: that the living must live, that the living must die, that autumn follows after summer, spring after winter, that there are the four elements, and happiness, and billions of catastrophes, that life is a reality, that it is a dream, that man lives by peace, that man lives by blood, in brief, what they will never know. . . .[8]

Such affirmations may seem in contradiction with the judgment of many critics for whom Giraudoux's theatre consists in works of the mind, their revelations far indeed from the commonplaces of the last quotation. Actually the misunderstanding about Giraudoux that reigned during the thirties can be reduced to the following: his method is complicated and baffling; therefore the idea expressed must itself be difficult to understand. And in fact Giraudoux's theatre offers quite the contrary. It is presented as an initiation to simplicity, in other words a reevaluation of simplicity through the detours that must be made in order to rediscover it. The objective is to exasperate the mind by an accumulation of intellectual subtleties,

8. Giraudoux, *Visitations,* Ides et Calendes, Neuchâtel and Paris, 1947. Translation by Bert M-P. Leefmans, *The Kenyon Review,* 1954.

to the point that an emotional adhesion beyond all comprehension will spring from the network of multiple lines that the intelligence has been following.

Knowledge of a certain order can be acquired only through the delirium of an inferior order. In certain religions the individual must subject his body to the most extreme violations in order to reach mysticism. Giraudoux's postulate seems to be that a manifest truth can be reached and experienced beyond intellection through a paroxysm of the intelligence. Preciosity, burlesque, humanist rationalism, and Aristotelian rationalism are actually so many means of making the mind so dizzy that it bows to the unchallengeable and striking fact of life. The spectator of good faith is expected to relive the adventure of Creation—the very Creation that the writer relived at the time of composition, that also of the director, from the blocking on paper to the performance—from ideas, form, or essences to the synthetic emotion of the human adventure.

In *la Guerre de Troie n'aura pas lieu* peace, represented both mythically and negatively by the title and the first line of the play (immediately challenged by the second, whence the drama):

> *Andromache:* There will be no Trojan War, Cassandra.
> *Cassandra:* I'll take that bet, Andromache.

is specified in the very first scene, then becomes "happiness," then "beauty"—all abstract notions—then the "sun" of that day, then evocative expressions like a "fisherman's house," the "murmur of seashells," and is finally, through a double ambiguity, embodied in a character, Hector. We thus go from what is most abstract in peace (its negative definition: the absence of war) to one man who will take its defense.

The concrete images remain vague enough for each spectator to give peace the face of his choice. The "fisherman's house," the "murmur of seashells," the sun that spreads its "mother of pearl" over the unspecified landscape all indicate a Mediterranean universe without particularizing it, suggesting its essence, from which the spectator can imagine his own fisherman's house, murmur, sun. Owl, station, train, birch tree, cat, silk, fur, hand, armor—Giraudoux's glossary always directs the spectator toward a certain concrete category, concrete feeling, concrete landscape. He never individualizes it; he is satisfied to emphasize its dominant feature. It is up to the spectator to bring about the final individualization. The Germany and France of *Siegfried* are deliberately clichés of the two countries, posters of the French or German railways; the fashionable young girl Judith is hardly more than a literary convention before she takes on the dimension of tragedy; the married life of Clytemnestra and Agamemnon is evoked by a "curly beard" and a raised little finger. There is nothing more concrete than those notations, yet nothing more open to all imaginations. In sparking his text with words that grammarians call concrete but which, in context, are no more than generic terms, Giraudoux launches the spectator out in the direction of a specific, even individual image. But he never actually imposes it; he lets the audience discover its own.

Once again in Giraudoux's works we have the inversion of a habitual approach. Where others impose a particular image from which the spectator is expected to extract generalizations, Giraudoux affirms the general at the beginning and demands not that the spectator imagine an illustration of that generality —the play itself fulfills that function—but that he provide some living correlative. In that respect, Giraudoux's theatre is one of the first complete or total theatres of the French stage. If the playwright devotes himself entirely to his text, the spectator must devote himself to the performance—in other words, his theatre excludes both passive auditors and unimaginative readers. It is not paradoxical to say that Giraudoux's plays are among those that are the most misunderstood when simply read. They are texts composed, "written," like a poem in dialogue, but destined to be spoken, performed, acted—texts which are, and were meant to be, the drama's fundamental means of expression, and consequently incorporates all of its structure, symbols, and ideas. But they become dramas, theatrical works, only when supported by the play of the flesh and blood actor and an appropriate staging. Indeed the most "written" plays are those which are truly grasped only when performed or imagined as performed. And that, Louis Jouvet understood.

Giraudoux claimed to have had two muses: Thalia before, and Jouvet after.[9] His theatre is a theatre of language—but of spoken and acted language. Moreover Jouvet was known as being anything but an unobtrusive director. Although a student of Copeau, and as respectful of the text as he, Jouvet used all the pomp of the scenic spectacle to make it live. A director who at the end of his career would make a special tableau of Sganarelle's last line in *Don Juan* or add the majestic spectacle of a tribunal at the end of *Tartuffe* believed in the importance of scenery and staging for reinforcing and adding life to the text. He did justice to Giraudoux's texts when he called on set designers such as Guillaume Monin (*Electre*), Léon Leyritz (*Intermezzo*), Pavel Tchelitchev (*Ondine*), or Christian Bérard (*la Folle de Chaillot*)—all otherwise designers of ballets or operas. When in his article on the director and in *l'Impromptu de Paris,* Giraudoux himself rose up against "staging," he meant to protest against the systems and theories of pure spectacle in which the text is sacrificed. But in the texts of his plays, he constantly indicated the recourse to stage devices and machines, their power of enchantment, and his belief in the actor and the audience.

Therefore when Clytemnestra delivers her well-known speech on Agamemnon's little finger and curly beard, it must be *heard*. Her dress, the tension of her body, the pillar she leans against, the grouping of the other characters and Electra's isolation must be *seen*. When reading *Intermezzo,* the phantom gives the impression of being merely a voice

9. Giraudoux, "le Metteur en scène," *Littérature.*

within Isabelle. When performed, his existence must be believed, for he is really standing up behind Isabelle, draped in his cape, in the semi-darkness of a Limousin evening.

Such is the difference between Giraudoux's plays and other theatres of language—certain dialogues in George Bernard Shaw's political plays, for example, for they are self-sufficient non-dramatic debates that have no need of staging. Actors, scenery, and staging are inseparable in Giraudoux. The text gives the fundamental drama, which is complete only when the three collaborators—the written text, the spectator, and the actual performance—are united. The meeting of all three is necessary to the incarnation of the symbol.

From *Siegfried* to *Pour Lucrèce,* a definite evolution can be seen in Giraudoux's art and thought. It was felt from year to year by drama critics such as Robert Kemp and Pierre Brisson and has been the object of many academic studies. The thematic content of the plays has oscillated from man to the supernatural and from Anglo-Saxon or Germanic culture to Mediterranean culture. After *Siegfried* came *Amphitryon 38;* after the adaptation of *Tessa, la Guerre de Troie;* after *Electre, Ondine.* The oscillation was accompanied by an orientation of the whole, during the course of which Giraudoux discovered tragedy, expressed it through myths and the intervention of various forms of divinity, hesitating all the while between the supernatural and the preternatural, and then let a particular theme invade his works—that of the war of the sexes, last expressed as completely humanized.

But one idea dominates his evolution: the idea that man will never live in peace because he is not alone, that God or the gods, social or psychological forces, the members of the other sex all set definitions before him which are different from his and which attract and repel him at the same time. There is no judgment on the part of Giraudoux; there are merely choices and ambiguities determined by the nature of each play. It is probably exaggerated to say with Jacques Houlet [10] that all Giraudoux's characters "win our sympathy in some way or other." But actually in the combat that takes place on stage between man and the gods, between man and woman, between France and Germany, between Hector and Ulysses, between Lia and Jean, our sympathies are not with either side but with the struggle itself as symbolized by the combat. So that beyond more or less individual definitions or essences, dividing and wrangling over the play's universe, a radically dramatic definition of man's condition is posed. Comedy springs from the triumph of human definitions (and as Georges May pointed out: "Giraudoux's men are expert at beating the gods" [11]); tragedy, from the triumph of forces which refuse man peace.

There has been great emphasis put on the fine formulas scattered throughout his fantasies and plays concerned with God or the gods. For example, Holophernes describes the universe as a place infested by the gods:

> From Greece to India, from North to South, there isn't a country which doesn't swarm with them, each with his vices, his odors . . . The atmosphere of the world for anyone who likes to breath, is that of a barrack of gods.

Here a pagan is speaking. For Judith and her people, Jehovah and his messengers alone "infest" the universe. Just as each hero carries his universe about with him, so each period, each culture, each genre carries its own gods about—those that can be touched as well as abstractions; in other words, the symbols of that which transcends the individual and attempts to snatch away his privilege of giving order and form to his own world: for a knight of the courtly novel, spirits and enchanters; for the inhabitants of Sodom, a proliferation of angels; for the French bourgeois of the Second Empire, imperatives of the

10. Jacques Houlet, *le Théâtre de Jean Giraudoux*.
11. Georges May, "Jean Giraudoux: Diplomacy and Dramaturgy."

44

bourgeoisie's vices and virtues. A secularization of the conflicts does not change the vision of the world and destiny underlying Giraudoux's plays. Metaphors and masks of man's condition vary, but both the situation of man and the poetic vision remain the same.

For in a world expressly constructed to satisfy the mind, there is no break between things and their essences, and the separation between essences leads to the exteriority of things. Worlds can be superimposed on the world, two worlds can occupy the same space at the same time, in the boldest desire of the mind: contradiction. For the individual who is well defined within his own nature, a bearer of his own universe, everything occupying that same space would thus seem supernatural. Woman is a monster for man, man a monster for woman. There is clearly a hierarchy of characters, from the literal-minded, who are willing to see only their own essence and universe, to the "elect," who plainly see the superposition and separation of universes, and accept it so as to be able to combat it, surmount it, or communicate with those other worlds denied or rejected by their fellowmen.

Destiny is the directing force of the election which places such and such character at a junction and gives him the lucidity to see in both directions: Florence between the President and Jérome, Judith between love and sanctity, Isabelle between the phantom and the Supervisor, Ondine between humanity and Nature, Siegfried between France and Germany. Destiny gives the elect just enough freedom to be in agony. Whatever the situation and world in which a man lives, there is always a transcendency—puzzling, repelling, or attractive—and represented by Giraudoux as a concrete and present universe, mixed in with the so-called normal universe but separated from it, like two faces superimposed on a photograph, yet always distinct.

According to Giraudoux,[12] the Frenchman, in a kind of

12. "la Tragédie et Bellac," *Littérature*.

moral and metaphysical Bonapartism, delegates tragedy to tragic heroes and does not identify with it. All of Giraudoux's characters are more or less delegates: his gardeners and soldiers are delegates of our gardeners and soldiers, his waiters, delegates of our waiters. Above them are the great ambassadors, who treat with the supernatural as equals and reveal its dangers, its charms, its grandeurs. Giraudoux's theatre is definitely a diplomatic operation, an open diplomacy, a machine intended to make men conscious of a destiny concerning them and transcending them at the same time, and to rid them of the debate by taking it on in their places.

Giraudoux treats man's condition in the same way as Talleyrand treated Europe: the hand that played with the destiny of nations was the hand of an artist. And if a lesson exists, it is a lesson of artistic perspective. Laurent Lesage [13] interprets the ironic distance established by Giraudoux as an inheritance of German Romantic stoicism. It can also be seen as a lesson for man in how to dominate his own condition, a metaphor of Pascal's thinking reed, of the feeble creature constantly threatened by the supernatural, in danger of being crushed by the universe, but always superior to that universe to the extent that he is capable of "thinking" his own oppression and making it an object of diversion by means of the mind and art. As a result, Giraudoux's theatre has often been reproached with coldness and a lack of pity. Yet through the "delegation" and the perspective furnished by intelligence, Giraudoux succeeded in avoiding that self-pity, so easily confused, in the theatre, with participation.

Despite the value of other methods and other results, Giraudoux has taken a privileged place in the history of the French stage. By avoiding purely psychological identification, too easily and superficially offered by the realistic play, he was the first French playwright to respond to the demands of

13. Laurent Lesage, "Jean Giraudoux, Surrealism and the German Romantic Ideal."

modern theatre and reach a large public at the same time. He transformed theatre into a feast, comparable to the passing of a Prince, surrounded by his pomp and ceremony, prisoner of his legend, and both separated from his people and bearer of their destiny.

CHAPTER 2

THE DOUBLE GAME: JEAN COCTEAU

The ease created by Giraudoux's presence on the French stage during the last years of the Third Republic was countered by an uneasiness produced by Jean Cocteau. Just as Gide's scandals were in contrast to Valéry's order, so, in the theatre, Cocteau's scandals were in contrast to Giraudoux's order. Giraudoux arrived on the twentieth-century French stage at precisely the time it was ready to receive him, as did Racine in the seventeenth century. Giraudoux's is a theatre of harmonious recreation, cleansing the spectator's soul, as it were. Cocteau began to write for the theatre in 1916, when the battle for reform was at its most acute. He started as a revolutionary and continued as a revolutionary. And we know that in general, any immobility, any rigidity was distasteful to him. If his works often give more the impression of a great to-do and confusion than of revolution, it is because his desire for complete change was opposed to an unquestionable narcissism.

To the conflicts and struggles of Cocteau's subjects and themes are added the unexpected contrasts of the works as a whole. His theatre would seem to have covered all possible genres, from the avant-garde spectacle to commercial cinema, everything that could be represented or played by actors of every category. Ballet: *Parade, la Dame à la licorne;* farce: *les Mariés de la Tour Eiffel;* opera: *le Pauvre Matelot, Oedipus-Rex;* fairy tale: *les Chevaliers de la Table Ronde,* the film *la Belle et la Bête;* pseudo-classical tragedy: *Renaud et Armide;* transposition of classical myth: *la Machine infernale;* naturalist-type dramas: *les Monstres sacrés, la Machine à écrire, les Parents terribles;* Romantic-type dramas: *l'Aigle à deux têtes, Bacchus.*

Such diversity of means gives Cocteau's works a disparate appearance, a sort of Jack-of-all-trades or amateur aspect that makes him seem rather like Georges in *les Parents terribles*. Cocteau has tried to perfect already existing genres and make them more effective just as Georges, having tried other experiments, wants to perfect the spear gun and make it shoot bullets.

With each work, Cocteau plays the game he has chosen to play. In theatre he plays at being a playwright. He accomplishes the necessary rites: advance interviews in the newspapers and, at publication, explanatory prefaces or analyses. The preface to *les Parents terribles* reveals that the play was written in a hotel room in Montargis and that the objective was to produce a play "which, far from serving as a pretext for staging, would serve as a pretext for great actors." His prefaces often give the impression that the work is an exercise in style, imposed by external circumstances. The "idea" of theatre comes first and varies according to the period, the year, the month. Every play is an example, a model, an illustration. Cocteau's works are presented as a group of occasional plays—to enhance actors or actresses, to satisfy a request from the Vicomte de Noailles, to scandalize a certain public.

Once he has decided to go along with such or such circumstance, Cocteau starts to work as if the genre of the play he is writing were the only one possible. In fact he is more actor than playwright. He identifies with his role, with every role that circumstances have led him to play in the world of letters; and he is an actor who gives himself completely and honestly to the role of the moment. Cocteau is a writer who lives in the literary moment, whether that moment be called *la Machine à écrire, Renaud et Armide,* or *Bacchus.* If Victor Hugo, according to Cocteau, was a madman who thought he was Victor Hugo, Jean Cocteau is an actor who identifies himself successively with the fictional ideal playwrights that the particular period would seem to demand. He plays minor parts as well as major ones, according to the need of the times. He is an understudy of genius. When there is a comedy lacking on the French stage, Cocteau is ready to plug up the hole. He provides an avant-garde spectacle when needed. To the Boulevard, which complained about the exhaustion of its great suppliers, he gave *les Parents terribles, la Machine à écrire, les Monstres sacrés,* just as for the Comédie Française he produced the new play in verse that no one any longer dared write, *Renaud et Armide.* He became Edwige Feuillère's Rostand with *l'Aigle à deux têtes,* just as with *la Machine infernale,* he was the first of his generation, even before Giraudoux, to reinterpret Greek tragedy because the new era needed a Racine. *Bacchus* shows a certain fatigue in that respect, for there he was a follower. The general impression is that Cocteau has always something to do, if not always something to say. The problems he would seem to pose are of an esthetic and even technical order, for he is more interested in the secrets of workmanship than in the actual material of the product.

If there is an evolution in Cocteau's works, it is based on a twofold movement: he wanted both to create fashions and revive them. In most of his prefaces he affirms the necessity of saying no to whatever is established, as soon as it is established. One must never become immobilized in a game. Once the rules are fixed, "the rules must be changed." [1] His is indeed the psychology of a great dress designer. And in his perpetual invention of new rules, Cocteau constantly refers back to a certain past—now a lost naïveté, that of primitive theatre or childhood; now the bygone age of the theatre of actors, the sacred monsters. The ancient tunic is made old-fashioned by knight's armor; the suit, by Second Empire uniforms. Just as Antoine was right to have imposed "real quarters of meat and a fountain" on a public used to painted objects, Cocteau was to consider it his duty as an artist to impose painted canvas on a public accustomed to real quarters of meat, or to reinvent

1. Prefaces to *les Mariés de la Tour Eiffel,* 1922; *les Parents terribles,* 1938; *l'Aigle à deux têtes,* 1946.

the Boulevard for a public that had come to demand modernist theatre.[2] He created the fashion by reintroducing his grandmother's and great-grandmother's dresses. The objective of such an operation is to keep the public's esthetic consciousness in a state of alert. However, a multiplicity of changes ends by resembling constancy. And in spite of the unexpected and the novelty, every one of Cocteau's plays can be recognized by a group of permanent features which might be called the writer's signature.

For Cocteau has more of a signature than a style. The handwriting is always the same, while the style changes. To whatever genre it may belong, a Cocteau play can be recognized by certain words, certain formulas, certain images, just as in some families, despite a difference in sex, age, physical appearance, and temperament, each member has a beauty mark on his left shoulder. The words "wonder" and "witchery," "charms" and "enchantment," "miracles" and "magic," each a part of the very flesh of his fantasies such as *les Chevaliers de la Table Ronde,* somehow or other work their way into the more or less realistic plays like *la Machine à écrire* and *les Parents terribles.* Every situation that is out of the ordinary becomes "a dream" for the characters—a comparison that stems from a cliché but one which Cocteau accentuates by extension. The characters ask to be awakened or not to be awakened, or they compare themselves to the dreams of someone else, as in *l'Aigle à deux têtes.* Moreover, symbols reappear: the thread (*Orphée, la Machine infernale, Renaud et Armide*); the mirror, either actualized (*Orphée,* the film *le Sang d'un poète*) or used as a metaphor (the lake of the Queen's death in *les Chevaliers*). These are but a few examples of a vocabulary and an arsenal of pass-key devices which constitute the superficial signature of Cocteau's works, just as a little star signs his drawings.

2. Preface to *les Parents terribles.*

The Double Game

On another level, we find that the milieu of nearly all Cocteau's plays is "the family." Doubtless it includes an idea of the couple in the manner of Giraudoux, but it also includes the idea of a household: the households of Orpheus, King Arthur, Jocasta, Yvonne, and Esther, all characterized by a feeling of bedroom slippers and slammed doors never found in those of Giraudoux's Alcmene, Clytemnestra, Lia, or Lucile. The novel *les Enfants terribles* and the play *les Parents terribles* have fixed the theme of family promiscuity at the center of Cocteau's works—a promiscuity of people (mother-son, sister-brother) and also of intimate objects. But even in the deliberately anti-naturalistic plays, Cocteau introduces a realism of intimacy through the mention of pieces of clothing, physical contact, and childish quarrels. In *la Machine infernale,* Jocasta promiscuously touching the young soldier in Act I; Jocasta and Oedipus, wearied by ceremonies, "letting themselves go" in the bridal chamber of the third act; Jocasta beginning to undress Oedipus; her dialogue with him on their wedding night—all suggest, beyond the play's tragic ambiguity and symbols, a whole universe of contact, underclothes, whispering, shut-in household scenes, family secrets. Therefore it is hardly surprising that the man who write *la Machine infernale* also wrote *la Machine à écrire.* In *les Chevaliers de la Table Ronde,* another "family" play, the great halls of King Arthur's and Merlin's castles change in the third act to the Queen's own room, where Guinevere appears in a nightgown, ready for a jealous scene that suggests Chrestien de Troyes as modified by Henri Bataille.

Might not those constantly reappearing rooms in Cocteau's theatre—rooms of the Queen, the wife, the mother—be reminiscent of Gertrude's room in *Hamlet?* Do not the bed, the chair, the disorder of intimacy and its somewhat sickening tepidness constitute for Cocteau the ideal place where love appears in all its dimensions: physical contact, incest, hate, the minute of truth? In any case, it is obviously one of his signatures, the other being a reference to magic, witchcraft, and miracles. Here again a comparison can be made with the signature of his drawings. The handwriting of the "Jean Cocteau" or quite simply "Jean" is soft and childish. It evokes the warmth of the breast; it is Oedipus crying "Mother!" The star accompanying it is a sign of the higher and occult powers mixed in with that intimacy and directing it toward the glory of catastrophe.

Intimacy and witchcraft often have a meeting point in the object—more or less ordinary—that lies about, goes astray, or behaves in unexpected ways. "Even the familiar objects have something suspicious about them," wrote Cocteau in his description of the stage set for *Orphée*. The objects that furnish his stage are therefore intimate or ordinary, but also magical. Whereas in *les Mariés de la Tour Eiffel* the phonograph and camera are magical (the camera produces an ostrich and a lion that eats generals), the rest of his works are strewn with object-witnesses, chosen amongst the most ordinary and suddenly gifted with supernatural powers: in *Orphée,* the horse (demoniac) and mirror (the door to death); in *les Chevaliers,* a flower pot (the flower speaks) and a bat (a carrier pigeon); in *les Parents terribles,* a bourgeois apartment (a gypsy caravan); in *la Machine infernale,* Jocasta's scarf and brooch (weapons of fate); in *la Voix humaine,* the telephone (a new weapon with which to kill women). Sometimes the language and sometimes its physical aspect accentuate the object's mystery or secret in a kind of expressionism rare on the French stage until Adamov and Ionesco.

The objects often acquire their powers through disorder. Out of their usual places, they seem stripped of their usual functions, diverted from their roles in this world, and free therefore to assume new functions. The incongruity of the object not in its proper place creates an uneasiness in the spectator which comes from the consciousness of pure unjustified being. The transcendency of being that appears when being is stripped of the habitual relationships established with it becomes magic in the hands of a poet, the sign of, or a door opening onto, the supernatural. Through not belonging, the being of things becomes strange. The point at which consciousness bumps up against an impenetrable transcendency—a fact or an exceptional or monstrous relationship—is the point at which the poet, by an act of faith, affirms that *there* the world of poetry begins and that the imagination, the poet's "deep night," is called upon to give perceptible content to the ensuing uneasiness. If need be, the poet gives the finishing touch that makes the strange seem stranger still. But he also takes refuge behind analogies. For the talking flower in *les Chevaliers,* he recalls that a plant that sends forth waves has been discovered in Florida; for the automobile that dictates his poems to Orpheus in the film *Orphée,* he evokes the car radios that transmitted B.B.C. code messages during the Nazi occupation.

An object which is not in its place can be poetic: a lion on the Eiffel Tower, theatrical costumes in a bourgeois house, even a stray shoe under an armchair. The same holds true for the characters. Cocteau tries to poetize them by isolating them, displacing them, making them somewhat foreign. On the simplest level, he does it by a disparity of class: Stanislas in the Queen's room (*l'Aigle à deux têtes*); Hans, the poor mad peasant, chosen as king for a week (*Bacchus*); the situation in *Ruy Blas* (Cocteau's film adaptation). In a more visual way, he disguises or masks the character in a decisive scene: Margo, in *la Machine à écrire,* is dressed up like Lucrezia Borgia during most of the first act; Esther, in *les Monstres sacrés,* completely covers her face with cold cream when Liane confronts her with cruel facts. The displacement is complete in *la Machine infernale,* in which Jocasta speaks and gesticulates like a foreigner. Cocteau did not use the device only to justify the speech of Elvire Popesco,[3] but, as in the other cases, to isolate

3. A famous Boulevard actress of Roumanian origin for whom Cocteau wrote the part. However she did not play it until the revival of *la Machine infernale* in 1954.

the character by an accidental peculiarity, or at least seemingly accidental.

In the same way, Cocteau hoped for revelations from certain coincidences, certain unexpected encounters. Just as Elvire Popesco was to give a more staggering meaning—unpredictable but hoped for—to the myth of Oedipus, so the music of Bach as background to the film *les Enfants terribles* was to furnish "accidental synchronisms" out of which the most original beauty would spring. At the beginning of every Cocteau play, a certain amount of chance, coincidence, and accident must be accepted in addition to the usual dramatic conventions: Orpheus' poetry dictated by a horse and his guardian angel in the form of a glazier; Jocasta's Roumanian accent; Stanislas as the image of the dead King. The process is similar to a combination of fairy tale illusion and surrealist experiment. Cocteau's world is made up of disparate beings and elements, each one generally familiar but isolated from its context, whirling about in a vacuum, fastening on to one another as if by chance, and thus perhaps creating poetry. Cocteau has said that the great writer is he whose "aim is straight." He himself gives the impression of hoping to aim straight while closing his eyes, like the characters of certain comic films who haphazardly shoot in the air and out of the sky falls a duck or a balloon. In that way, Cocteau hopes to shoot down the blue bird.

More than a vision of the world, it is a device, and a device that can lead to every extravagance—legitimate to the extent that the incongruity of the combined elements is a protestation against the superficial coherence of psychological theatre or the theatre of ideas, and also against the traditions surrounding myth and certain great subjects. The poetry of *les Mariés de la Tour Eiffel* consists in replacing traditional coherence by an inner chance that is quite contrary to the logic of everyday reality. "The scenes fit together like the words of a poem," says Cocteau in his preface. Here the poem would be a surrealist *divertissement* or, to be more explicit, a collage. Its interest lies both in its amusing absurdity and its challenge to accepted forms of poetry or painting. Cocteau counts on "the part that belongs to God" to make the symbol emerge, just as a chemist's apprentice might haphazardly choose two substances, mix them together in a test tube, and hope for an explosion. Of course there is the danger of his obtaining no more than a bit of smoke and a change in color. Underlying that kind of operation is the hope that the audience will ask two questions, for which the answers are all prepared: Why? —Why not? and What will come of it? —We shall see.

Cocteau's experiment in *les Mariés* in 1921 might seem old-fashioned today, for it is essentially a document, a polemic argument that took place during a quarrel, now established in history. It does not have the weight of either Jarry's *Ubu Roi* or Apollinaire's *les Mamelles de Tirésias,* in which the revolution in form was accompanied by a true theme. Yet *les Mariés,* in the intransigency of its conception, is still a call to order every time a resurgence of naturalism in the theatre begins to exercise its charms. It remains a warning against psychologism, earnestness, and want of imagination.

The plays that follow, from *Orphée* to *Bacchus,* and whatever the genre, reaffirm the poet's right to search for a synchronism of chance between elements drawn from the familiar world and the most exalted forms of myth or art. The Parisian vulgarity and banter of the demon Jinnifer in *les Chevaliers,* the duality of Jocasta and the Sphinx in *la Machine infernale,* the great themes of incest and death embodied in Boulevard characters in *les Parents terribles* are most striking examples of it. But do the shocks thus provoked have real dramatic value? There is no doubt that they create a tension between the play and the audience (surprise, indignation, irritation). However the determining factor is largely "the part that belongs to God," with the result that the juxtaposition of disparate elements may be rich in living tensions or turn out to be sterile, the spectator's interest being caught up in the play's ingeniousness or absurdity rather than in the drama itself.

A theatre of exorcism, Cocteau's works drive the demon out so effectively that there is hardly time to see him. The spectator is usually too busy watching the exorciser's pirouettes and incantations to think about the person possessed. Whence the clear division of public and critics into raving admirers and rabid disparagers, into those who see Cocteau's works as the reflection of a deep and intense drama and those who see Cocteau as the entertainer of a certain high society with a taste for anarchy.

> Three managers organize the publicity. In their terrifying language, they tell each other that the crowd takes the parade for the inner spectacle, and they grossly try to make the crowd understand it.
>
> No one enters.
>
> • • • •
>
> The Chinaman, the acrobats, and the little girl come out of the empty theatre. Seeing the managers' supreme effort and failure, they try, in their turn, to explain that the spectacle is given inside.

Such, in general, is the scenario of the ballet *Parade,* produced in collaboration with Picasso, Erik Satie, Diaghilev, and Leonide Massine. Besides its value as a manifesto, it has a theme that might serve as a symbol for the whole of Cocteau's works: Cocteau keeps his public outside. The true spectacle of the inner circus remains forbidden, despite the poet's innumerable invitations to enter. And perhaps that inner circus is no more than an absolute vacuum, as Eric Bentley has suggested.[4]

Yet beyond the parade, beyond the enormous differences of style and tone that are so many theatrical variations of an

4. Eric Bentley, *In Search of Theatre.*

outer ceremony, there is the suggestion of a real drama, if not its total realization. Almost all Cocteau's plays lead toward the same resolution. They are often directed toward a violent death and the hero generally appears more like a victim of the drama than the tragic master of his fate. Victims of either magic spells or very special circumstances, Cocteau's heroes submit to action more than they direct it. In *les Parents terribles* it is not Yvonne who is responsible for Madeleine's lie, but Georges and Léo; in *les Chevaliers* many of the characters are replaced by a demon who takes on their appearances; and particularly in *la Machine infernale* the caprices of the gods and destiny are so emphasized that Oedipus' heroism disappears. Oedipus did not solve the Sphinx's riddle; she gave him the answer out of love. And although he puts out his eyes at the end, it is not so much his own act as it is in Sophocles.[5] During Cocteau's play, the weapons themselves (Jocasta's brooch and scarf), from the very beginning, are impatient to put out Oedipus' eyes and strangle Jocasta. And in the third act there is a kind of rehearsal of Oedipus becoming blind when he looks into Tiresias' eyes and thinks he is blinded by pepper. In short, Cocteau emphasized Oedipus' mechanical victimization more than his tragic heroism.

Here, Cocteau is eminently representative of modern drama, which draws as near to tragedy as possible, yet most often remains on this side of it. Tragic heroism for the Greeks consisted in going all the way through an ordeal, to the point of giving any final acceptation the value of a challenge, and finding true grandeur in the catastrophe itself. Today this conception is replaced by a taste for victimization, still colored by Romanticism.

Cocteau uses the basic elements of tragedy in his dramas: the misunderstanding, a source of tragic irony, and the play of supernatural forces or obscure powers. Yvonne is mistaken

5. "As for the hand that struck my eyes, it was mine and no one else's." *Oedipus Rex*, line 1330. See Bernard Knox, *Oedipus at Thebes*, Yale University Press, New Haven, 1957.

about the meaning of her love for Mik just as Oedipus is mistaken about the oracle and the encounters in his life, and the interiorization of fate and its expression in psychological terms detract nothing from its transcendency. But either the characters, following in the path of fate, stop just on the edge of the revelation that might have elevated them (Yvonne dies without having really got to know herself, in *les Parents terribles*); or the development of the action remains outside the character, who is victimized and then liberated without having had any determining effect on the drama (King Arthur, in *les Chevaliers,* does no more than talk about the forces that "intoxicate" and then "disintoxicate" him); or, as is most frequently the case, the characters accelerate the final movement and precipitate their own deaths in gestures that are more evasive than fulfilling (Solange's suicide in *la Machine à écrire,* the anticipation of Hans who kills himself, in *Bacchus*).

Although the precipitated denouements are far removed from classical tragedy, they have two great merits. One, their theatricalism is effective. The foreshortening, the elements of spectacle, the effects of surprise and shock do create an unquestionable climate of finality. The spectacle is carried away by an increasingly rapid whirlpool of scenic movements and at the end death is imposed, so to speak, on the spectator's nerves. Two, they reveal a conception of freedom which is Cocteau's own. In the preface to *les Mariés de la Tour Eiffel,* Cocteau wrote:

> One of the photographer's lines could be used on the title page: *Since these mysteries are beyond us, let's pretend to be their organizer.* It is our line par excellence. The conceited man always finds refuge in responsibility. Thus, for example, he prolongs a war after the phenomenon that had been its deciding factor is over.

Freedom would then be shown in the acceleration or slowing down of the necessary developments, in their foreshortening or extension. Freedom is Cocteau's "pretense" and the others' "conceit." And Cocteau has no illusions about his own characters. When at the end of *Bacchus* Hans cries out "Free . . . ," his way of dying should be seen not as "tragic death par excellence, both fated and chosen"[6] but as a pretense, a voluntary illusion. Hans' final freedom is in fact abstract. It consists only in anticipating an already determined event. In the same way, the Queen's command "Say that I wanted it" in the third act of *l'Aigle à deux têtes* seems merely a verbal claim, for Stanislas' suicide—the very reason for her own—was not part of her plans.

Therefore what Cocteau's plays reveal is not a traditional tragic vision, but a particular conception of destiny very near to fatalism, wherein the best man can do is to live "as if" he were capable of controlling his fate. That "as if" can be found in all the eloquent affirmations, costumes, grand gestures, and at the extreme limit, in art itself. In *la Machine à écrire* many inhabitants of the city claim, at one point or another, to have written the anonymous letters. The play explains that in making the claim they hope to get out of the mediocrity in which they are imprisoned. They want to be recognized even in crime and their desire is so powerful that they end by believing their own lies. Actually their mythomania picks up the "pretense" and "conceit" of the preface to *les Mariés*. Caught in a development of events that is beyond them and for which they are not responsible, they want to have themselves put in prison so that everything will happen *as if* the scandal was their own work. In short, the only escape from fate is in the lie. And the game of lying must be played to the very end, that is, all the way to total illusion, until the mask of freedom is seen as the very flesh of man. Man's only recourse is to deceive himself and others.

Death by suicide, in Cocteau's works, is the highest form of human pretense. By precipitating death, it often appears as an

6. Pierre Dubourg, *Dramaturgie de Jean Cocteau*, p. 157.

escape. The character disappears before the last illuminations of his ordeal. He wants to testify before it is too late and makes himself the martyr of certain values (poetry, love, grandeur, humanity) at the very moment that those values may be shown as impossible. As soon as the character realizes that the world has tricked him, he answers with the definitive trickery of suicide. He neither triumphs nor makes his peace. He retires. The deep and despairing cry of Cocteau's works is in the agitation of man who is caught and either ignores the fact or succeeds only in reconstructing a higher ignorance in the form of illusion. But although gilded by language and adorned with all the devices of mind and imagination, the trap remains merciless. By means of theatrical devices, Cocteau has invented a masked ball and he is the first to proclaim its vanity.

Cocteau's heroes—pure, still not disillusioned, preys to circumstance—are victims of chance, victims of a *fatalitas* often similar to that of melodrama. They believe that they benefit from it until, having gone too far in the game, they are seized with an unbearable mistrust which leads to a voluntary illusion. Cocteau's universe is not one of tragedy but of danger. The cosmos surrounding the characters is not that of a great moral order in the Greek manner, in conflict with man's affirmation of himself. It is a Coney Island contraption, a lay-out of pitfalls. In *les Chevaliers* the characters are deceived by a demon who takes on the appearances of several of them, and the Grail that appears is a false Grail; in *les Parents terribles* mother love hides incest; in *la Machine infernale* everything is a trap or a threat, from Jocasta's scarf to the young girl who is a mask of the Sphinx. Those who fall into the traps—who are marked out for them—are the naïve and the pure in heart: poets, idealized adolescents, dewy-eyed revolutionaries. Whence the melodramatic aspect of Cocteau's theatre. Parallel to the hero of Byronic gloom or the fated Romantic, his hero can be recognized by a sign, a coincidence, or phrases with double meanings which he utters without quite knowing their significance. We might cry out *Fatalitas!* during *la Machine infernale* in which ghosts and ambiguous dialogue transform the *Tyrannos,* caught by Sophocles at the height of his glory, into the hero of an adventure novel; or when during a storm in *l'Aigle,* a young revolutionary, who just happens to be the dead King's double, takes refuge in the Queen's room; or during *les Parents terribles* when Mik, a good son and good lover, finds himself not only the object of incestuous love but his own father's rival. Characterized by adolescence—a state of both grace and malediction, and a combination of impulsive acts, ignorance, purity, disorder, and youth—Cocteau's heroes are to a certain extent "going forces" in the Romantic manner, and "going" in a treacherous universe filled with every danger. Actually the adjective "Romantic" does somehow describe Cocteau's works. The variety of forms, the esthetic debates surrounding the plays, the justifying abstractions of the subject matter (poetry, youth, impure order, pure disorder) only partially disguise the underlying theme of isolation, an isolation of the individual destined for better and for worse. In *Scandal and Parade*[7] Neal Oxenhandler emphasizes the theme of the *poète maudit,* the cursed poet, found throughout all of Cocteau's works. The ambiguity of benediction-malediction, generally identified with adolescence, is also, directly or indirectly, identified with the situation of the poet. Orpheus—*poète maudit;* Stanislas—*poète maudit;* Galahad—*poète maudit* at the end of *les Chevaliers* when the birds sing "Pay, pay!" They are poets like Ruy Blas (it was no accident that Cocteau adapted Victor Hugo's *Ruy Blas* for the screen) or Hernani, with a vague touch of Rimbaud. Who has cursed these poets? Society, without any doubt, and also the supernatural powers that play with the poet, giving him privileges in order to deceive or trap him more successfully.

The poet constantly feels himself in danger of death. Cocteau, accused by Mauriac of having dragged the Catholic

7. See Bibliography.

Church in the mud with *Bacchus,* answered that such accusations can only come from a man who belongs to the race of those "who kill poets." [8] Yet whatever Mauriac's bad faith in attacking him, he was not aiming at Cocteau, the poet. He only meant to protect the Church from any scratch, however slight. Cocteau's vigilance is of the same order as his characters' mistrust. For him, Mauriac became identified with Hans' accusers, with Orpheus' Bacchantes, with "impure order." The same motives pushed him into taking Jean Genêt's defense in the courts. Cocteau is a man perpetually on trial, either by himself, through the poets of his time, or through his characters. Doubtless he exaggerates the trial; after all, he has been elected to the French Academy. But in fact, any feeling of being hunted, any individual anguish can become a model for a more universal anguish. It would seem that Cocteau came to a stop between the rather Romantic individual complaint and universalization, which he replaced in part by all the surface effects of his contradictory esthetics.

The problem of the cursed protagonist is complicated by the fact that the young hero in each of his plays, often played by Jean Marais, cannot be considered individually. Cocteau also counted on Yvonne de Bray, Elvire Popesco, Edwige Feuillère. The female role (mother, sister, queen) is just as important in Cocteau's plays as the leading male role, except perhaps for Eurydice in *Orphée,* who is a bit pale and simple-minded.[9] Because of a kind of allegorical redistribution of qualities that somehow evoke Tennessee Williams and, in certain cases, Jean Genêt, Cocteau's hero can only be truly understood as part of the couple, young man-older woman. The poet-martyr's identification with his persecuted or rebel hero is obvious, but so is his identification with the feminine mask. *"I* am Yvonne," Coc-

8. See *Théâtre de France,* No. 2 (season 1951–52), Paris, Les Publications de France, 1952.

9. In the film *Orphée* Death was the strong feminine mask, fundamental to all of Cocteau's drama.

teau might have said, paraphrasing Flaubert's "*I* am Madame Bovary." All more or less Jocastas, Cocteau's women are at once incarnations of the poet's feelings with regard to the young hero, and women-obstacles, now an outer obstacle (mother, wife, lover), now an inner one ("le Fantôme de Marseille" in *Théâtre de Poche*).

The comparison with Tennessee Williams seems even more evident when we consider that Cocteau chose to adapt *A Street-car Named Desire* for the French stage, and that Tennessee Williams attempted an adaptation of the Orpheus myth in *Orpheus Descending*. Obviously the heavy sexual atmosphere of Williams' works is foreign to Cocteau's, or at least considerably relieved in the major plays. Yet the general pattern—the duos, even the trios—are analogous. The unity of the couples reveals that they are but two faces of one basic individual—an eagle with two heads or with two sexes, as it were. In minor works such as *le Fantôme de Marseille,* the hero remains undivided by also playing the part of a female impersonator. In fact the hero in Cocteau's dramas and certain of Tennessee Williams' plays is not one character but a couple, a divided hermaphrodite who tries to possess himself—an often impossible desire, and always tormenting.

The idea of the hermaphrodite can be seen in the complicity of intimacy so characteristic of Cocteau's atmosphere: the complicity of Yvonne and Mik, of Jocasta and Oedipus, of Maxime and Margot, of Maxime and Solange, of the Queen and Stanislas, of Hans and Christine, of Guinevere and Lancelot, parallel to that of King Arthur and the false Gawain. In Cocteau's theatre there are always at least two who are marked out—marked out for poetry, grandeur, disorder, or love. Even the fairies or the Sphinx want somehow to absorb the young hero, who is as beautiful as an angel, or rather, in Swedenborgian terms, as half an angel.

Cocteau does everything he can to set up obstacles between the two poles of the divided hermaphrodite, making the union either criminal or impossible. In *l'Aigle à deux têtes* and *Bacchus* the distance is established in the form of social or political incompatibility in a given civilization. In *les Parents terribles* and *la Machine infernale* it consists in a difference in ages, but mostly in a mother-son relationship, making any attempt at union monstrous incest. When one of the poles is part of the supernatural (Renaud and the fairy, Armide; Orpheus and Death, particularly in the film), there is what might be called a metaphysical incompatibility. Might not the hermaphrodite be a metaphor of the "difficulty of being" in a universe where the traps of nature are mixed in with social taboos? The key to the agony is given in a short scene, generally cut, of the film *le Sang d'un poète,* in which the hermaphrodite uncovers the lower part of his body and discovers a sign reading: "Danger of Death."

That monstrous touch of fate serves as an archetype for the metaphors of danger and universal fatality which constitute the unchanging hidden drama in Cocteau's works. Each story consists in the search for union, realization, equilibrium, right up until the last scene, when an unexpected meaning breaks through in the form of catastrophe, a price to pay, a fatal incompatibility. The rest is surface effect. By means of a kind of baroque or rococo disproportion, the surface effects conceal the drama's underlying structure and are in fact taken for it—an obtrusive "parade," intentionally created by Cocteau who, through the diversity and exuberance of his talents, wanted both to disclose *and* to mask the danger in order to give the true equivalent of man's condition.

In *les Chevaliers de la Table Ronde* the demon Jinnifer is never seen. He can be perceived only by his "signature" (a certain vulgarity of language and humor) and by his fundamental malevolence. Between the two stretches the whole domain of physical appearance, situation, and parts to be played. The same is true for Cocteau's plays themselves, in which the most superficial and the most profound are the only constants. Danger, like Jinnifer, plays the most diverse parts. In the same way that the Knights feel uneasy before the false Gawain and the false Queen, so the spectator is disturbed and apprehensive before Cocteau's apparent dramas. Metaphors of destiny's traps, his plays themselves are traps. The spectator should be seized with the same mistrust before them as Cocteau is before life.

Mistrust is characteristic of Cocteau's sensibility [10] and creates a primitive and somehow pre-tragic terror in his works. He never intellectualizes his fear but preserves it in its integrity, in its extreme discomfort. Theatre is one of man's maneuvers to appease a threatening Nature or super-Nature—an illusory maneuver, since despite all the embellishments and digressions, the universe can only be portrayed as implacable. Whereas Giraudoux resolved the problem of tragedy through intelligence, Cocteau, completely involved in a world for which the time of brilliant solutions is past or yet to come, does the dance of a man who is condemned to death, with no appeal possible. His masquerade is a staggering metaphor of the hesitation of a consciousness before its condemnation. Man can be seen innocently claiming freedom or the realization of values, desperately clinging to those desires, plunged in a defeat which is masked by a voluntary illusion. In a parallel way, the playwright himself plays an analogous double game. He puts all his effort into raising the exalting or blinding illusion to the rank of reality while preserving enough illusionism to keep the reality from ever being reached.

Success—a synthesis of the hermaphrodite, the triumph of poets or lovers, the realization of a total and happy equilibrium, excluding all hazards or perils—is not of this world. It is in a beyond where Orpheus and Eurydice, Guinevere and Lance-

10. Even recently, in the weekly French paper *Arts* of November 19-25, 1958, Cocteau wrote: "Ink has become dangerous in a period when the slightest sign might well be badly taken. That is why I am taking refuge . . . in a manual craft [pottery] which demands nothing more than a piece of work well done."

lot, Patrice and Nathalie (the Tristan and Isolde of the film *l'Eternel retour*) are reunited. The price for union is death. And even then, an entire staircase separates the dead bodies of Stanislas and the Queen, Yvonne dies without Mik, Maxime abandons Solange. In this world everything must be paid for and the deal is transacted above man and without his consent. Galahad is condemned always to leave what he loves in order to keep the purity that makes it possible for him to chase out Merlin.

A grim and anguished theatre, full of surface glitter that is no more than an illusion of esthetic satisfaction, Cocteau's plays are outwardly like entertainments of the twenties and thirties. He has used all the devices of the entertainment, from avant-garde forms to the Boulevard, in order to express the meeting between the illusionism of that time and the personal and sincere perception of a basic dimension of man's condition. Cocteau searched the present and a recent past for all the masks imaginable. Clowns, Music Hall stars, the favorite actors of the bourgeoisie and other classes are all buffoons in a masquerade addressed as much to the Prince de Beaumont as to the masses who attended vaudeville theatres during the time of the Popular Front. What gives Cocteau's theatre its value is its cry of warning addressed, whatever may be said, to all men.

Added to that is his fidelity to an uncompromising idea of theatre. He is a modernist not only when he concretizes psychological or metaphysical phenomena on stage, with the freedom of today's poets, but also in his "Boulevard" plays. Even *la Machine à écrire,* generally considered his worst play and one that he himself repudiated, is infinitely superior to plays of the same genre in that, while continuing to play the Boulevard game to the very end, Cocteau goes beyond the document on life in the provinces and succeeds, through dialogue and action, to actualize a theme of pure theatre: that of illusion, as both mask and instrument of the inexorable destructibility of man.

Cocteau has a love of the theatre which is evident from his

general declarations, but which can also be found in the conception of his plays themselves. A metaphor of illusion, theatre should be presented with all the signs of illusion. At certain moments, the reality of what unfolds on stage must be forgotten so that the spectator may once again become conscious of the actor's number. The acting of Jean Marais, formed by Dullin but mostly by Cocteau, does not ring true because it should not ring true, for he must constantly maintain that distance which is the very definition of theatre and makes it possible for the spectator to believe and not believe at the same time. The same can be said for the stage sets (often designed by Christian Bérard) and the texts themselves. In *les Parents terribles* the characters constantly remind us that they are acting out a play—vaudeville, drama, or tragedy, depending on the moment and situation. Allusions to dreams and magic, now represented by living beings or objects, now evoked by metaphors of language, should also be interpreted in the sense of a diversion from the real. What happens on stage is never absolutely true, despite appearances. Each play is presented as a trance or comedy, throwing man into a story that is fictional or dreamed up by some god.

A Protean theatre, it is the faithful image of a Protean universe. The number of forms that the traps of the universe can take is infinite; so are the forms taken by man's illusory defenses. The meaning of reality is finally lost in the game of lies and counter lies. Through an intransigence recalling the Baudelairian dandy, Cocteau, as the only possible affirmation of his identity, succeeded in immobilizing two elements of the confusion: theatre and the emotion of fear. His double game is tragic even though individually, his plays are not. It is a recognition, a voluntary act. For Cocteau, writing a play is taking man's part—but he takes it in all lucidity, for by resorting to devices and descriptive illusion, he affirms that he defends a lost cause.

CHAPTER 3

THE UNIVERSE AS PARABLE:
PAUL CLAUDEL

Paul Claudel's dramatic works are certainly the most ambitious of all French theatre. As an attempt to take in time and space, they can be compared only to one other gigantic work, Victor Hugo's non-dramatic *la Légende des siècles*. Both poets wanted to synthesize man's past and bring out its meaning. But whereas Hugo, the Romantic, tried to respect historical time and crowned his vision with humanitarian dreams, Claudel cast over our history the eye of an eternal God, capable of telescoping time, and having grasped the globe as a unit, he set up the Cross. This epic work is an accounting of the world and its history, with history being explained in terms of destiny. The supernatural is not localized; it informs the whole. A meaning is not revealed through time; it is given in advance. The one great symbol of all symbols is that of the Christian Cross.

We are very far indeed from the magic of *les Chevaliers de la Table Ronde,* the room in *les Parents terribles,* the columns of *Electre,* even the sky of *Sodome et Gomorrhe*. The plays of Cocteau or Giraudoux are sufficient unto themselves. Claudel's theatre is not. It takes on its complete meaning only when integrated into an infinitely vaster drama, that of the Christian universe. In some ways, Claudel's works are made up of fragments of *the* Drama par excellence and in that respect are forever incomplete.

In his preface to Paul Claudel's *Théâtre* Jacques Madaule shows how the place of Claudel's works, in relation to a dying civilization in the first half of the twentieth century, is similar to that of the works of Homer, Virgil, and Dante, in relation to their own times. Claudel is the poet who sings of a world in which a cycle of history has come to an end. *Le Soulier de satin* and the trilogy of the Turelure-Coûfontaines: *l'Otage, le Pain dur, le Père humilié,* mark Europe's material and spiritual supremacy over the world. The twentieth century marks the beginning of another conjunction of forces, another civilization. The order of the world under the Cross at the end of the nineteenth century is comparable to the order of Dante. It has its Paradise, its Purgatory, its Hell. Everything is clearly in its respective place: popes, kings, antichrists, sacrifice, lust, politics, materialism. Claudel was the poet of the end of a world. Born at the height of Europe's power, a witness to the upheavals at the beginning of the twentieth century, conscious of European grandeur as well as its vices, he tried, as it were, to evaluate that enormous fragment of history. On the threshold of a new world, he stopped to sing and devoted himself to meditations on the Bible. His dramatic works as a whole are an answer to Valéry's well-known formula: "We civilizations know now that we are mortal." Claudel became the Bossuet of one of those civilizations. He eloquently stylized its most significant moments, and gave them eternal meaning guaranteed by the Catholic God, that is: a civilization is planned by God, its realization on earth is transitory, but through its figurative value, it participates in eternity.

From the very beginning, from the minute the curtain goes up on a Claudel play, the poet's dogmatic and uncompromising position must be accepted, for to the merest detail it dominates his vision of man and history. Claudel was a Roman Catholic, and a fervent one ever since his profound mystical upheaval in 1886. Doubtless Giraudoux's essentialism and Cocteau's contrived universe must also be accepted. But their works were not meant to illustrate their "philosophies," which merely provided the drama's inner structure. In Claudel, anecdote and drama are deliberate illustrations of a doctrine. His works are didactic—not demonstrations, but pure and simple affirmations, for faith does not allow of discussion. Every one of Claudel's plays is a parable meant to illustrate concretely a lesson given in advance.

To be sure, his works would necessarily have two publics. A Catholic and non-Catholic audience would see the plays in different ways. For the first, the plays' explanation of the world is the only true explanation; for the second, it is the metaphor of a possible explanation. For the first, the analogies are *real;* for the second, they are concrete content given to the general feeling for analogism or to the mind's and heart's need to discover an illusion of intelligibility in the universe. There is no doubt that at a Claudel play, a wholly and deeply Catholic audience would actualize the dream of today's playwrights: a union of theatre and religion comparable to that of Aeschylus' time—the drama expressing the destiny of a collectivity in terms of the belief that is the very flesh of that collectivity. But our epoch is characterized by a dispersal of beliefs. Claudel's audience—that of the Théâtre de l'Oeuvre, the Comédie Française, the Théâtre Marigny, or the Théâtre de France—is necessarily mixed. To certain spectators, Claudel's drama presents truth itself, embellished by poetry; to others, and in the same way as any poetic theatre, it is a very beautiful metaphorical hypothesis. For some, it is history clarified; for others, a fantasy. Through intention and didacticism, Claudel's drama divides the spectators into believers and esthetes.

Yet his theatre exists beyond its intentions. Many of Claudel's admirers are non-Catholics. Their appreciation is somewhat like Renan's of the life of Jesus. Christianity, through its dialectic of salvation, is essentially dramatic. Beyond the doctrine itself, the drama may be considered as one of the best Western metaphors of man's condition and Claudel's theatre brings it to light.

The whole of Claudel's work has a structure which makes it into a kind of "Divine Comedy," with the principal plays grouped almost chronologically into three cycles.

The first is "l'Arbre" or "The Tree," a collection of the first or second versions of his first plays, written between 1894 and 1898 and including *Tête d'or, la Ville, la Jeune Fille Violaine, l'Echange,* and *le Repos du septième jour.* Related to that cycle are *Partage de midi,* 1905, and *l'Annonce faite à Marie,* 1910, the last version of *la Jeune Fille Violaine.* A trilogy follows: *l'Otage,* 1909, *le Pain dur,* 1914, and *le Père humilié,* 1916. The last cycle consists in *le Soulier de satin,* completed in 1924. The title, "The Tree," would actually be suitable for Claudel's works as a whole, for the group of plays just mentioned might be considered as the trunk to which numerous branches are attached. For example, a dramatized narrative like *le Livre de Christophe Colomb,* 1927, belongs to the cycle of *le Soulier de satin,* but constitutes, along with *Jeanne au bûcher,* 1935, a lyrical and allegorical meditation on an exemplary destiny, just as *l'Histoire de Tobie et de Sara,* 1942, is on a book of the Bible. In the same way, the earthy comic vein which comes through in most of the plays, particularly in *le Soulier de satin,* is exploited for itself in the farces *Protée,* 1926, and *l'Ours et la lune,* 1917.

In Claudel's evolution as a playwright, the dominant movement is that of an increasingly clear and specific incarnation of the Idea in a given moment of history. The use of history is inherent to the Christian doctrine, which is based on events and dogmas expressed through a chronicle. Every moment of the chronicle is eternal as well. In his plays, Claudel wanted not only to bring out a universal Meaning and show how that Meaning is embodied in possible anecdotes, but to incorporate it in the actual past of the collectivity to which it belongs.

The first part of Claudel's works, "The Tree" and connected plays, establishes the basic themes, occasionally linking them to a moment in history, but mostly treating them for them-

selves: the themes of conquest and pride (*Tête d'or*), government and faith (*la Ville, le Repos du septième jour*), Grace
through evil in the adventure of the couple (*l'Echange, Partage
de midi*), sacrifice and miracle (*la Jeune Fille Violaine*).

In such plays, his characters are one with a universal inner
category and practically admit, themselves, that they are symbols. Thus Claudel avoided the particularizing so dear to naturalistic and realistic theatre, but sometimes at the price of an
absence of life never quite filled by either picturesque settings
or the concrete vigour of certain images. This is especially
flagrant in *la Ville,* in which the great scenes harden into
stylized debates between Poetry, Disbelief, Femininity, etc.—
abstractions that are hardly concealed by the characters' names
and masks. By means of true allegorization, the poet tried to
escape from his subjectivity by translating his inner conflict into
the most general terms, objectifying it through the great commonplaces of the intellectual crisis at the end of the nineteenth
century.

Even in *Partage de midi* the metaphorical ballet danced by
De Ciz, Mesa, and Amalric around the Woman, Ysé, stems
from that method. In *l'Annonce faite à Marie* as well, the two
couples, Pierre/Jacques and Violaine/Mara, dominated by the
figure of Anne Vercors, all settled down in the shadow of
Monsanvierge, give the anecdote the value of an allegory, in
which each character coincides with a vocation, the vocations
obviously arranged by the poet in order to illustrate a truth
given in advance.

Yet the two plays transcend hyperbolic allegories like *la Ville*.
By referring to history, they avoid abstraction. There Claudel
recognized Christianity's historicity, the fact that every epoch
has its specific forms of incarnation. The miracle of a child's
resurrection, reproducing the birth of Jesus on Christmas night
(*l'Annonce faite à Marie*) is situated precisely at a time when
that miracle would be acceptable, the Middle Ages, whereas
the first version of the same theme took place at a rather vague

moment somewhere between the Renaissance and today. In the same way, the modern circumstances in *Partage de midi* give life to the drama of the couple, torn between the spirit and the flesh.

With the Turelure-Coûfontaine trilogy, Claudel used actual historical events as the subject of his plays. The great themes are not merely stated but embodied in a given moment of history: the fifty-odd years between Pope Pius VII's abduction to Fontainebleau (1813) and the unification of Italy (1860–71). The vicissitudes of the Papacy and the Church dominate the plays, and Napoleon's fall, Louis XVIII's return, the colonization of Algeria, the division of Poland, the Italian War, and general social upheaval are all determining events and dependant for their ultimate meanings on the fate of the Church. The protagonists are not only participants but truly makers of history.

In these dramas, Claudel has almost completely refused to indulge in the usual tricks of the historical genre. At no time did he ever claim to present a faithful reconstruction of events. The characters who play with the fate of the world, aside from the popes and kings, are imaginary beings with fanciful names. Between 1815 and 1870, everything happened *as if* a family called Turelure-Coûfontaine had played a determining role. True, the Baron Toussaint Turelure was probably patterned after Joseph Fouché. But Turelure is a poetic creation based on certain of Fouché's fundamental characteristics, developed or simplified. Turelure is the ideal agent of a particular policy that had been imperfectly embodied in figures of the Revolution and Empire such as Fouché. Claudel deals with early nineteenth-century history in the same way as the writer of *la Chanson de Roland* dealt with an episode of the war of Charlemagne.

The trilogy thus represents an attempt to give the French stage a "historical tragedy." The meaning of the events is the reality; the events themselves, only a sign. And the meaning

justifies all the distortions of so-called historical truth.[1] Since
the meaning here is the Catholic Mystery, the tragedy would
be more comparable to Spanish drama than to Aeschylus or
Shakespeare.

By actually using the Spanish drama as a source of inspiration, Claudel reached the high point in his art with *le Soulier
de satin*. There, he used the method with infinitely more
breadth and audacity, and with greater success as well. As the
period was remote, Claudel was able to modify historical facts
more freely, telescope the centuries, "manipulate them like an
accordion, at will." And where the events of the trilogy remain
limited in space (Europe), *le Soulier de satin* is made up of a
whole network of actions which envelope the entire earth.
"The stage of this drama is the world," wrote Claudel in one
of his first stage directions. The movement of his theatre has
been not only to make the flesh of history and the spirit
coincide, but also to exhaust the meanings of the word "universal": philosophical and physical, under the aegis of the
mystical meaning, Catholic.

The idea was to grasp the moment at which that total experience existed, both on a religious and a physical plane. At only
one period in history was it possible, the period during which
Catholicism winning the battle of the Counter-Reformation
and the achievement of great discoveries coincide. No doubt
nineteenth- and twentieth-century man possesses the world in
a more complete way—but, in the eyes of the Catholic poet,
that world is not as satisfying as the world of the Baroque age.
Protestant sects are established in Germany, England, and

---

1. "The playwright's art, like the painter's, has its freedoms," affirms
Claudel in his introductory note to *l'Histoire de Tobie et de Sara*. He
explains how he used those "freedoms" when he adapted the deutero-
canonical *Book of Tobias*. He eliminated characters and added others,
once he had extracted the deep meaning of the story, with the help of
a quotation from Saint Matthew, and had acknowledged Sarah as
representative of the human soul. He applied the same method to
actual history.

America; rationalism has corrupted and split most societies, in fact ours is a completely divided globe. That of the Counter-Reformation was also, but the struggle was going in the direction of unification, the great Empires were Catholic, the Cross was advancing and pushing back the frontiers of Hell (the Protestant world) and Purgatory (the Far East). Claudel chose the period because at that time every human gesture was defined in relation to Roman Catholicism. The whole surface of the globe was either fighting Rome or working for Rome's triumph. It is probable that, except for Dante writing *The Divine Comedy,* no poet has ever had as much the feeling of writing a total work as Claudel during the composition of *le Soulier de satin.* Every quiver of the characters' flesh is directly and obviously bound to the eternal truths of the Church. And since it concerns the entire world and all the men of that world, of whom we are descendants, Claudel's drama shows, as it were, that all of us, no matter whom, all twentieth-century theatre-goers, are bound through our common past to that Church. Even if we are its enemies, we are defined in relation to it, and not it in relation to us. Thus *le Soulier de satin* has the scope of a universal epic.

An epic becomes drama when the accent is put not only on the greatness of the exploits but on the inner and outer conflicts of the heroes as well. Every nuance of the hero's most personal inner life is indissolubly linked to a tremor of the entire universe. Suggested in the somewhat overwhelming allegory of *Tête d'or* and developed in *l'Otage,* such interaction was fully exploited by Claudel in *le Soulier de satin.* The tormented adventure of Rodrigue and Dona Prouhèze is in itself a great drama of love and faith, but in addition, the fate of our whole universe depends on its every pulsation. Obviously the relation is not a naïve one of cause and effect, as in the historical plays of Scribe or Sardou. It is one of reciprocity in the play of symbols which make up the skeleton of the visible universe.

That universe itself is dramatic because of the epic simplification which brings out great fundamental conflicts and tensions, such as the distribution of Good and Evil, True and False. Contrasting with a profusion of concrete, colorful, and vivid details are clear and distinct divisions among the great principles and great values. Indeed, Claudel's universe is one in which no doubts are allowed.

His theatre on the whole consists of a simple drama: a conflict between shadow and light enriched by the Christian dialectic. But it is finally that dialectic which brings in all the complexity of human destiny. For while Claudel's drama is built upon the clarity of a basic universal conflict, it is also built upon the complications of the roads to follow within the conflict. There is no doubt as to values or mysteries; but in the course of what leads to the revelation of those values, there is painful hesitation and a complex struggle. And while there is no doubt as to the duty to please God, there is a problem of choice as to the way to please Him most. Such is the subject of *Partage de midi, l'Otage,* and *le Soulier de satin.* Suffering springs from the fact that in order to do one's best, one has often to do the worst. And doing the worst, the heroism of acceptance, and the victory that consists in *wanting* to do what one does reluctantly all constitute sacrifice. In fact Claudel's drama often appears as a long sacrificial rite.

After the fiftieth performance of *le Soulier de satin,* Claudel wrote: "Sacrifice . . . somehow provokes the Divine part. By willingly withdrawing, we make room for an action, stimulated as it were, of Grace, we are playing on the side of the All Powerful for an enormous profit." [2] This is actually a kind of Pascalian wager, but the wager is terribly complex. Violaine's

2. *Le Soulier de satin,* Club du Meilleur Livre, Paris, 1953. Appendix, page 20.

way, as well as that of Ysé and Mesa, Sygne, Dona Prouhèze
and Rodrigue, is made up of detours. Of course the face of
evil is always recognizable: it is Mara, Amalric, Turelure, or
Don Camille. But that evil is necessary. There is no purity
without impurity, no Paradise without Hell, no salvation without sin or apparent sin, which would mean that Claudel's
works are authentically Christian in emphasizing the corruption of Creation after Adam's fall. But the detours imposed by
sacrifice are often what would seem like a passage through Hell
—a passage that has little to do with traditional ethics. For
example, Sygne de Coûfontaine's way of salvation lay through
betrayal; Mesa's and Ysé's, through betrayal *and* their indirect
murder of De Ciz. Claudel's Christian dialectic requires that
strong souls be humiliated by means of the most profound
abasement.

Sacrifice is more especially complicated as it involves one individual who sacrifices not only himself but others, and requires a choice, complicated by the fact that the terms are
masked:

> This notion of sacrifice is tightly bound to the great Chris-
> tian idea of the *Communion of Saints,* in which it would
> be naïve to imagine the inoffensive workings of a benevo-
> lent society. Religion's commandment: 'Love one another!'
> has more of a relation to nature's commandment: 'Eat one
> another' than one would think.[3]

The conditions for the salvation of a soul are cruel when looked
upon from this world. And many critics have not failed to
become indignant.[4] But there is no doubt that such cruelty

3. *Ibid.*

4. Joseph Chiari (*The Poetic Drama of Paul Claudel*) protests against
the cruelty that Claudel attributes to God and refuses to believe that His
designs were that distorted or that merciless. In fact, Claudel's God is
hardly more unrelenting than the Greek Nemesis.

saves Claudel's Christian theatre from sentimentality and the easy good conscience of certain optimistic sects.[5]

In *Strait is the Gate* André Gide drew a moving and ironic portrait of a Calvinist sacrifice. Claudel demands much the same sort of sacrifice from his heroes. But in Claudel not only is the gate strait but several pass through at the same time— and without irony:

> There is deep mystery and an infinite source of tragedy in the fact that we are the condition of eternal salvation one for the other, that we alone carry within ourselves the key to the soul of such and such of our brothers, who can be saved only by us, and at our own expense.[6]

Claudel's dramas are built upon the idea that souls are destined one for the other or elect one another. To that extent, not only is the sacrifice of oneself necessary, but that of certain others. Ysé has the key to Mesa's soul, and Mesa, the key to Ysé's, and the union of those two souls is well worth the sacrifice of others. The union cannot be immediate; for were it, it would be only a trap. It is, on the contrary, in the refusal of that union on earth, in the trial of separation, and through that trial, that the souls destined one for the other will be led to exemplary acts which will save worlds (*l'Otage, le Père humilié, le Soulier de satin*) and save themselves at the same time. Providence, now through outer obstacles, now through the action of the characters themselves, provokes and reinforces the separation. Ysé is already married; she goes with Mesa, but leaves him for Amalric so that they may be more powerfully reunited at the moment of death. Dona Prouhèze is already married, but when she is finally free to marry Rodrigue, the letter she sends him goes astray between the con-

5. See Henri Peyre, "The Drama of Paul Claudel."
6. See above, note 2.

tinents. And in *le Soulier de satin* the problem is further complicated by the fact that two men need Dona Prouhèze: Don Rodrigue and Don Camille:

> Whence the importance of Don Camille's role. He needs Prouhèze more than Rodrigue does. He needs something in Prouhèze that is beyond Rodrigue's desire. A Prouhèze detached from any human attachment, preferring nothing to the eye of God, whatever it may be, the pure star in the ray of her Creator! It is that Prouhèze, that Prouhèze alone who is the condition of his salvation. . . .[7]

In these more or less complicated adventures, based on reversals of attitude or often surprising situations, but all connected to a rather simple basic model, there is quite obviously a lesson. Claudel wanted to bring out the ambiguity of certain vocations, the nature of perfect love which lies in God and not in the flesh, and God's hidden benevolence, masked by a cruel and unjust destiny, which makes it possible for souls to unite in perfection or quite simply be saved. It would be a mistake to see any Jansenism in that severity and absurdity. For Claudel vigorously repudiates the Jansenist notion of predestination as well as the affirmation that only very few will be saved. Yet not only does he reject all complacency and would, "like Mauriac, rather assert that Christianity enters into souls in order to divide them,"[8] he emphasizes the absolute individuality of destinies and vocations. While it is true that Grace is possible for all men, there is no question that certain men—and they alone—are marked out for the highest and most agonizing adventures. And it is they who become dramatic heroes.

The adventures of Dona Prouhèze, Rodrigue, and Don Camille can be lived only by them. Every anecdote is individual, that is, unique and possible only with such or such

7. *Ibid.*
8. Henri Peyre, *op. cit.*

protagonists and no others. There is no anecdote that is universal in itself; souls are not interchangeable. When Claudel writes that "we alone carry within ourselves the key to the soul of such and such of our brothers," he implies "and no other." In Claudel's theatre, each one answers "with a particular name, his own! *Adsum!*" thus making Claudel's religion a source of drama—first because it uses Christianity's notions of agony, renunciation, inner conflict, and "Providence's circuitous ways," but also because it emphasizes the singleness of destinies and considers the characters as irreplaceable. In a universe where the poles of Good and Evil are already defined in all orthodoxy, each man, torn between the attractions of one and the other, lives his inimitable destiny, dated historically but representative of an eternal truth. An epic theatre in its choice of extraordinary characters—extraordinary in their political positions or richness of adventures, in the dimensions of the space they occupy and the transformations they bring to the world—Claudel's works are also, and perhaps especially, a theatre of the individual.

As the individual is never alone, his vocation being to open the soul of another, to sacrifice himself for one or several others, the drama is always the double one of love and action. The adventure is lived by strong, passionate beings who act and are acted upon at the same moment, in the same gesture. Christianity's paradox, a source of heresies and schisms, is the conflict between freedom and predestination. In Claudel freedom is manifest and arrogant, even sometimes very Corneillian in tone. The characters are always free to damn themselves. By giving her satin slipper to the Virgin, Dona Prouhèze partially gives up her freedom: "But when I try to rush toward evil, may it be with a lame foot!" Man is free to miss his vocation. Sygne de Coûfontaine was perhaps meant to save Pope Pius VII by marrying Turelure, but as the Priest Badilon told her: "You alone must do it of your own will."

Yet the conflict in Claudel is less that between what in man is free and what predestined than the struggle between all in man "which miserably clings to things, one by one and successively" and "what is most essential, God's image." It is the continually reaffirmed difficulty of that choice which, beyond any dogmatism or controversial judgement, has provided Claudel with a lay public, in its creation of a lyrical pathos close to that of Greek tragedy. A theatre neither of doubt nor of anguish, but of a rather Corneillian agony and effort, Claudel's works, by rejecting the complacency of easy devotion and with the help of Catholicism's enormous and magnificent arsenal, presents an image of individual man whose paradox is to be implacably himself and at the same time always something other than what he is.

A public that might be put off by a systematic asceticism finds that Claudel, in his passage from the world to the supernatural, does not exclude the world but rather embraces it. The carnal universe is the place of action, the theatre of the struggle for salvation. Although Claudel's judgement on anything that is not Catholic would sometimes seem injurious, he does not dismiss those "enemies" or "successive things." They are always present, transfigured but preserved in a kind of baroque integration, somehow "saved" by the symbol they carry within themselves. There is nothing monastic about Claudel's renunciation. Amalric's sensuality is necessary to Ysé's and Mesa's adventure, just as noise and confusion, colored plumes, the Chinese, and the great farcical masks of the Spanish Empire are to Rodrigue's. Don Rodrigue is perhaps humiliated, mutilated, and stripped bare at the end of *le Soulier de satin,* but the play itself is not. The poet takes an obvious pleasure—and often a pagan one—in playing with such material. That vigorous part of his temperament may have drawn him toward Hell, but it put rich blood and gluttonous life into the carnal world of his theatre.

The conflict between Christian renunciation and richness of spectacle would seem to provide excellent theatrical material.

And yet Claudel's plays have been slow to conquer the general public or even be performed.

To the reader, a Claudel play often seems devoid of any consideration as to the conditions and possibilities of performance. Claudel refused to bow to the usual restrictions of the stage. Or at least he never facilitated the director's task. Moreover, in writing a work of the length and spectacular complexity of *le Soulier de satin*, he was little concerned with the physical resistance of actors and spectators alike. Claudel wrote for the stage, but for a stage that had not yet been constructed.

Today most of Claudel's dramas have been performed; the texts are no longer considered "unperformable." For the notion of what theatre is has been considerably enlarged since 1890 because of the anti-naturalist reaction, on the one hand, and because of the discovery and partial assimilation of conceptions far from those of Western theatre since the seventeenth century: Greek staging, medieval staging, Balinese, Chinese, and Japanese plays and staging. Claudel, performed very early in his career in avant-garde theatres, has gradually conquered an increasingly large public and has finally made the Comédie Française and commercial theatres. There is no doubt that his success since the 1940s has been due in part to a war-time and post-war religious revival, but mostly it is due to the theatre's progressive acceptance of texts that had long been considered unperformable.

The great test was the Comédie Française's production of *le Soulier de satin* in 1943. In this instance the meeting of Claudel and Barrault was decisive. Claudel's most scenically difficult play was performed after a few changes and with enormous success. Then the Comédie Française and Louis Jouvet did new stagings of *l'Annonce faite à Marie*. Barrault brought back *l'Echange* and introduced *Partage de midi, le Livre de Christophe Colomb,* and most recently, *Tête d'or*. The Paris Opera put on *Jeanne au bûcher*. And the T.N.P. produced *la Ville*, while one of the little theatres staged *Protée*.

Claudel, at first avant-garde or reserved for a chosen few, has become an eminently successful playwright.

Barrault was enthusiastic about Claudel's works largely because the idea of "total theatre," found in Antonin Artaud and in the theories of Barrault himself, is illustrated or embodied in plays like *le Soulier de satin* and *Christophe Colomb*. Claudel is "unperformable" according to nineteenth-century standards because his works absorb, with little discrimination or practical sense, all the possible enlargements of our conception of theatre. His experiments with ballet and pantomime (in *l'Homme et son désir* and *la Femme et son ombre*), his partial although real knowledge of the arts of the Far East, his translation of Aeschylus' *Oresteia* all enabled him to escape from a limited conception of theatre. His use of music, puppets, and cinema completes the list of his devices. Through disrespect for the theatre, Claudel appears today as one of its most authentic liberators.

To take only one example, Claudel's use of the film screen is particularly effective. It serves not only to juxtapose two actions that are distant in space—something which has often been done in social problem or detective story plays—but to actualize the symbol. In *Christophe Colomb,* as in *l'Histoire de Tobie et de Sara,* the symbol appears as both real and endowed with another nature—the two-dimensional nature of the motion picture image. The spectator is provided with the multiple sight of God. While the stage is the world, the screen reveals the deep meanings through close-ups. Thus in *Christophe Colomb* the sailor's death in Columbus' arms is, *at the same moment,* seen in its entirety—with the movement of bodies and the surrounding space, and in its intimacy—in the enlarged detail of the protagonists' expressions. In that way, both dimensions of the event are portrayed. Every death, every act is private and can be revealed only at close range (a view never before provided by the theatre) and in an intimacy which contains the true adventure of souls. At the same time, in the context of the action, that act involves a universe of gestures, a world of adventures and of boats plowing through space. The cinema has been used in the theatre in the opposite way: real actors act out the private drama, while the screen enlarges the spatial world and presents the mob scenes, without ever portraying the same character in the same action at the same time. It was Claudel and Jean-Louis Barrault who understood that the space suggested by the stage itself is the universe, and the feeling of intimacy or divine indiscretion is provoked by the motion picture close-up.

This is but one example of the "totality" of Claudel's drama, a totality as much on the scenic level as on an ideological level. Music, ballet, and pantomime are used in the same spirit of theatrical imperialism, with theatre absorbing all the arts and uniting them in the actualization of a unique and exhaustive work, in the same way that the Catholic vision accounts for the entire universe.

The Claudel-Barrault collaboration, even more than the Giraudoux-Jouvet collaboration, is one of the major events of the modern French stage. To read or hear Barrault, one might think that Claudel played the part of the Father whose Word was embodied by the Son, Barrault. Here the *mystique* of theatre is merged with true mysticism. "Our souls became homothetic," wrote Barrault concerning his collaboration with Claudel. Barrault was not merely satisfied with staging the enormous first version of *le Soulier de satin*. He himself cut a certain amount and suggested many changes to Claudel. The agreement between poet and director arose from a common vision of life and theatre: the taste for a universe in its totality, that is, in the simultaneity and figurative relation of the visible and invisible; the sacred character conferred on two means of expression par excellence, the Word and the Gesture; the conviction that one and the other, while representing transcendency, spring from the body itself, from its rhythms and organic pulsations, so that a link is established between the creature (all flesh) and the Creator (pure Logos or pure Meaning). Claudel threw himself body and soul into Catholicism, and with an impetuousness and almost pagan vigor, corresponding to the passion and cult of Life that has carried Barrault along during his entire career. Claudel's "baroque" was exactly what was needed to charm the complex mixture of intense sensuality and spirituality characteristic of Barrault's art, and vice versa.

In theatre such as both Claudel and Barrault wanted, language—the Word—is lyrically expressed, according to a calculation of rhythms and intensities and even pitch, which is close to the operatic recitative.[9] It is a kind of sacred recitation (occasionally interrupted by coquetries, platitudes, or vulgarities) which keeps the drama, even ones that seem earthy like *le Pain dur,* constantly in the perspective of its ultimate meaning, the divine. One of the constant tensions of such theatre is therefore the unchanging relation between the body (whose pulsations are perceptible in gestures and language) and the supernatural—between the breath of man's lungs and the breath of the Creator. And the Gesture in this kind of dramatic liturgy is of major importance. It is indissolubly itself and the meaning it symbolizes, like the gestures of a priest during Mass. Claudel never hesitated before tableaux more allegorical than dramatic, if they were apt to strike the imagination by the clarity of a meaning suggested by the body's position: Coeuvre putting his foot on Lala who is stretched out at his feet (*la Ville*); Violaine kissing a leper (*l'Annonce faite à Marie*); crucifixions, crawling around on stage (*Tête d'or, le Soulier de satin*); and particularly, a symbolic use of the hands (Ysé's and Mesa's hands at the end of *Partage de midi,* the double shadow in *le Soulier de satin,* the hand of God in *Christophe Colomb*). Although Claudel was sometimes little concerned

9. The Comédie Française printed an edition of *le Soulier de satin* which indicates, in the actual typography, the values of every syllable in the text.

with the possibility of staging his suggested tableaux, he still demanded them throughout his works. During the staging of *le Soulier de satin,* he wanted Barrault to keep him informed as to the slightest details of the spectacle, he wanted to participate in their preparation, and he actually set up the staging of *The Oresteia* on paper. The whole visual aspect is essential in Claudel's works. Color and moving bodies represent the visible world which cannot be ignored since it is a vehicle for the invisible, the perceptible support of higher meanings. His theatre is not only a theatre of language and gesture, but also a theatre of spectacle—and, in the case of *le Soulier de satin,* what the French call "the great spectacle" (sumptuous costumes and décor, crowds, machines), which up to then would seem to have been reserved for the cinema and children's operettas at the Châtelet.

Finally, Claudel's theatre maintains the state of theatrical "double consciousness." Deliberately poetic and anti-naturalistic, it presents an imaginary universe which the poet asks us to accept both as a real universe and as a fabricated object, a man-made creation. The fantastic and even absurdly comical aspect of proper names in the most serious plays is already a signal. But in *Christophe Colomb* and especially in *le Soulier de satin* Claudel most obviously exploits the notion of dramatic *play:* what happens on stage is the product of human devices and should not be taken too seriously. No doubt "the poet," as Jacques Madaule points out, "takes God's point of view, and that is why he often feels like laughing at the most pathetic moment." But it is also because in a Christian perspective theatre is indeed presumptuous in trying to compete with Creation, and to avoid sacrilege it must be given an aspect of farce and be made to mock itself. It would seem here as if the Church's traditional distrust with regard to theatre led Claudel to avoid any Promethean pretensions in his art. Given his ambition for totality, the contrast produced is one of the strongest in French theatre, especially in *le Soulier de satin.*

The Universe as Parable

In that gigantic drama with "the stage as the world," the Announcer, in his rather heavy jesting and nonchalance with regard to the characters and the actors themselves, evokes a mixture of Pirandellian devices and fairground theatre. It consequently lowers the whole to the level of an improvised masquerade and so keeps alive the consciousness of its human fabrication, inseparable, in true theatre, from any deep participation in the unfolding drama. Everything happens as if Claudel's personal conflict between his temperament, tremendous pride, and Christian humility had been the source of that somehow supplementary but always necessary tension.

The combination of a drama and a scenic display that is both self-conscious and inseparable from the drama's symbolism is helped by the Christian doctrine of the immanence of Meaning in the Sign, the paradox of the presence-absence of God. It is difficult today to attend the performance of any attempt at a modernized Mystery-play without thinking that such an attempt had already been far more successfully carried out by Claudel. Claudel's theatre is an aggregate of devices, audacities, and truly functional discoveries—one of the rare moments in French theatre when innovation does not seem experimental.

Claudel borrowed the key of the world from Christianity, carved it, decorated it as a good craftsman would, and presented it to his public with the imperturbable certainty that it was the only key possible. The universe appears as a comedy that God puts on for Himself, with men for actors and endowed with just enough freedom to give the impression that they may ruin the spectacle.

But there is more. Claudel's epic drama and the actual history of humanity have, fundamentally, one point in common. They are both parables of the Drama of divine love, told to God and man, and repeated indefinitely. For the comedy is essentially a drama of love. God suffered and was crucified out of love for man who betrayed Him. The betrayal poisoned the reciprocal love of God and the first man, and only by the sacrifice of one and the other can that love, that union in love, be restored to its perfection. Thus earthly adventures are adventures of love, which always contain the moments, progressions, and reversals in the history of the relations between God and man. Each man is a unique person, just as Christ was a unique person; each individual sacrifices himself for another, just as Christ sacrificed himself for every man in particular—and in every hero's sacrifice, Christ's sacrifice is repeated.

In what, then, does this drama of love consist outside the Christian doctrine? It is first of all a metaphor for the dual feeling attached to the flesh—a source of ecstacy and dissatisfaction at the same time. It is also a metaphor for the feeling of transcendency: the world is transcended by its own meaning. It is the embodiment of a paradox—that of the feeling of immanence—for transcendency is within man. And finally, it is the idea that through the detours of love, through the very suffering that it inevitably leads to, through the dialectic of renunciation, the true essence of love and of self will be attained "at the same time and indissolubly."

PART II

BACK TO MAN

CHAPTER 4

THE AGONY OF SOLITARY SOULS: HENRY DE MONTHERLANT

In all the plays of Henry de Montherlant there are but two instances of scenic supernatural: the apparition of the Infanta's Shadow in the third act of *la Reine morte* and the death mask at the end of *Don Juan*. Otherwise we see and hear nothing other than men struggling at the level of man himself—no supernatural, no ghosts or demons or angels, no gods, no magic. Montherlant's poetry does not lie in the scenic embodiment of metaphors or of beings normally situated beyond our perception. Nor is his theatre a portrayal of the conflict between man and higher realities. Without affirming or denying the existence of such realities, it is the portrait of man's struggle with himself, caught between his own nature and values that he either finds in himself or thinks of in supernatural terms. In other words, Montherlant's works are a return to psychological theatre. Metaphysics is never dealt with in itself, but only to the extent that it is the object of a character's consciousness.

Montherlant is the first to use a psychological vocabulary with regard to his plays and his characters. Pride, esteem, hate, scorn, sadism, love, purity of heart are terms he uses constantly in his prefaces, postscripts, analyses, and answers to critics when he explains his characters' adventures and problems. He describes the Infanta of *la Reine morte* as "a neuropath like the King." In 1954, in the postscript to *la Ville dont le Prince est un enfant,* he wrote: "People speak to us of 'psychological theatre' as a certain form of theatre. For me there is only one form of theatre worthy of the name: psychological theatre." [1]

1. All references are to Montherlant's *Théâtre,* Bibliothèque de la Pléiade, Gallimard, Paris, 1954.

What interests Montherlant in *le Maître de Santiago* is not the hero's struggle or relationship with God. It is the inner mechanism of the psychological phenomenon of faith, its combination with intransigence, and the ambiguity of abnegation and pride. Whereas Claudel's *le Soulier de satin,* performed at the time Montherlant was writing *le Maître,* is a Catholic play, Montherlant's work is a play *about* Catholics. Claudel's play is similar to the Spanish *autos sacramentales;* the hero's supernatural destiny is objectively affirmed. Montherlant, who writes about the same period and the same atmosphere, at no time treats the supernatural as such. He describes an emotional and intellectual attitude to it.

Another of Montherlant's concerns, and one that he has reaffirmed several times—often to defend himself against the critics—is that of "the imitation of life." By that he means that no rule of composition, no preestablished principle of what a dramatic character must be should turn the playwright away from the faithful reproduction of psychological flux, its surprises, even its incoherence. "Unity of style? Never heard of it. There is no unity of style in life," he wrote concerning *Celles qu'on prend dans ses bras,* a play in modern dress, in which the Spanish-like tone is mixed with very Parisian vulgarities and occasional farce. As to the sudden turn-about-face of Georges in *Fils de personne:* "That instability *is* life," he said in 1943. For Montherlant, man is essentially a psychological mechanism whose workings do not follow a logical development. He can be described in terms of classical psychological categories (and not in those of what Montherlant calls "dime store psychoanalysis"); he is made up of contradictions; he surprises others and surprises himself. And the objective of theatre is to bring out those workings with the help of exemplary anecdotes.

Such psychologism and fidelity to life might have led to a more or less naturalistic anecdotal theatre, similar to Boulevard productions of the twenties and thirties. And the refusal to integrate the discoveries of modern psychology, obstinately holding to a general "intuition," might have turned what was meant to be a uniquely psychological theatre into a simple repetition of supposedly eternal themes which have in fact been long since reinterpreted and transcended. Even the French classical writers of the seventeenth century who were convinced that "everything has been said" treated man from a point of view quite new for their time and used categories that were developed by Descartes, the Jesuits, or the Jansenists. Indeed in a play like *Celles qu'on prend dans ses bras,* Montherlant, through fear of dime store psychology, fell into a type of psychology midway between *vaudeville* and Porto-Riche. Yet the greater part of his dramatic works transcends the application of his two principles, and the return to man that he represents does not mean a pure and simple return to a form of theatre which has had its day.

There is no doubt that Montherlant clearly refuses certain techniques of traditional realism, devices which go back to the eighteenth-century bourgeois reaction to classical language. He believes in the necessity of a theatre of language and, like Giraudoux, of well-written language, without the "spaced periods" so dear to Diderot and the naturalists. "People call a play that is well written 'cold.' What they want are a great many spaced periods," wrote Montherlant in his *Notes de théâtre.* In the same text he complains about actresses who feel the need to add "ah!"s and "oh!"s, "but"s and "well"s to their scripts. He rejects the pauses and interjections used to make the script seem true to life, for the truth and life he seeks cannot be situated at the level of a photographic or documentary copy of human behavior. Montherlant's notes and prefaces also show his concern with finding a good balance between conventional or impersonal acting and methodical "characterization." Certain actors "do too much," others not enough. In acting as in language, one well placed "ah" is effective, one detail of behavior is suggestive. A repetition of "real details" falls into verism and turns the attention away from the drama toward scenic realism.

In spite of such comments, Montherlant's interest in actual staging is rare and could hardly be compared to Cocteau's material love for the stage and its tricks, Claudel's theatrical imagination, or Giraudoux's true knowledge of actors and directors. He is far more interested in the literary quality of his plays than in the actual problems of theatre. And in fact he sometimes even prefers to ignore theatre:

> My taste [for theatre] has diminished even more since the war, as it were. I have not been to the theatre *once* by choice since 1919, although the duties of society (friends' openings) or someone's insistence have led me there four or five times. It is not disdain for the art, but seeing a play performed always gives me a weaker impression than the one I had reading it.

Such was his feeling in 1929 as expressed in the preface to *l'Exil.* In 1954, in the postscript to *la Ville dont le Prince est un enfant,* he concluded: "Whoever says theatre (performance) also says loss of time. I had already lost much time with *la Ville*—from the minute it stopped being only a *volume.* . . ." In his explanatory texts, Montherlant alternates from one state of mind to another—an alternation similar to that by which he explains certain of his characters—now devoting long pages to the work of an actor or the story of how one of his plays was produced, now claiming to disregard anything that is not the text itself.

His plays are ambiguous in the same way. There is no doubt that Montherlant writes for the stage, but there is also no doubt that the characters speak—well and a great deal—much more than they act. They stand opposite one another and pass the time describing and analyzing themselves or describing and analyzing each other. The *tirade,* frequent in Montherlant, is sometimes a logical discourse as in Corneille, sometimes a narrative as in Racine. But, where the *tirade* in Racine and Corneille is the source of action or transformation of character, in Montherlant it is essentially the analysis of an emotional state of indecision. The first two acts of *la Reine morte* constitute a prolonged state of expectation during which King Ferrante probes within himself. The end of the third is marked by a decisive act: Ferrante has Inès killed. Similarly all of *le Maître de Santiago* is the analysis of a state of refusal. Alvaro spends his time describing and justifying his attitude by giving a portrait of himself and of others. The final conversion of his daughter is the only "act" in the play. The same is true for *Fils de personne,* an analysis of a particular situation which lasts up until the final sacrifice.

Yet a Montherlant play does move. It is fundamentally the portrait of a soul, but a portrait relative to, and at the moment of, a crisis, a choice to be made. The most active of his plays in that respect is doubtless *la Ville dont le Prince est un enfant.* The Abbé de Pradts' decision to authorize Sevrais' and Sandrier's friendship is a serious act and sets off a whole train of action. The resulting scandal due to a misunderstanding, its shaking effects, the head of the school's decision, and his explanations at the end of the play represent a dialectic of situations which, without taking anything away from the psychological portrait, adds an outer dynamism that is missing from certain of his other plays. However those others are just as dramatic. Their treatment of one apparently static situation is frequently found in French literature, mostly in the novel (*Adolphe, Dominique,* certain of Gide's novels) but also in theatre (Racine's *Bérénice,* Sartre's *Huis Clos,* to take extreme examples).

In *la Reine morte*—the portrait of an old king whose political plans are undone by his son's secret marriage—and in *Fils de personne*—the portrait of a father disappointed by his son's mediocrity—the heroes, because of the misbehavior or shortcomings of others, are forced to examine their own consciences.

Nothing is resolved during most of the play despite a certain amount of secondary action, but as a result a permanent state of tension is maintained. For static and repetitive as the analysis often is, it is always *against* others. It leads to analyses and counter-analyses until finally all the characters are covered, with the analyses always in relation to the basic conflict. The very repetition of the hero's fundamental attitude produces a cumulative effect which makes the decision or final action seem like the necessary explosion at the end of a continually mounting tension. In *Port Royal,* a play in which everything has been decided in advance, so to speak, the entire subject matter consists in the nuns' and the archbishop's growing knowledge of themselves and of each other. Each one hopes for a compromise from the other, but each one is just as certain that he himself will never come to terms. The play is made up of that increasingly clear confirmation of two opposed intransigencies.

A clear distinction must be made in Montherlant between the action itself, often within, in the classical manner, and the action on stage. *Malatesta,* considered by Montherlant as the counterpart of *le Maître de Santiago* and in which he presents a hero as eager for life as the hero of *le Maître* is for nothingness, is an agitated and lively play. But this "pagano-Christian salmagundi," as Montherlant himself calls it, does no more than show the hero's character in all its facets by means of a few adventures. Malatesta's expedition to Rome to assassinate the Pope and his residence there under guard is only meant to keep him in a state of having to perpetually ask for recognition. The necessity of Malatesta's death does not come from within his own character, as do the final actions of Ferrante, Alvaro, or Georges. A lively portrait of an Italian Renaissance adventurer, with his pride, his appetites, his cultural and ideological confusion, *Malatesta* is a series of intensely dramatic scenes that mark out a mad adventure, but the resolution of the drama is not created by an unbearable increase in tension, nor by a cumulative effect leading to an explosion. It is created by a murder which comes from the outside. Malatesta is poisoned by his biographer. Montherlant's more satisfying plays —his linear and least agitated ones such as *Port Royal* and *le Maître de Santiago*—resolve the drama by means of the elements of the conflict itself and leave the spectator with the impression of having taken part in the flow of an intense and implacable action.

Therefore, and contrary to Claudel, Montherlant is most convincing in his austerely constructed works. It is in such plays that he is most successful in giving a portrait of the man who is somehow at the end of his rope and who liberates himself by a definitive act: murder or sacrifice.

For Montherlant's theatre is chiefly concerned with the man who can bear it no longer, the man who is already aging, who has lived out his life, whose first loves are long past, whose children are born and grown, whose tasks in politics, war, or a profession have been accomplished. In fact his heroes are getting older and older: his Don Juan is sixty-six, his Cardinal in *le Cardinal d'Espagne,* eighty-two. Montherlant gives the leading role, and sometimes the only important one, to the "old King" of tragedy.

Some particular circumstance leads the aging man to watch himself live; thus he becomes dual and dramatic, for he struggles between what he is and what he wants to be, what he seems like in his own eyes and what he says he is, and of course what he seems like to others. Each of Montherlant's characters has a strong tendency to talk about himself, to describe his own figure. Malatesta, Ferrante, Georges, and Alvaro quite naturally spend their time probing into themselves, explaining themselves to themselves, justifying themselves. But an incident always intensifies the tendency. For example, the more Malatesta feels frustrated in not receiving the recompense or recognition that is his due, the more vigorously he draws his own portrait. "I" is one of the more important words in

Montherlant's plays. All of his heroes would seem to be constructed around the remark: "How can they do that to me? Me, who . . ." and they're off! Their own portraits or their own analyses are ways of explaining that they do not deserve their misfortunes—like the Infanta when she is humiliated by Don Pedro's avowal, and King Ferrante when he is hurt by his son's disobedience; like Alvaro when he is asked to go and seek his fortune in the new world; like Georges when his son shows his vulgarity or when that same son is about to be taken from him; like the Abbé de Pradts, faced with young Sandrier's "betrayal." Their indignation when faced with injustice is an impassioned reaction, almost immediately justified by moral considerations. Montherlant's portrait of man is that of a being in which there is little distinction between passion and ethics. The hero who is hurt not only suffers but considers himself the embodiment of a moral value.

The element of "ethics" in Montherlant's plays has led to great confusion among critics as to the meaning of the plays, a confusion kept alive by certain of Montherlant's own comments. He sometimes seems to want his theatre to preach the greatness of souls, yet he often denies that he has any intention of moralizing. In his preface to *Pasiphaé* Montherlant declares that in his "imaginative works," he wants "to be both a moralist, that is, one who makes a study of passions, and a moralizer, that is, one who proposes a certain ethics." The fact that, since 1938, Montherlant would seem to have changed his mind, claiming in articles and letters that he emphasizes character study at the expense of the moral lesson, does not keep his public and critics from seeing moral propositions in his works. For in the plays themselves, the characters express themselves in moral terms. They claim to be on the side of Good (greatness, purity, intransigency) and mix maxims in with the analyses they make of themselves and others. But do the maxims express the characters' ethics only, or Montherlant's as well? Are they meant to complete a character's portrait or make him into a model?

Almost every dramatic work implies an ethics and calls for a judgement on the part of the spectator as to the value of such or such behavior. But other values generally transcend the judgement. For example, to the extent that the spectator identifies with Phèdre in her personal tragedy, in which a whole web of complicated emotions envelopes the character, he accepts the idea of the crime against which she struggles so as to give his entire attention to the beauty and pathos of the struggle. Montherlant clearly aims at a modern equivalent of the classical struggles, but in his characters' inner conflicts he puts particular emphasis on the ethical values they affirm—with the result that the audience often has the impression of being asked to approve of certain values rather than be moved by the pathos of the conflict itself.

The ethics proposed by his heroes is not the currently accepted "vulgar ethics," considered by Montherlant as a "codified opinion of the moment"—not a social ethics, but an ethics of the individual. Although as a good student of Barrès, he implies that France and man will be saved by a cult of the ego, he is fundamentally less interested in the results than in the code of morals itself. His heroes are conscious of being supermen. They are convinced that they are of "superior quality" or among the "elect," like the Jansenist nuns of Port Royal. The world is thus divided into two ethical groups: men of good quality and men of bad quality. Montherlant's heroes belong to Gobineau's category, the "sons of Kings." For some, they represent a continuation of a Corneillian heroism; for others, a resurgence of Stendhalian egotism in degraded form.

Fils de personne and its sequel *Demain il fera jour* are striking examples of the ambiguity of Montherlant's attitude with regard to the moral significance of his works. In the first play, Georges Carrion is entirely involved in the cult of human quality, and just as Ferrante in *la Reine morte* sends his son to prison "for mediocrity," so Georges ends by letting his son go off to danger and possible death because he is disappointed in him. As the son Gilou is presented as a little fool, sometimes sentimental, sometimes indifferent, and interested only in movie magazines, Georges' disappointment might well seem legitimate and he attracts the spectator's moral sympathy. In *Demain il fera jour* the same Georges Carrion really sends his son to his death, but this time out of fear. He needs a guarantee that will save him in case the victorious Resistance movement decides to pick a quarrel with him. Montherlant explains the character's transformation as follows:

> Georges has collapsed. He has seen the Occupation and he predicts the consequences: his incentive is shattered. In another respect, nothing remains of his love for his son: the spring has run dry. The champion of *quality* will go so far as committing a frightful act. In 1941 he sacrificed his son to an ideal. In 1944 he sacrifices him to his own fear. And it is the same man.

The hero, compared to a "samurai" in the first play, and also called a "Jansenist free-thinker," now shows himself as "vile under the influence of fear." Montherlant lengthily explains the psychology of his degradation and rightly defends himself against accusations of incoherence or improbability. Actually the two plays and their justifications throw light on many important aspects of Montherlant's drama. There is no doubt that it consists in an ethics of "quality" and "greatness" and that such an ethics is an ideal proposed by the writer. But something else leads Montherlant to explode those values, as if he himself believed that they were no more than abstractions, a kind of moral dream that he imposed on his characters and which he is the first to deflate:

> The double faces of Malatesta and Georges, so different from what they think they are; of Ferrante, so different from what he wants to be. Georges no more defends a certain idea of man, no matter what he says, than Ferrante defends the reasons of state, no matter what he says.

Thus the idea of man with which Georges would have liked his son to coincide and which seemed to be the motive for his behavior, is merely an illusion or, in any case, a false motive. And on the contrary, it is his fear in *Demain il fera jour* which is real.

Certain of Montherlant's comments seem to suggest that his theatre represents the drama of the individual who is mistaken about the motives for his acts, more than the conflict between those who live according to an ethics of human quality and the mediocre world that surrounds them. Actually the drama is one of pride or, to use the vocabulary of classical psychology, one of an attempt, out of self-love, to justify ourselves in our own eyes and in the eyes of others. Montherlant's heroes are not really great men; they are men who want to see themselves as great.

Montherlant's comedy *Brocéliande* clarifies the meaning of his works even more than his own explanations. The protagonist Persilès, a rather timid bourgeois, starts to speak like a hero as soon as he believes himself a descendant of Saint-Louis. His illusion of aristocracy transforms his attitude. He becomes haughty, convinced of his superior quality, avid for purity and grandeur. His supposed superiority consists essentially in its affirmation, for in fact it is based on an illusion. In this very amusing comedy, Montherlant mocks his own serious heroes. They, also, affirm their superiority in language, using a vocabulary of grandeur, but the motives for their actions are quite another thing. Alvaro's Christian intransigence in *le Maître de Santiago?* Rather a desire for nothingness, a surrender to "nada." Philippe de Presle's and Geneviève's patriotic heroism in *l'Exil?* Rather passionate friendship and maternal love. Ferrante's grandeur and regal intransigence in *la Reine morte?* Rather the lassitude of an old tired king.

There comes a time in many of the plays when the character breaks down. In a moment of weariness, he relaxes and confides in a third person. Such moments are interesting both dramatically and psychologically. They disclose the character's hidden motives, and they are excellent theatrically in that they represent an unmasking. The mask of greatness and moral exigency is removed, revealing a face that is marked solely by emotion or passion. Here Montherlant is in the classical tradition of the search for truth, the unveiling of souls, the psychological undressing that is fundamental to action in the works of Racine or Molière. Montherlant's first play *l'Exil*, written in 1914 and never performed, presents his method in a most obvious and elementary way. The young protagonist Philippe de Presle, at first cynical and hostile to wartime obligations, then impatient to enlist, reveals—both indirectly throughout the play and directly in a long scene with his mother at the end of Act II—that his attitudes and comments are not motivated by any solid principle but solely by a passionate friendship for Senac. In a parallel way, his mother's patriotism falls apart when Philippe talks of enlisting. The hearts of Montherlant's heroes are like blank pages on which passions are expressed in moral terms.

When Ferrante confides in Inès and the young page Dino del Moro in *la Reine morte*, when the head of the school confides in the Abbé de Pradts at the end of *la Ville*, when Christine gives in to Ravier at the end of *Celles qu'on prend dans ses bras*, each one exposes himself and shows that his haughty tone is no more than a cover for a whole obscure mechanism. In a note written in 1954, "En relisant *la Reine morte*," Montherlant explains Inès' murder in terms of Ferrante's masculinity, his sadism, and his disgust with life and children. During most of the action, the heroes are of bad faith, by the playwright's own admission. The moral values they claim to embody are an objective more than an attainment. Their ethics is not an absolute, but an ambiguous state of consciousness.

In this respect Montherlant has much the same attitude as La Rochefoucauld in the seventeenth century, who did not deny the courage of certain acts but investigated the motives behind the attitudes of courage and charity. And he discovered that ethics is not a motive but a result, that there are essentially no moral intentions, only bursts of passion justified *a posteriori* by the characters' rationalizations or the outer sanction of appearance.

Everything happens as if Montherlant, in choosing the subject matter for his dramas, went out in search of the great spectacular acts which history, custom, or the heroes themselves explain in moral terms, and then devoted his play to unravelling the reasons for them. Every act has two meanings, and the play discovers the real meaning, the original meaning, contained in the characters' psychological makeup. His method is the reverse of Sartre's in *Huis Clos* or *les Mains sales*. Sartre presents an action in terms of its significance, which comes *after* the action. For Montherlant, man is a dramatic being, swinging between his values and the determinism of his psychology. He occasionally succeeds in living in the rarefied atmosphere of his principles, but his agony comes from the fact that he refuses to acknowledge the very source of those values.

Montherlant does not belong to the race of unobtrusive writers who let their works speak for themselves. Even more than Cocteau, he surrounds each of his plays with analyses, prefaces, postscripts, answers to critics, written sometimes many years after publication or performance. He comments upon his own works better than any critic has been able to do. He analyzes them from the inside out, and supports his arguments with his own maxims or those of his characters. He is not a writer who cuts the umbilical cord once the work is submitted to the public.

In spite of the fact that he denies putting himself into his works, it is clear that he remains very close to them. His insistence in choosing solitary heroes who claim to be discouraged by the current way of the world, who vehemently cling to the idea of superiority, and who then show how their motives are not always as noble as their attitudes or at least more passionate than moral—such insistence reveals the temperament of Montherlant himself. His theatre might be considered as the masquerade, perhaps not of his actual ideas and passions, but of his inner struggle. In the conception and construction of his plays, he often gives the impression of hesitating as much as his characters. He uses them as spokesmen, through a kind of identification with certain of their outbursts, and then dissects them, judges them, and turns against them. At a performance of a Montherlant play, the spectator takes part not only in the sudden changes and metamorphosis of an entirely objectified work, but in two tangled dramas: the character's and that of the writer who struggles with him, identifies with him, tries to reject him, and more or less succeeds in all respects.

Montherlant sometimes gets rid of his actual subjects in the same way as he does his characters, with cruelty. He completed *Fils de personne,* an ambiguous play, with a short Boulevard comedy *Un Incompris,* "a counterpart that borders on caricature," "a little work that also brings out uncertainty, which is what we should feel concerning the very nature of heroism," and with *Demain il fera jour,* in which Georges changes from being heroic to being despicable. In the same way, *Brocéliande* might be considered a kind of sacrifice through mockery—this time a sacrifice of all the works preceding it. The movement seems to be a double one: the hero, who sacrifices everyone mediocre, is finally sacrificed in turn by the writer, who makes him grotesque or despicable.

The double sacrifice reveals an exigency which is never satisfied—an exigency and a fear. The exigency is that of always being aware of oneself; the fear, that of being taken in, caught, hurt. One must be able to answer for oneself at every moment: whence the extravagant rationalizations, whence the destruction of the very content of those rationalizations. If the attitude seems contradictory, there is always a ready answer: so is life.

Although such an attitude makes the audience uncomfortable when it is applied to the relationship between the writer and his characters, it gives the characters themselves, seen objectively, an unquestionable richness, a true dramatic ambiguity, and, because of their dilemma, a tragic dimension. The hero is a sacrificer like his creator, and his act itself, which should prove the integrity and authenticity of his chosen values, in fact shows the non-moral motive for his attitude.

Certain critics, and Thierry-Maulnier in particular,[2] have noticed that Montherlant's heroes' sacrifices of others are somewhat similar to exorcisms. By killing or exiling the person they consider as weak or mediocre, they think they have killed or driven out their own weakness or their own mediocrity. Such would be the case of Ferrante when he imprisons his son or has Inès de Castro killed, and of Georges when he lets his son go off to possible death. Montherlant seems to subscribe to the interpretation and adds to it elsewhere with a theme he is partial to in his novels: the bull fight. Thus his heroes' sacrifices have ritual value, and the ultimate meaning of the whole should be sought beyond the often over-simple moral maxims, in their cynicism, beyond the analysis of a classical psychological device, in an attitude of magic. Just as the matador immolates his own animality or fear by killing the bull, so heroes like Ferrante and Georges sacrifice, through others, that part of themselves open to tenderness, abandon, indulgence, even happiness.

Such characters are reflected in the others. They see in others their own temptation, the face of what they do not want to be but what in a kind of way they are. The tragic irony comes from the fact that in sacrificing what they do not want to be, that very dimension of themselves becomes perceptible or acknowledged. *La Ville dont le Prince est un enfant* is once again the richest and most subtle example of the process. The play's setting itself, a Catholic school, is favorable to the casting

2. Quoted by Montherlant in note no. 4, *Fils de personne*.

of spells. The teachers who work not only on their pupils' minds but on their souls, the religious coloring given to all feeling, all emotion, all affection, the ritual of friendship among students or students and teachers—all make it possible for the writer to transcend the conflict between a moral attitude and its psychological motivation and move toward a rather strange poetry made up of both the most murky elements and the greatest purity. The Abbé de Pradts, expelling Sevrais so that his favorite pupil, Sandrier, may be removed from what he believes to be Sevrais' bad influence, learns, in what is a kind of backfire, that Sandrier is also to be expelled so that he will no longer be under his own bad influence. Sevrais' expulsion reveals that the Abbé was unknowingly in the same position as the child he had accused. Thus without realizing it, he was making Sevrais pay for his own weakness. The play's setting is favorable to self-analyses and reciprocal confessions, and makes it possible for the writer to play with all the subtleties of his characters' bad faith, up to the final elucidation.

The dialectic of sacrifice is not present in all of Montherlant's plays. But it is frequent enough to throw light on his works as a whole. Montherlant's characters become rigid within an image of themselves, an image to which they can attribute qualities of greatness, magnanimity, purity, lucidity, or brilliance. The motive for their rigidity is the Pascalian "self-love" which, "unable to destroy truth in its essence, destroys it as far as possible in his own knowledge and in that of others." [3] So that the greatness of Montherlant's characters does not lie so much in their ideal, or in the rules of action they propose—sometimes tempting, sometimes tiresome or naïve— but in the intensity of the very drama that tears them apart. Their greatness is theatrical not human. They succeed in being admirable through so persistently trying to coincide with a proposed image, and more especially as they occasionally, in the course of the play, succeed in convincing their creator him-

3. Pascal, *Pensées,* trans. W. F. Trotter.

self. Moreover the images they hold up for themselves may be detestable, but they are rarely dull. The grotesque arrogance of the hero in *Brocéliande* like the mystic renunciation in *le Maître de Santiago,* Ferrante's regal haughtiness like the Abbé de Pradt's cult of beautiful souls are suggestive of highly colored theatrical attitudes. About the only exception is Ravier in *Celles qu'on prend dans ses bras,* whose contemptuous sneers are as distressing as his psychology in love.

Beyond the real value or truth of the image man holds up for himself—and that image varies from Don Juanism to mystic asceticism, from a totally humanistic life to complete renunciation—Montherlant offers us a definition of man independent of the concrete content furnished by ethics, politics, or even individual passions. It lies in the notion of effort toward a certain self-realization. In the course of his works, the effort is sometimes taken seriously, sometimes shown as illusory, sometimes considered for itself beyond all judgement. Man is not fundamentally political or charitable or religious or capable of love. All those characteristics are secondary. He is first and above all a being who strives toward a chosen image. The hero is he who strives the most vigorously, the most steadfastly, and often with the most cruelty.

There is nothing metaphysical in the idea; it belongs to the order of psychology. For what is under consideration is not the objective itself, but man's movement toward it. And Montherlant's description is of man in that pose.

French critics are clearly divided over Montherlant. It is never easy to find an impartial judgement concerning him. Either the critical essays devoted to him are the works of admirers blinded by their enthusiasm, such as Jacques de Laprade, or of ferocious disparagers. It is interesting to note that foreign critics, who are more apt to consider the works in themselves and not in their immediate relation to the French scene, and who seem especially sensitive to their grand style, are high in

their praise. For Eric Bentley, Montherlant's works represent
"a grown-up theatrical art." [4] For John Gassner, Montherlant
is "the most authentic genius for dramatic writing discoverable
in France after 1940." [5] And indeed his theatre is both ambitious and serious. Montherlant expects a great deal from his
public. He writes plays that require a taste for great style and
a capacity for constant attention. His characters express themselves in classical French, clear and elevated (excepting the
vulgarities of *Celles qu'on prend dans ses bras* and *Don Juan*),
a language of unquestionable dignity and precision. However,
the beauty of form is often a mask, and some particularly fine
speech which seems to give the key to the play's subject, in
fact gives the key to a false subject, the true appearing further
on. The ideal spectator for a Montherlant play is therefore he
who does not accept the characters' explanations outright but
who is capable of admiring their quality without immediately
jumping to conclusions.

Montherlant has often complained about the incomprehen-
sion of both critics and audiences. Yet because of his over-
subtlety in analyzing the characters and his attempt to show
that the true meaning of the action does not lie in the characters' own comments about it, his intentions end by passing
unnoticed. Quite recently, apropos of *Don Juan*, Paul Gui-
mard [6] laughed at those who, in describing the play, use words
like "catch a glimpse of," "secretly," "perhaps," "without seeming to." Yet Montherlant meant the audience to "catch a
glimpse of" the tragedy hidden within the farce. But by completely reducing a mythical character to his most elementary
motives, he submerged the play's hidden intentions in a vulgar
farce. The legendary rebel and seeker of the absolute or
Molière's arrogant free-thinker becomes quite simply a sixty-
six year old lecher. Montherlant's meaning comes through in

4. Eric Bentley, *In Search of Theatre*, p. 48.
5. John Gassner, *Masters of the Drama*, p. 722.
6. *L'Avant-scène*, No. 188, January 1, 1959.

a change in the play's tone when Don Juan and Ana meet, and also at the end when the death mask worn by the hero sticks to his face and becomes one with it. A tragic dimension is restored to the character, who is the prisoner of a vulgar and grotesque sensuality but a lucid prisoner. Yet it would seem that the attempt here of pushing man's incoherence to the extreme only makes the play itself incoherent. The French critics of 1958 found it no more than a painful farce that does not hold up.

Montherlant has always inserted a hidden element in each play which is in fact the key to the play's meaning. Robert Kemp, at the time of *Port-Royal,* spoke of "well-covered poison" with respect to the analysis of the one nun's disbelief which subtly but definitively orients the play's meaning. There Montherlant did not break the work's esthetic harmony. But that is doubtless one of the dangers of his art. The misunderstandings that constantly attend his works do not come from the difficulty or obscurity of the actual subject matter but from the veil he throws over his subjects in order to "imitate life."

Once the spectator has understood, he has only to play the writer's game. He will then recognize one of man's faces, that of his solitude—not a whining solitude, waiting to be repudiated, but a solitude that is so vigorously accepted it ends by seeming to be chosen. It is reinforced by a contempt for others, the price attached exclusively to the ego, and the construction of a whole system of values (which vary according to the play) to justify it. Great gestures, acts, values, and language are all meant to glorify it, exalt it. His is an authentically ironical vision of man, since it is inseparable from a doubt as to the basis for the solitary hero's grand attitudes and a doubt as to the meaning of the final revelations. For in wanting to remove that very doubt, men perform the definitive acts that reveal the deep ambiguities of self-love.

CHAPTER 5

FROM ANGUISH TO PLAY:
JEAN ANOUILH AND
ARMAND SALACROU

Both Anouilh and Salacrou were discovered by directors who headed the reform to purify French theatre and who were in search of new talent to fulfill their objectives. Lugné-Poe gave Salacrou his chance in 1925 with *Tour à terre* and Anouilh his with *l'Hermine* in 1932. Salacrou was then adopted by Charles Dullin, whereas Anouilh, having finally conquered the public with *le Voyageur sans bagage* (produced by Pitoëff in 1936), was most often performed by André Barsacq, Dullin's former set designer.

Both became successful playwrights, capable of satisfying the tastes of an ordinary as well as an intellectual public. Yet neither represents a compromise between a high idea of theatre and facility. Their theatre is rather an accumulation, a result of most of the accepted attainments of the early twentieth century.

Salacrou and Anouilh started out from two very different dramatic concepts. One has only to compare *le Casseur d'assiettes* or *le Pont de l'Europe* (Salacrou: 1923, 1925) with *l'Hermine* or *Jézabel* (Anouilh: 1931, 1932). Salacrou's beginnings are quite close to the surrealist experiments, modernist construction, and the theatre of dream. Imaginary countries, circus fantasy, and dream projections are woven into very freely constructed and wordy plays, where the poetry is often interrupted by discussions on the meaning of life and love, in a style more parodic than ironic. The early plays of Anouilh are, on the contrary, extremely bitter and dismal dramas, akin to naturalism, but a naturalism in which brutality is greatly intensified. Each playwright gradually modified the form of his plays by borrowing from esthetics contrary to his own. And both ended by producing a composite genre, generally based on naturalism, but in which the forms borrowed from poetic drama bring the necessary theatrical distance.

Although the evolution of both, on the esthetic or purely theatrical level, is obvious, it would seem that the human drama each writer expresses today has always been at the core of his works. Salacrou's *le Pont de l'Europe* deals with a Frenchman, king of a distant country, completely turned toward his past, in search of his dead loves or trying to reconstruct what would have happened had he given in to his true aspirations. This attempt to understand the flow of past time, the "why"s in face of the irremediable, make up the entire subject matter of later plays like *l'Inconnue d'Arras, Dieu le savait,* and *Sens interdit*. Meditations on what is ended are accompanied by a doubt as to the meaning of the past and an indecision as to the present. That attitude, together with poetic disorder and "the play within the play" in *le Pont de l'Europe,* has led critics to evoke *Hamlet* apropos of Salacrou's first plays. Since then Salacrou seems to have been more and more disillusioned, with the result that his poetic escapes have become rare, a sometimes cynical realism has triumphed over the dream, and when imagination gives the work a non-realistic form, the imagination is more intellectual than poetic. From 1923 to 1952, in *le Pont de l'Europe, l'Inconnue d'Arras,* and *Sens interdit,* the fundamental question remains the same but the poetic answer is replaced first by a Pascalian anguish and then by a sinister burlesque, whereas the non-realistic form, which at the beginning had created a universe of fantasy, becomes purely functional, a device necessary to a demonstration.

When we consider Anouilh's first plays, we also find the central drama that directs all his works. His characters are on the defensive from the very beginning. They all have a deep wish for purity or happiness, in any case for an absolute, and the realization of that wish is prevented by the surrounding world which is sordid, illusory, and brings about the defilement of anyone who accepts making a compromise with it. In this type of theatre the hero has no recourse but flight. Such is the case of Marc in *Jézabel* or Thérèse in *la Sauvage.* Then Anouilh lost his earnestness, added a theatricalist consciousness to his dramatic skill, and his solutions from then on are increasingly dependent on theatrical convention—either childish and comforting, like Gaston's departure with the little boy at the end of *le Voyageur sans bagage,* or spectacular (that is, where the force of the image is stronger than the realism) like the death of Frédéric and Jeannette in the rising tide in *Roméo et Jeannette,* or the deliberate anti-realism at the end of *Eurydice.*

Anouilh wrote his first "Pièce Rose," *le Bal des voleurs,* in 1932 although it was not produced until 1938. His second, *le Rendez-vous de Senlis,* was written in 1937. His discovery of fantasy and game and the use of devices borrowed from non-realistic theatre helped him escape from the naturalism of his first "Pièces Noires." But as in Salacrou, the central subject has not changed. For both playwrights, the weight of reality, the experience of man in the world of men is still to this day the core of their works.

On the most superficial level, the greater part of Anouilh's and Salacrou's plays deals with the immediate problems of the man of today. Both denounce the existing order of things and the corruption and misery hidden behind it. Whether they attack advertising or the cult of the French Revolution, family values or politics, they solidly anchor their subject matter in a contemporary context.

In addition to plays situated in the present time, a universal myth like that of Anouilh's *Antigone* is closely linked to the problem of the Resistance and collaboration in the 1940s, and Salacrou's *la Terre est ronde,* a historical drama dealing with

Savonarola's dictatorship in Florence, is clearly a description of a Fascist state. Even in the details contemporary allusions are obvious: the guards in *Antigone* are twentieth-century policemen, the family scenes in Anouilh's *Becket ou l'honneur de Dieu* have a very current bourgeois flavor.

Anachronisms or basic distortions refer the spectator to the most immediate elements of his own universe. But such allusions are actually denunciations: the guard in tragedy is no different from the modern prison guard; one reflects on the other. The somewhat sordid and grotesque aspect of the present is related to the crimes of antiquity which make us shiver; and the great crimes of antiquity also involved a certain amount of the sordid and grotesque. Thus the anachronism is double-edged, and two accepted concepts are denounced.

Even within the present, both playwrights often use another device of double de-mystification. They borrow from established genres (*vaudeville,* bourgeois comedy or drama, eighteenth-century comedy) and switch over in midstream to the opposite genre, or they show, through forms meant to maintain the public's good conscience, all sorts of reasons for having a bad conscience. Anouilh's *Ardèle ou la Marguerite* has the form of a *vaudeville* but leads to a double suicide and very sad discoveries indeed. Conversely, Salacrou's *l'Archipel Lenoir* starts out like a cruel naturalist play, supposedly tending toward a collective murder, and ends up as a farce. By using devices of this kind, Anouilh and Salacrou confront the public with an established and satisfying modern mechanism, only to more successfully destroy the motives for satisfaction. Therefore an ordinary spectator is at first pleased to find himself in the presence of a traditional type plot and characters or precise allusions to contemporary problems. But, at the same time, he is shaken in most of his opinions and in his tendency to be satisfied with himself and his world. The traditional genres are shown to be false, the allusions are found to be accusations.

On the level of elementary politics, Anouilh's satire might

be considered as tending toward the right, Salacrou's toward the left. But both go far beyond political positions and current concerns and touch on fundamental human attitudes. In their choice of forms and themes, both seem led by a desire to deflate illusions that are characteristic of our times, no doubt, but which are also of greater scope. When they throw suicide into a farce, they put the whole idea of comedy in question. When they see through the farcical game of conjugal infidelity or the Romantic idea of grandeur in unhappiness, bourgeois values of order or the cult of humanity, they succeed in questioning an entire concept of human nature. Basically, what seems funny is actually pathetic, what is reputedly ennobling is in fact degrading, what touches the heart is often grotesque or disgusting. In Anouilh and Salacrou, the mission of theatre —the art of illusion par excellence—is to denounce illusion.

With respect to unhappiness, Anouilh has taken a conspicuously anti-Romantic position. Never in French literature has there been a more repetitious and vigorous denial of Alfred de Musset's formula: "Nothing makes us so great as a great sorrow." In *la Répétition,* for example, most of the characters suffer or end by suffering. Their suffering, created by jealousy, wounded pride, unsatisfied passion, etc. is either held up to ridicule (as with Villebosse) or presented as a source of moral decay and ignoble acts (Hero, and the Countess herself in her schemes to destroy Lucile). Generally in Anouilh suffering leads to shame and acts of moral and physical self-destruction. The same can be said for poverty. The myth deflated here is not that of the emotional suffering which ennobles the victim but the myth of the virtuous heroism of the poor. As early as *l'Hermine,* the hero Franz admits that "Poverty made my youth into a long period of pettiness and disgust." Poverty leads Anouilh's characters to petty calculating, rancor, bitter dreams. And when the poor take refuge in dignity and intransigence, they become spoil-sports, they upset the game, become hateful through an excess of purity, and are the ruin of the others, like Julien in *Colombe*.

Destroyed also, although sometimes only partially in that the plays leave it unresolved, is the theme of the one and only love. When Anouilh puts two young people together for the first time, they may fall in love at first sight and make most impassioned speeches about the eternity of their love (*Eurydice, Roméo et Jeannette*). But then they have to commit suicide quickly before their love degenerates, before the impurity of others and their own temperaments can show them the vanity of their dream. Or else love is part of an unreal *divertissement* like *le Bal des voleurs, Léocadia,* and *l'Invitation au château*, in which the playwright's technique itself emphasizes the fantasy of the final happy marriage. There are no united and happy couples in Anouilh's theatre. All the mature couples who appear on stage are always plunged in a farcical situation and treated rather lightly or with an accent on the situation's sordid or bitter aspect. The only ones who escape, until a new passion comes along, are the couples who have established a "good friends" relationship (*la Répétition, Ardèle*).

The couple is hardly treated with more indulgence by Salacrou. *Un Homme comme les autres* shows all the hypocrisy and dissipation of married men; the charming infidelities so dear to *vaudeville* turn *Histoire de rire* into a mournful melodrama. In *Sens interdit* Salacrou picks up the idea of a world where time is reversed and life is lived backwards. He presents couples who impatiently await the time of their youth when they will not yet have suffered or been deceived, when they will make the discovery of total love. His device is comparable to Anouilh's in *Colombe,* in which after having shown Colombe's corruption and the vanity of Julien's illusions as to the eternity of their love, he abruptly takes us back to the past and ends his play on their first romantic meeting, a meeting that was madly joyous and full of the two young people's greatest hopes.

We thus find in both playwrights the acknowledgement of moments or periods when things or human beings are as pure, passionate, sincere, and true as we should like to believe them. But the moment is always one in which nothing has yet been accomplished: childhood, its friendships and dreams, the first days of love. Anouilh and Salacrou are obsessed by the notion of degradation in time, but there again they reject the Romantic attitude in that they do not accept the idea of a spiritual eternity (in the heart, memory, or "form") of things that have disappeared. Memory does not make things relive. It consists essentially in regrets. According to them we remember the past; we don't live in the past. And when we try to reconstruct it from fragments, we sink into the grotesque, as in *la Valse des toréadors,* or into despair, as in *l'Inconnue d'Arras.* No Proustian ecstacy, this!

A theme common to both writers is that of the "little boy that I was." When childhood is evoked, it generally seems open to all the great ideas or all the great passions. It also carries within itself the seeds of the corruption to come, as soon as there is a relationship between two people. Then begins the jealousy, the longing. A vague memory of Jean-Jacques Rousseau hovers over this conception: two children are the beginning of a society, therefore the beginning of corruption; it also contains the idea that observation and imitation of the adults' corrupt society leads to the degeneration of children (Toto and Marie Christine imitating the adults in *Ardèle*).

Often the characters actually remain children. But then the situation is not livable. One cannot be both a child and an adult. In Salacrou, the struggle results in an unbearable anguish. In Anouilh, the persistence of the child in the adult leads to catastrophe. The catastrophe may be admirable, as in the case of "little Antigone"; or it may consist in incoherence, passion, and murder, as in the case of the "little boy" Henry II in *Becket.* In other words, the corrupting world is definitely not for them.

Yet there is more in Anouilh and Salacrou than a bitter portrait of reality, whether it show contemporary depravity or universal illusions. Both have a vision of the world which goes far beyond a theatre of denunciation and satire. And it is here that they separate.

Salacrou suffers from an obsession which might be described by the well-worn term "cosmic." In all his plays, limited as the anecdote itself may be, there is always a feeling of great celestial space. The very title *la Terre est ronde,* for a drama which is set in Florence at the time of Savonarola, is revealing. The action takes place in 1492, and through its relations with the departure of Columbus, destined to prove the truth of the title, a parallelism, otherwise rather facile, between Savonarola's dictatorship and certain events of the 1930s, takes on its full meaning. In his other works, less Shakespearian in form and ambition, Salacrou always uses that sense of the cosmic as a reference or in the form of a metaphor. For instance Jacques, at the beginning of *Une femme libre,* is installing a reduced model of the entire solar system in the house. *Un Homme comme les autres* is filled with expressions like "my passing over the earth," "we live in a lost world," and man's destiny is compared to the activity of an ant hill. In other words, the play's anecdote, no more than a fairly banal situation in itself, is constantly seen, and by the characters themselves, as if from another planet. The word "earth" is often capitalized in *l'Inconnue d'Arras,* men are again compared to small animals (birds and flies), the infinity of successive generations is suggested, the stars "which remind men that they are on an earth among other earths" are evoked. In *Une Femme trop honnête* the ironic lines constantly remind us that the action of the play has almost no importance "seen from on high" or put into its place "in the Milky Way." In all the plays a kind of Voltairian glance from the outside falls upon men, who are considered as small relative beings, lost in space and subjected to the implacable indifference of universal determinism.

In his essay *Mes Certitudes et incertitudes* [1] Salacrou explains his philosophical position. It can be summarized as an acute hyperconsciousness of universal determinism, causing the desire for liberation through faith. As Salacrou has never found such liberation, he wavers between anguish and despair, provoked by the implacability of the absurd, and a kind of wisdom that consists in living *"as if* [his] flesh were not a collection of small molecular structures, *as if* [he] were master of [his] decisions. . . ."* As for his participation in left-wing political activities, it seems meant to give his "life, which has no meaning, a temporary usefulness."

This position is reflected in his plays, where action is the meeting point of chance happenings, of independent causal series. The characters are astonished at their destinies, their transformations, the small place they occupy in a universal, spatial, and temporal context. They constantly look back and struggle with the notion that things could not have happened otherwise.

What in most of his plays saves Salacrou from naturalism is a kind of amplification of naturalism. Man considered as the product of nature and various determinisms is not exactly the central point of his works. The actual center is situated in the conflict between determinism and a desire for freedom. More than dramatic stories told in naturalistic terms, his plays are a hopeless protest against determinism, the portrait of prisoners who vainly struggle in their chains. When they imagine a possible freedom, they are called to order by remarks such as: "The free man's game is the only game that amuses God" (*l'Inconnue d'Arras*). In *Dieu le savait* the characters hesitate between a totally mechanistic vision of the world and faith in a Calvinist God who knows everything in advance and predestines all beings. On the whole the anxiety created by his theatre is therefore metaphysical. It is akin to what one feels reading Pascal's comments on man without God, formulas

1. Armand Salacrou, *Théâtre*, Vol. VI.

such as: "The eternal silence of this infinite space terrifies me." The principal tension does not lie in the relations between characters but in the relations between the characters' lives and the cosmos.

Given the naturalist aspect of the dialogue, it is understandable that Salacrou, in order to bring out the true meaning of his plays, was led to state it directly, sometimes using the most elementary forms of the problem play. That is, he places his characters on stage, not for a Giraudoux type debate in which poetry transcends the demonstration, but for a kind of contradictory discussion or statement of the playwright's ideas on determinism. When Hector and Ulysses, in Giraudoux's *la Guerre de Troie,* weigh war and peace in a dialogue that will change the world's fate, the emotion is created by the importance of the conflict, the evocative power of each declamation, a ceremonious representation of man's danger. When the characters of Salacrou's *Dieu le savait* discuss freedom, determinism, and predestination, their discussion—individual commentaries on an anecdote—adds nothing to the play's action, reveals nothing that we don't already know about the characters, and represents nothing more than itself. The arguments are therefore listened to for themselves and not for their dramatic value, and instead of theatrical participation in an image of our destiny, the interest is non-esthetic, separated from living experience, and lies in the polemical value of reasoning. Although, for that reason, *Dieu le savait* is Salacrou's least successful play, the rest of his works are full of commentaries and philosophical affirmations, sometimes purely satirical but often edifying and demonstrative, making the theatre at certain moments seem like a speaker's platform.

Indeed therein lies both the power and the limitations of Salacrou's theatre. Life is no more than what the naturalists have shown it to be, and in all honesty Salacrou must remain at that level. Yet he would have liked it to be something else. He has shown it in the poetry of his early plays. However if the objective of theatre is to reveal the truth, that "something else," given Salacrou's attitude, can only be shown in the characters' discussions. It is an abstraction, an object of intellectual speculation. The emotion we feel in Salacrou's works comes from the spectacle of a play nailed to the ground, with all its attempts to arise broken by the playwright's implacable lucidity.

Anouilh transcends psychological realism, not through a consciousness of cosmic anguish but through the combination of an ethics and a poetry of theatre which is his own.

Critics have expounded on the search for purity through sordidness in Anouilh's works. And, true, the play of corruption and purification is a constant theme in his theatre. His plays abound in symbols of purity such as simply the title, *Colombe,* or phrases like the line repeated by most of his young heroines: "Here I am, naked under my little linen dress." The contrast between such precarious purity and the surrounding sordidness is a conflict which gives Anouilh's bitterness its dramatic aspect.

But the play of purity and sordidness is ambiguous. Taking *Colombe* as an example, we find that the purity Julien wants to impose on Colombe is withering and deadly, whereas the corruption she undergoes in the company of actors makes her live and brings her happiness. In general, the accuser, thrown by Anouilh into his world of shame, is controversial. He is subject to contradictory judgements and is far from being a paragon of virtue and justice.

Such ambiguities remain in the category of the realist portrait, and Anouilh could have stopped there. In fact he did in his first plays. But in the course of his writing, he overcame the naturalist conflict with its moral implications by rejecting the conflict itself. In his great plays the hero finally transcends good and evil through an increasingly clear refusal to play the game of life. His refusal leads to two extreme solutions, often combined in the same play: the tragic catastrophe brought about by his abstract *no* and the substitution of the game of theatre for the game of life.

Antigone, at the beginning of the play, has buried her brother for very precise motives, similar to those of Sophocles' heroine. At first sight the subject of Anouilh's *Antigone* is the conflict between two "laws" and the painful choice it imposes on exacting or responsible people.[2] But in the course of the play, the conflict between political realism and a refusal to compromise is not resolved by the choice of one as against the other. Creon demolishes Antigone's reasons. Her final "no" is less a refusal to collaborate with Creon's politics than a rejection of any collaboration with the conflict as a whole, that is, with life itself.

Antigone's extreme attitude is representative of the higher refusals of Anouilh's other great heroes, who are presented in more specific contexts. The world as seen by Anouilh is a machine for corrupting man, lowering him, keeping him from being a man. His dramatic hero is he who is conscious of the situation, caught between the obligatory degradation of life and a will to escape from it. Sometimes the hero succeeds in a grotesque way like General de Saint Pé in the "Pièces Grinçantes"; sometimes he discovers that his dignity lies in absolute negation.

In *l'Alouette* the Inquisitor is one of the possible symbols of the universal conspiracy against man. But when faced with Joan of Arc, he is forced to acknowledge:

> There will always be a man to hunt down somewhere . . . who will finally be caught and killed and who will, once again, abase the Idea at the height of its power, simply because he will say *no* without lowering his eyes. (*Full of hatred, he hisses between his teeth looking at Joan.*) The insolent breed!

2. It was this aspect of *Antigone* that was picked up by the critics and audience at its first performance in Paris in 1943: a choice between the resistance to an order considered unjust and collaboration with it.

Antigone's or Joan's insolent attitude is also that of Thomas
à Becket in *Becket ou l'honneur de Dieu,* a play which might
be considered the height of Anouilh's production to this day.

On one level, the historical drama is a pretext for very contemporary allusions, sordid family scenes, denunciations of
political corruption, whether applied to a disillusioned King of
France or to a kind of clownish Pope. On another level, the
play is a tragedy of passion. The mechanism of unrequited
passion in Henry II's friendship for Becket is shown in all the
complexity of the game of love and hate, despair and jealousy.
There are times when Henry II behaves like one of Racine's
heroines. Very symbolically, the barons who go off to murder
Becket walk to the rhythm of his heart beats. But that passion
has a most Anouilhian function: it destroys the illusions which
are the very structure of the characters' world. On the other
hand, it appears to be based on illusion itself to the extent
that it is unrequited: Becket's friendship for the King is of
quite another nature. Becket is beyond the sordid and beyond
love. As the King's friend, he plays the part of a fellow libertine
and he plays it well. Yet what interests him is not debauchery
but perfection in debauchery. When the King appoints him
Archbishop, all he does is to be the perfect Archbishop—a far
cry from Eliot's Becket in *Murder in the Cathedral.* There is
no question of God in Anouilh's play, but rather the *honor*
of God:

> *The King:* So you've begun to love God? (He shouts)
> And you haven't changed, pigheaded boy,
> you still don't answer when someone asks you
> a question?
>
> *Becket* (*gently*): I have begun to love the honor of God.

In the conflict between the honor of the King and the honor
of God, Becket's choice is not motivated by any logic:

> *Becket:* I shan't try to convince you. I shall only say
> no.

The King:	But you must be logical, Becket!
Becket:	No. It's not necessary, my King. One has only to do, absurdly, what one has been entrusted with doing—and to the very end.

And "absurdly" is the word for it. Becket never for a moment gives a thought to what he considers a duty. It is an imperative given without justification and which places the hero beyond any psychological or sociological vision. Such an attitude is doubtless one solution to the problem of life which is unlivable, but a desperate one. For as life is necessarily vile, choosing "absurd" purity is actually choosing against life, killing oneself or having oneself killed in the name of that "no" which is both the honor of man and his annihilation.

Anouilh's comedies, his "Pièces Roses," "Pièces Brillantes," and certain "Pièces Grinçantes," emphasize another kind of solution: theatre itself. It is presented in the form of fantastic and contrived denouements such as the end of *le Voyageur sans bagage* or of *la Valse des toréadors*. In the first, the hero escapes from his real past by acting out a lie with the help of an unexpected and Heaven-sent little boy; in the second, the plot is nonchalantly resolved by a conventional device from classical comedy: the farcical discovery of hidden filiations. Even more clearly, at the end of *Hurluberlu,* the hero—after both his conspiracy to save France and his marriage have failed —has no other solution but to act in an amateur production, and the curtain comes down on the beginning of a play within a play.

In fact all the works of Anouilh are filled with that kind of theatricalism. The comedies are masquerades: Joan of Arc in *l'Alouette* acts out her past life; *Antigone* is presented as the staging of a tragedy. Every one of Anouilh's plays, except for perhaps his very first, are dominated by a theatrical vision of life.

In the comedies the characters—either bored or disgusted—

live masked most of the time and play at living a certain conventional or extravagant destiny. In contrast to the young girl, "naked under her little dress," in search of a purity that is impossible in this world, there is the rather mad old lady, laden with jewels and lace, masked, lucidly playing a part which saves her from despair. Many of Anouilh's characters are counterfeits, from Lady Hurf in *le Bal des voleurs* to Ornifle in *Ornifle ou le courant d'air*. Their motives are clearly neither ambition nor shame, but the fear of being bored or of suffering. Madame Alexandre in *Colombe* is a perfect symbol of this "hypocrisy" in that she is an actress. But even characters like Tigre in *la Répétition* or Messerschmann in *l'Invitation au château* live masked, each in his own way.

Consequently the subjects of a good part of Anouilh's plays consist in justifications of the mask, attempts to unmask the characters, and even pure exercises of virtuosity on the theme of the mask. The theme is exploited in a more or less physical way depending on the play's degree of seriousness. In *le Bal des voleurs,* Peterbono and his two friends disguise themselves by means of costumes. In the first act, Peterbono and Hector change costume and identity three times, and Gustave, four. In other less fantastic "Pièces Roses" and in the "Pièces Brillantes," a poor young girl is generally disguised as a rich one: Amanda in *Léocadia,* Isabelle in *l'Invitation au château.* The costume party in *Pauvre Bitos,* one of the "Pièces Grinçantes," becomes a pretext for Pirandelloish effects and the basis for an allegory intended to explain the revolutionists during the Reign of Terror as well as the psychology of the 1944–45 purge. In *la Répétition* the heroes, disguised in Louis XV costumes for an amateur performance of Marivaux's *la Double Inconstance,* are themselves involved in a cruel adventure of libertinage and passion similar to *les Liaisons dangereuses.* In *le Rendez-vous de Senlis* Georges is actually neither masked nor disguised, but he hires professional actors in order to create a family for himself.

Anouilh uses the device of the mask to get a double effect. First of all he brings back one of the essential and original elements of theatre: the assumption of someone else's identity or physical appearance which begins the very moment an actor pretends to be himself and another. One of the purest and most effective forms of theatricalism consists in producing a kind of chain of false identities, as in Beaumarchais' *le Mariage de Figaro,* in which a young actress is both herself and Cherubin, a young boy who during the play passes himself off as a girl. In many respects such theatre would seem to consist in superimposing masks on a face or in taking them off one after another, just as clowns manage endlessly to remove their multi-colored vests. Truth plays hide-and-seek on stage. And Anouilh has brought the game's spectacular aspects back to the French theatre of today.

On the other hand, he has also presented an ironic vision of life, for his characters are closest to certain truths when they consciously assume a mask. Not until he performed Marivaux did Tigre discover a passion he no longer believed himself capable of. Not until they disguised themselves as revolutionists during the Reign of Terror did the characters in *Pauvre Bitos* reveal their deeper selves. Not until she wore theatrical costumes and gave in to the artificial life backstage did Colombe discover her true gaiety. In *l'Invitation au château,* when Madame Desmermortes sees Isabelle—a poor girl hired to play the part of a mysterious rich girl—mingle with her guests at the ball, her comment is: "She's the only one who doesn't seem to be acting a part." Anouilh thus introduces an authentic dramatic effect: the revelation of the true through the false and because of the false.

Even a serious play like *Becket* is informed by that vision. Thomas à Becket, like most of Anouilh's characters, can only play his part well when he wears the costume symbolic of the part. By putting on a monk's habit or an Archbishop's sumptuous robes, Becket succeeds in identifying himself with the honor of God: a serious masquerade, but a masquerade. And it is through playing the parts that Becket finds his truth and his own honor.

In a play like *Becket* the close link between the refusal of Anouilh's heroes and the theatrical vision of life becomes clear. In fact they are inseparable. Whereas Salacrou recalls Pascal's anguish, Anouilh states Pascal's theme of *divertissement:* man tries to save himself from anguish by identifying himself with a role, with a game. Where there is game, there is a negation of earnestness. But the earnestness is restored in a higher form when there is total identification with the role, as in the case of Antigone or Becket. In the last analysis Anouilh's theatre is ambiguous: man's defeat in face of life, but his victory as a total actor, on whom neither Creons nor Inquisitors nor passionate kings can have any real hold.

The consequences of such an attitude are dual. On the one hand, it is the source of multiple theatrical effects, either original or borrowed from all that is obviously theatrical in the Commedia del'Arte, Shakespeare, Molière, or Beaumarchais. On the other hand, it gives enormous rights to theatre, since it is not only a metaphor of life but also a solution. Unexplained flash backs, juggling with time and space, a whole arsenal of devices which might be described as toned-down avant garde are not based on magic or the supernatural. They are pure theatrical freedom. They represent no more than the playwright's way of telling a story—in other words, the indefeasible power of theatre itself.

Salacrou also used modernist conventions to escape from a naturalist type construction. But, given the philosophical basis for his plays, his devices become simple working hypotheses. The mixture of flash back and allegory in *l'Inconnue d'Arras* is an example of Salacrou's method. Ulysses, the hero, relives his life in the one second separating the moment he shoots himself from that of his actual death. His wife, friends, and mistresses all appear, but the character-memories free themselves, become independent of the psychological hypothesis and involved in an action which is obviously no longer either a reminiscence or its development by Ulysses himself. Juxtaposition of past and present, sudden and integral reappearances of the past, dialogues between the dead and the living are presented neither as an image of the beyond nor as a solution to man's agony but as a spectacular means for otherwise impossible debates which demonstrate the play's thesis. Salacrou's devices, no more justified by psychology or the supernatural than Anouilh's, explain rather than resolve. For one the theatre is an end in itself; for the other, it is a means.

Since the war Anouilh's popularity has far exceeded Salacrou's and he is currently considered a combination Giraudoux-Boulevard playwright. There is no doubt that Anouilh's inventiveness, range of expression, scenic color and variey are far more enchanting than Salacrou's austerity and rather slow moving rhythm. Even when dealing with sordidness, Anouilh is picturesque or ironically amusing. Salacrou avoids brilliance. In many respects, a comparison between the grace and sparkle of one and the somewhat dull hardness of the other is unfair. But it is justified to the extent that together they are representative of what is best in today's theatre of bitterness and lucidity.

A satire of the modern family, customs, and politics, of false values, incoherence, hypocrisy, and the resulting confusion in individuals has been the most frequently used theatrical material from Edouard Bourdet's out-dated comedies to Marcel Aymé's violent attacks. Anouilh and Salacrou have assimilated and reinterpreted modern disenchantment, ranging from the bankruptcy of official values to the negation of God. They may not have phrased it in terms of a new philosophy, as did Sartre and Camus, nor have they expressed it in an absolutely revolutionary form, as did Beckett and Ionesco. But they have transcended purely psychological drama and brought out, beyond specific and limited conflicts, a certain definition of man and of drama itself.

Lost in a world where there is no answer, men somehow struggle, each on his own level, in the anguish of knowing that they are caught in an absurd mechanism or in a masquerade. Indeed the heroes cry out but in vain; they refuse their condition, with the final result being the stake, prison, a decadent old age, or just a draft that blows them away. Nothing remains but their consciousness of the situation and their pride in being able to say no to it, useless as that may be. Whether the "no" be in Antigone's unjustified attitude or in Joan of Arc's certainty, in Ulysses' suicide or the deliberate decision to laugh of *Une Femme trop honnête,* it is always the center around which the drama is organized. The play in itself is a protest. It is both a rebellion and a game, hence the symbol of an ambiguous victory.

CHAPTER 6

MAN AND HIS ACTS: JEAN-PAUL SARTRE AND ALBERT CAMUS

Anouilh makes a theatrical game out of disgust, cowardice, the torments of love, and the struggle of man, torn between his rather ignoble nature and a few higher aspirations. His theatre in itself would seem a kind of revenge on a socio-psychological prison. In Salacrou's plays the prison is placed in a Pascalian context. Man's acts, although situated within history, seem to have meaning only when considered in the light of eternity. But man, in his search, is finally brought back to man by the simple facts of suffering, age, and death.

Sartre and Camus give final form to this return to man.[1] Their originality consists in achieving it without going back to a scientific viewpoint, a vision limited to psycho-physiological determinism. What might have resulted in a neo-positivism—considering the collapse of our supposedly transcendent and absolute values—appears, on the contrary, as an affirmation of man's privileged metaphysical position. With the added notion that philosophy is more an object of action than of speculation, more a part of life than a play of ideas, the medium for existentialist thought became quite naturally a work of fiction: the novel or theatre.

Starting from the principle that man is alone before man and the fact that such a situation is understandable or conceivable only in terms of action, Sartre and Camus have tried to

1. Germaine Brée and Margaret Guiton, in their book on the contemporary French novel, *An Age of Fiction* (Rutgers University Press, New Brunswick, New Jersey, 1957), similarly described the *novels* of Sartre and Camus as a "return to man."

create a type of theatre in which the concrete representation of life and their own philosophical concepts are absolutely inseparable. Given their basic philosophical positions, the dialogue is indissolubly linked to physical *acts*. The plays are crammed with action or the expectation of action. Whether the play takes the form of an historical drama (Sartre's *le Diable et le Bon Dieu*), an allegory (Camus' *l'Etat de siège*), a kind of semi-detective story (Sartre's *les Mains sales,* Camus' *le Malentendu,* even Sartre's *Nekrassov*), or a series of debates (Sartre's *Huis Clos,* Camus' *les Justes*), the spectator is held by the expectation of rebounds, the promise of extreme and definitive acts, the surprise of certain dramatic effects, and the double question: What's going to happen? How will it turn out? Sometimes both writers do end by creating a rush of physical happenings that border on the unreal. Camus' *Caligula,* for instance, might seem like an arbitrary catalogue of acts of cruelty and madness. Hence the adjective "melodramatic" as applied by some critics to their plays.

As treated by Sartre and Camus, physical action, generally violent, takes on a new value in that their basic philosophy consists in destroying the importance traditionally accorded to motives. What really counts are not the reasons for an act but the act itself, its present significance, and the significance it gives to the characters and the world. In other words, the search for the psychological causality of an act is either shown to be vain or replaced by an investigation of the act's significance.

This does not mean a total rejection of motives. Although explanations may be reduced to a minimum, they are indeed necessary, for the acts are not gratuitous. Caligula himself, in Camus' play, does not gratuitously make an experiment of the gratuitous. He is pushed by a "need for the impossible," the "need for something that is not of this world." Yet the motive is only very briefly presented and in such terms that it seems more metaphysical than psychological. In certain cases the spectator, used to long verbal explanations, is possibly baffled.

Especially in *le Malentendu,* Martha's need for escape, leading to her murdering the wealthy clientele of the Inn in order to get money, is explained rather sketchily and always in the same terms. Here Camus' reaction to what is usually thought of as "psychological theatre" is particularly clear. A traditional writer would have easily taken up most of the play with long digressions on the psychology of suffocation, the misery and dismal mediocrity of Martha's life, etc. Camus merely sums up those digressions in an image of the sun and the sea. For the true subject of the play is elsewhere: in the absurd and fatal conjuncture of Martha's acts and her brother's almost unexplained behavior.

Even in a retrospective play like Sartre's *Huis Clos,* in which the acts are in the past and the characters try to evaluate them, emphasis is not put on discovering why, through what determinism of the world and men, the characters happened to commit their crimes. When they try, as Garcin occasionally does, they fail to reach any conclusion. The subject of the play is a study of the different ways in which men "bear" their acts. When any psychological causality is brought in, it is only as an a posteriori rationalization of the characters themselves. It is no more than a present state of consciousness. The same is true for *les Mains sales,* in which the long flash back that makes up the greater part of the play contributes nothing more than plain facts, and no explanation. The meaning of Hoederer's murder is given only in the present and through Hugo's decision. In *les Séquestrés d'Altona* as well, the hero is so tortured by the possible historical *significance* of his monstrous war crimes that he takes refuge in madness.

It has often been pointed out that Giraudoux's characters have hardly any pasts and are completely open to their futures. With a very different vision of the world, Sartre and Camus present much the same attitude. What counts for them is the project an act represents or its meaning in the present—a meaning which changes according to the agent's choices and the interpretation of other people. Of course for the existentialists, a concrete situation requires that a certain *nature* be taken into account. In general, no existentialist ever dreamed of denying given elements such as a man's body, sex, age, social class, temperament. And that weight, along with a consciousness of it and the effort made to objectify it or reject it, is inseparable from the subject of *les Mains sales, le Diable et le Bon Dieu,* or *les Séquestrés d'Altona.* To use the existentialist vocabulary, all freedom is *en situation;* but as Sartre and Camus want to bring out the irreducible element that distinguishes man from the rest of the world, their interest lies more in its manifestations and creations than in the mechanism of "natures" or "essences," which are considered as secondary. Such emphasis in theatre means a complete reversal of the treatment of action. Acts are no longer considered as products but as inventions.

Therefore an act is seen as a creation, almost as unique and irreplaceable as a signed work of art, and at the same time as both a source of drama and drama itself, not only at the moment it is committed—when it implies a struggle and a choice —but even afterwards, in man's effort to clarify the relationship between it and himself. Sartre's characters' frequent use of the expression "my act" emphasizes the idea of it being both an outer object and a reciprocal bond between man and what he does. His plays are investigations of the different relations of man to his acts, whether he tries to rid himself of them (which is impossible, whence Estelle's painful tragedy of bad faith in *Huis Clos,* Franz's escape into madness in *les Séquestrés d'Altona,* and Heinrich's devil in *le Diable et le Bon Dieu*) or completely assumes them. Without denying all the excuses that science gives for his behavior, man is considered in the perspective of the formula: In any case, whatever I do, *I* am the one who does it.

If the formula is taken as a central point, the existentialist theatre opens out around it and examines the ethical and political extensions it implies. Men are considered as having no excuses, as from the start it has been accepted that man is thus distinguished from the rest of the world.

As a result, the play's intensity depends largely on the seriousness of the acts committed. Everyday acts, taken one after the other, can be successfully used in the novel, as in Sartre's *la Nausée.* But dramatic economy demands that the weight of dilution be replaced by the shock of concentration, and the effect is produced through a violent or monstrous act. Indeed we are back to the ancient, Shakespearian, or classical conception of exemplary and extreme acts. If it is true that every act brings man's very being into question, murder, where even an illusion of reparation is impossible, is the best means of bringing it into play. Moreover Sartre and Camus, in the belief that great violence is a sign of the times, use murder in all its forms. As death is the situation par excellence for bringing man's being into question, whether the tragedy be private or collective, to kill or be killed is the symbol of man's greatest problem.

The more horrible the act, the more the individual, who always acts *alone,* begins to "question." Malraux, in *la Condition humaine,* had already described the solitude and anguish involved in murder. Sartre and Camus bring the greatest violence and the deepest solitude together in their situations. Solitude in this case is what separates the would-be murderer from the arguments in favor of the murder. For instance, in *les Mains sales* Hugo begins to like Hoederer whom he wants to kill for political reasons; and Kaliayev, in *les Justes,* had decided to throw a bomb at the Grand Duke until he saw children in the carriage. Emphasis is put on the isolation of each individual in his action or his suffering, in a vision of the world where, to use Roquentin's terms in *la Nausée,* there is obviously no "communion of souls"—for, as he says, "I have not fallen so low." My suffering is *my* suffering just as my murder, even in the case of collective action, is *my* murder.

The isolation of man in action is often symbolized by the

choice of heroes whose basic situations are exceptional. Orestes' background has made him a stranger to all the cities in Greece (*les Mouches*); Hugo is a young bourgeois in the Communist party (*les Mains sales*); Goetz is a military leader and a bastard born of a nobleman and a peasant (*le Diable et le Bon Dieu*); Lizzie is a prostitute on the fringe of American society (*la Putain respectueuse*); Nekrassov is an adventurer (*Nekrassov*); Kean is a great actor (*Kean*); Caligula is an emperor (*Caligula*); Kaliayev is a poet (*les Justes*).

Often there are more specific reasons for the choice of certain characters. In *les Mains sales,* for example, Sartre was speaking directly to the young bourgeois Frenchmen attracted by Communism at the time. But in general, the characters' exceptional situations are meant to express, in the form of a hyperbolic metaphor, the similar agony of any man faced with himself. They are not meant to imply that humanity is naturally divided into heroes and the superfluous rest of mankind.

The agony here is metaphysical. Although the hero may be acting out of passion or in the name of a value, what suddenly strikes him is the bare fact of his own existence and the dizzying vacuum of the nothingness it implies. Whether the hero be Sartre's Garcin, Goetz, Hugo, or Camus' Caligula, his hopeless discovery is that the world is absurd and his acts the unjustified creations of his freedom.

"You are no more than the sum of your acts," says Inez to Garcin in *Huis Clos*. The traditional idea that man commits such or such act because he is thus and so, is replaced with its opposite: by committing such or such act, man makes himself thus and so. Nothingness to start with, man spends his life giving himself an essence made up of all his acts. And it is through acting that he becomes conscious of original nothingness. The anguish that grips him is provoked by that nothingness, that absence of justification, and the metaphysical responsibility which makes him the creator of his own essence.

The idea is alien to many minds. It is uncomfortable, to start with. But more important it eliminates the notion of human nature, a fundamental concept in Western thought, and treats human destiny in itself as meaningless and useless agitation, in other words, absurd. The dramatic hero also finds it difficult to accept, and the conflict between his awareness of the absurd and his need for justification constitutes the strongest dramatic tension in Sartre's and Camus' works.

Once the hero accepts the idea—if he does—a second dramatic conflict becomes apparent: what is he to do now? The choice is simple. Either he can fall back into blindness and bad faith, that is, into a belief in reasons, eternal essences, the value of established orders, human or divine, with a meaning given in advance; or he can assume his acts and his life, fully aware of the world's absurdity, and accept the crushing responsibility of giving the world a meaning that comes from himself alone.

In his first play, *les Mouches,* Sartre showed the transition from frivolous freedom to the discovery of terrifying metaphysical freedom. He also showed that the discovery is unbearable (Electra's collapse) and at the same time how, unbearable as it may be, man can save himself and others when he assumes his act, as Orestes did.

Orestes is an apprentice, just as Caligula is to a certain extent in Camus' play and Goetz in *le Diable et le Bon Dieu.* Except that Orestes is in the privileged position of not being from anywhere and participating in nothing. When Jupiter tells him about the crimes of Clytemnestra and Aegisthus, he answers: ". . . I couldn't care less. I'm not from here" (Act I, scene 1). A bit later, when he begins to dream about the lives of men who are anchored in one place, with their possessions and their worries, he feels a touch of regret but continues all the same to congratulate himself on what he calls his "freedom": "Thank God I am free. Oh! How free I am. And what a superb absence is my soul" (Act I, scene 2). There Sartre, with the help of the Greek myth, skipped a certain number of stages. His hero is already outside the blind conformity of collective behavior.

Having begun life with the illusion of disengagement taught him by his cosmopolitan pedagogue, Orestes, at the cost of a great struggle and a double murder, succeeds in creating the "royal way" that leads him to assume his own acts. In addition to his pedagogue's impossible frivolity, he has to avoid two temptations: the attitude of the oppressed social group, convinced that their oppression is in the order of things, and its correlative, the alliance with a divine order, symbolized by the terrifying and grotesque figure of Jupiter. In other words, he must avoid the freedom of the "spider's web that floats ten feet above the earth at the mercy of the wind" (Act I, scene 2), as well as the human and divine traps that transform man into something determined, into "stone" (Act III, scene 2). By murdering his mother and her lover, Orestes discovers that an act is nothing more than an enormous and obscene presence, a parasite of man, both exterior and possessive. Orestes is the hero who understands that the act is his and only his. He also understands that it has outer consequences: a tyrant's death frees the oppressed people, whose bondage stemmed only from the tyrant. But as far as the act itself is concerned, only the agent can determine its weight, only the agent bears the burden. *Les Mouches* is a sumptuous metaphor intended to show men that responsibility is not synonymous with guilt, that the world of men is made up of the impact of actions, whose meaning comes only from the men who committed or suffered them. The play also indicates that the plague (and here we partially rejoin Camus) exists only to the extent that men accept it. The plague is in fact no more than the imposition of responsibility on others from the outside, and man has the power to counter that act with a contrary act.

This point of view has brought true overtones of tragedy to the theatre of Sartre and Camus. Their heroes love life. They have no particular desire to die, nor do they seek any glorification in death. But they prefer death to a degradation of the man within them. They fall from a high state in that, whether emperors or proud terrorists, they are reduced to suicide, prison, and physical or moral torture. And the catastrophe is always accompanied by an awareness which makes them superior to that which crushes them. However their awareness does not imply the recognition of a superior order but rather a recognition of man as the one and only value.

On that level, Sartre's and Camus' plays can be divided into two categories: those in which emphasis is put on the agony itself (*le Malentendu, Huis Clos*) and those in which both writers, succumbing to a kind of proselytism, seem to want to prove that the only way of really being a man among men is to assert one's freedom by rebelling against established orders, mere masks of the absurd (*l'Etat de siège, les Mouches*). In the second category, the theme of the efficacy of action prevails over that of its absurdity. In *l'Etat de siège* the hero dies but his revolt continues and sea air purifies the pest-ridden city. Whereas in *le Malentendu* Martha's suicide leaves a bitter impression on the spectator. Not that her death is useless, for it has the ultimate value of a protestation; but at the end of the play, the world closes in on Martha's testimony just as the river water covers her body. Yet in both cases, whether the action is effective or only a desperate protest, the basic tragedy and heroism are the same. And the writers' intentions were the same: to bring out, from behind the false face of humanity, man's true condition.

Here the return to man excludes a tableau of everyday life and mediocrity. Men are not truly men in their petty and niggardly daily acts but rather at the moment the idea of man is heroically brought into question through themselves. Consequently when everyday banalities are suggested, it is only to emphasize their *inauthenticité,* that is, their power to dehumanize the individual by blinding him to his own freedom.

The portrayal of beings and situations at their most ordinary and average constitutes a complete misunderstanding of humanism. Sartre's and Camus' humanism makes a distinction between a false humanity, which doubtless merits being portrayed but not as the true definition of man, and a true humanity, which in the world today can be found in any individual at moments of great crisis or in extreme situations. At such times man really wonders what he is. What counts is the portrayal of man, stripped of his pettiness and "the most man possible"—that is, not positively defined but rather suspended between possible definitions. For man can be defined as being outside any definition and at the same time bewilderingly in search of one. The best means of concretely expressing that point of view is the portrayal of characters caught in a paroxysm of situations and acts.

While both the existentialists' and Camus' way of considering the relation between man and his acts is profoundly dramatic in itself, the addition of a supplementary element, bearing also on the basic philosophy, makes the plays of Sartre and Camus not only dramatic but theatrical as well.

In the three chapters devoted to Albert Camus' theatre in her recent book, *Camus,* Germaine Brée comes back time and again to the theme of the play within the play and the characters' own staging of it. The "play" that Caligula deliberately puts on as an answer to the blind performance of the Roman patricians and humanity in general is the most striking example. In *le Malentendu* the action is made up of two opposed scenarios: Ian's return to his homeland—both written and played by him, and the scenario of melodramatic murderers enacted by Martha and his mother. The Plague in *l'Etat de siège* stages his own arrival by sending a comet into the skies of Cadiz as a Prologue. He then transforms the décor and forces the people to play parts, stipulated in advance, in a vast allegory of oppression and dehumanization. Even the heroes of *les*

Justes are cast as actors who are conscious of the roles assigned to them, wear disguises, and work out the staging for a political assassination. Thus Camus' characters are made up of those who write their own dramas and play the parts of their own choosing, and those who are subjected to a scenario written by others.

Sartre also seems to have had a similar theatrical vision in most of his plays. The characters in *Huis Clos* act out precisely the drama expected of them by the powers of Hell; Goetz is the stage director of Good and Evil in *le Diable et le Bon Dieu;* Jupiter and Aegisthus organize the collective spectacle of men and the universe in *les Mouches;* the leading characters in *Nekrassov* and *la Putain respectueuse* are made to play parts written in advance by the powers of this world; and the problems of the actor himself are portrayed in *Kean,* an adaptation of Alexandre Dumas' play.

On the whole, such references to a theatre of life give an especially theatrical savor to the works of Sartre and Camus. Their devices are somewhat comparable to those of Cocteau and Anouilh but the implications and significance are different. Rather than provide a solution to life by living "as if," the use of an imposed scenario or a play within the play is meant to furnish a means for action. The job of the stage director consists in assigning a place and a function to everyone and everything in relation to a given end and a plan of the whole. Defined as part of a whole, things and individual beings must sacrifice their spontaneity and freedom. The tension thus created generally results in an explosion of the elements outside the game or of anyone who freely refuses to enter in. Sometimes the stage director's order wins (*la Putain respectueuse*); most often the unpredictability of the absurd (*le Malentendu*) or of freedom (*les Mouches, les Mains sales, le Diable et le Bon Dieu, l'Etat de siège*) reduces man's scenarios and the metaphoric scenarios of the gods to nothing; and on occasion the individual or private self, the person who answers for his own fears, loves, etc. stands out at the height of the action as isolated and separated from the over-all plan (*les Justes, Morts sans sépulture*).

The great directors are the oppressors, the liberators, and the experimenters. Jupiter and Aegisthus, the Plague, the American senator, and in certain respects the Communist party, belong to the first category; the revolutionaries and Martha in relation to herself, to the second; Caligula and Goetz, to the third. In other words this particular form of second degree theatre, as compared to that found in other works, is not presented as an esthetic solution of the absurd, but as a metaphor of the oppressive order as well as the necessary means to explode its lies and injustices. Whether mask or anti-mask, it takes the form of a scenario written in advance and, through a necessary antithesis, evokes the themes of freedom and contingency. Anouilh also used the device in *Antigone, l'Alouette,* and other plays in which the heroes refuse to play the game of a scenario written in advance. But Anouilh's solution lies in the play itself, in the very theatricalism of the conflict, whereas in Sartre and Camus theatrical creation is always a means, never a reconciliatory end.

In *le Diable et le Bon Dieu* Goetz is an extraordinary actor who identifies with the roles of his choice. Several times during the play, he is called "buffoon." He acts for an audience: God. He finally discovers that his "play" has been no more than a bloody farce and that the spectator he counted on was missing. From the balcony of the sky, only a gaping emptiness looks down upon him. Just as in Camus' play Caligula tried to be pure Evil, Goetz tried to be one hundred per cent Good. Both are inventors and challenge the order of the world. What their social experiments leave them with is emptiness and negation. A desire for the absolute in the name of man leads to the destruction of man and the loss of humanity. As Germaine Brée points out, such imposition of the absolute is much the same as the Plague's absolute and abstract order in *l'Etat de siège*.

Having brought their heroes to the experience of nothingness and the consciousness of a universe without hope and
without illusion, both writers found it necessary to reintegrate
life. In *Caligula* Cheréa, who "lives within the truth, without
hope and without delusion . . . , recognizes the relative human order in which reign 'those truths of the flesh' that are
lived and not demonstrated." [2] Others return to life through
the concrete tasks imposed by urgent problems: Goetz finally
agrees to use his talents as a military leader by helping the
peasant rebellion; Diego, in *l'Etat de siège,* succeeds in convincing his fellow citizens to open the doors of the city in
order to let in the sea air.

The basic conflict then is threefold: the comedy of a world
of illusions (false justifications) as opposed to the theatre or
anti-theatre of those who seek the absolute, and both opposed
to the plain fact of existence as it is lived or to be lived, both
individually and collectively. In Camus existence as such is
expressed more or less allegorically in the character Cheréa in
Caligula and the Mediterranean richness of certain images in
l'Etat de siège and *le Malentendu.* Sartre expresses it less poeti-
cally in Hoederer's vitality and relation to objects in *les Mains
sales,* Hilda's love in *le Diable et le Bon Dieu,* and *Nekrassov*'s
gaiety. But as it is most often outside the play, it can only be
alluded to. Man's unchanging tragedy lies both in the search
for it and in the tension between the first two elements of the
conflict.

Despite great similarities in basic philosophy and theatrical
vision, Sartre and Camus differ profoundly on the esthetic level,
just as in a comparable way *la Nausée* differs from *l'Etranger,*
or *la Peste* from *les Chemins de la liberté.*

Sartre's dramatic universe is nearer to realism or traditional
naturalism. Eric Bentley [3] points out the fact that *Huis Clos*

2. Germaine Brée, *Camus,* p. 167.
3. Eric Bentley, *The Playwright as a Thinker.*

is essentially Strindbergian in tone and a drawing-room comedy in form. And indeed three Boulevard melodramas can easily be made out of each of the three characters' lives: a frivolous young lady who killed her child, a rather nasty lesbian who led her friend to suicide, a pacifistic journalist who deserted in time of war—all psychological dramas with social implications and perfect material for a "well-made" play. Even the setting for each drama is suggested: the lesbian's room with its gas stove, the newspaper office with the editors in shirt sleeves, the elegant room in Switzerland with its windows giving on to the lake. Sartre deliberately chose three rather typical news items and kept certain "true" details—that is, their naturalist color.

When Camus chooses a news item (*le Malentendu*), he chooses an exceptional one and then strips it of anything that might evoke everyday life. Moreover he eliminates any familiarity or banality from the language. His characters all speak the same language—a kind of stylized and intense common denominator, which wipes out any naturalist implications behind their purified intentions and feelings. Whereas Sartre, although he brands his characters with his own images and syntax, fills their dialogue with expressions and devices that closely copy naturalist "reality." One has only to compare the hangman's lines in the fourth act of *les Justes* with those of Hoederer's bodyguards in *les Mains sales* or the guards of Apollo's temple in *les Mouches*. In the case of characters who would normally use slang expressions, Camus keeps the slang to a minimum, while Sartre deliberately uses it as much as possible, along with syntactical ellipses.

The same holds true for form. In Sartre there are frequent references to traditional or familiar genres: *vaudeville,* drama, historical drama, etc. The décors themselves are conventional: real rooms, real garrets, real German countryside. Even a fantastic setting like the Second Empire drawing room in *Huis Clos* is fantastic because of its realism. The Barbedienne bronze statue, the Louis Philippe couch, and the bricks that obstruct the window are scenically effective only if they look real and are not artistically suggested. In that respect, Sartre has contributed considerably less to the development of theatre than Camus, who eliminated most references to familiar genres, aimed at a very special economy in his settings as well as language, and launched out into experiments of highly stylized total theatre.

Yet Sartre had reasons for what he did. He wanted first to get the spectator on familiar ground and then gradually bring him into existentialist drama, far from his familiar ground. In *Huis Clos,* for instance, the naturalism of each character's "case" and the realism of language and décor create an image of the beyond that is acceptable to audiences accustomed by films and theatre to seeing death represented in very earthly forms. But the true subject of the play is revealed on a third level. It is neither in the anecdotal interest of a few adventures or perversions, nor in the modernist pathos of the allegory of Hell, but in the relation of one consciousness to another, in the search for a definition of the self with the help of others, in the realization that the presence and judgement of others is necessary and yet leads to an impasse.[4] On that level the whole takes on all its meaning, and we discover that the play is not a metaphor of Hell but that the image of Hell is a metaphor of the hopeless suffering of individuals in search of their definitions in the eyes of others, yet constantly brought back to themselves.

Garcin's reticence in telling about how he deserted and especially how he physically fell apart at the time of his execution is an excellent subject for a naturalistic psychological drama: the pacifist has a shameful secret; he acted out of cowardice. And part of the dialogue is directed toward that drama, but at one point it turns away from it and moves toward an ex-

4. *Huis Clos* was first published in *l'Arbalète,* No. 8 (Lyon, 1943) as *les Autres* or the Others.

istentialist perspective. Once it has been established that an inquiry into the motives for an act does not reveal the act's meaning, Garcin's hopeless tragedy lies in the fact that he is unable to determine the meaning of his life by himself and is condemned to live between two women—one totally indifferent to the question and the other who, needing "the suffering of others in order to exist," decides that he has been cowardly and is thus satisfied with the spectacle of his shame.

Sartre's plays lead the spectator from the universe of perception, common sense, and psychological or esthetic habits to an existentialist conclusion, often difficult in its newness. What Sartre shows essentially is that his vision of the world is inherent in the normal universe. His method consists in bringing it out progressively. And often the progression itself makes up the greater part of the play.

Les Mains sales is presented as a politico-detective drama, based on a simple question comparable to the suspense-provoking questions in melodrama: Why did Hugo kill Hoederer? The suspense is all the more acute in that the spectator knows that Hugo's life depends on the answer. We take part in an investigation and a trial. The actual investigation, which takes up six of the seven tableaux, is in the form of a flash back concerned only with the simple fact of Hoederer's death and leaving the murder committed by Hugo in all its ambiguity. Sartre played the game of the detective story melodrama according to the rules but he stopped short of melodramatic satisfaction. The "secret" we are supposed to uncover is not uncovered and we understand that it is impossible to uncover it. In a sense the naturalistic melodrama destroys itself under our very eyes, leaving hero and spectator open to whatever lies ahead. Having finished his long demonstration and created the necessary vacuum, Sartre can then go on to lead both spectator and hero into the true subject of his play. In the last fifteen minutes we discover that the meaning of Hoederer's murder does not lie in Hugo's reasons for it, which in any case remain ambiguous.

Hugo's true motive is the one he chooses *afterward* when, fully aware of the situation, he determines—through his own death—the meaning of the situation and the value of Hoederer's life and his own. Somewhat the same gradual transition takes place within Goetz and the spectator in *le Diable et le Bon Dieu,* although its dialectic is not as clear because of the play's enormity.

In Camus' plays also, spectator and hero are led to make a common discovery, and the element of detective story suspense, the interest in what will happen next is one dimension of his theatre. But the level of the play's true subject is given straight away. There is almost no transition from one vision of the universe to another. *Caligula* begins with the emperor having just discovered the world of freedom and the absurd. Had Sartre written *Caligula,* he would doubtless have shown the hero making his decisive discovery in the first act, beginning with Drusilla's death and going on to show how Caligula was shocked by it and how it led up to his final experiment. In Camus' play the curtain goes up on an imaginary world whose dimensions are given from the very beginning and once and for all. Hence the dual impression of classical economy and intransigence.

Camus' uncompromising esthetics is based on a symbolic vision, far indeed from Sartre's. The Germany of *le Diable et le Bon Dieu,* deformed and stylized as it may be, *is* Germany during the period of the peasant revolts; whereas the Rome of *Caligula* has as little reality as the Naples of certain of Molière's comedies or the Poland of *Ubu Roi.*[5] Sartre takes an historic event and brings out its significance. Camus starts with a general dramatic conflict and then embodies it fictionally. Symbol prevails over locality. Thus despite a few clear allusions to the present state of Spain, the Cadiz of *l'Etat de siège* represents as imaginary a locality as the North African city in his novel *la Peste.* It is quite simply a city in a dry sun-scorched country

5. Despite Camus' research. See Germaine Brée, *Camus,* p. 146.

near the sea, which enables Camus to make use of his familiar myths.

While Sartre generally first tells a story, rich enough in realistic elements to be self-contained, Camus constructs a poetic allegory based on a conflict. In her book on Camus, Germaine Brée points out that Camus' most obviously anecdotal play, *le Malentendu,* "is entirely symbolical." In *Caligula, les Justes,* and *l'Etat de siège* the traditional creation of characters is replaced by the symbolical embodiment of possible attitudes to a dramatic conflict. And consequently Camus lays himself open to the traditional criticism of allegorical literature, the contrived embodiment of ideas or entities. But in all esthetic sincerity and by means of an immediate stylization of dialogue and characters, Camus does present his plays as intellectual creations from the moment the curtain goes up.

Less popular than his other plays but more ambitious and perhaps closer to the "modern tragedy" he sought, *l'Etat de siège* represents a synthesis of Camus' esthetics and general ideas, combining the philosophy of acts and extreme situations with a certain form of symbolism. In his preface Camus explains how Jean-Louis Barrault, inspired by Artaud, was haunted by the meaning and symbol of the plague and wanted to create a play around it. Camus, having just published his novel *la Peste,* was the obvious man to write the script. In this case the symbol was given first. Since he had already worked with it on several levels in his novel, Camus' job consisted in making the maledictions that crush man coincide with the physical ravages of the plague. The metaphor is not spontaneous; it is the result of a collective effort including three minds: Artaud, Barrault, Camus. *L'Etat de siège* is characteristic of Camus' art in that it is the development and extension of a simile he had already worked out. It is a theatrical exercise on a given subject: organized totalitarianism is the plague of the modern world.

The plague itself is embodied in a rather portly man in

uniform who takes over the government in Cadiz with the help of his secretary, Death. The symbol is obvious and becomes all the more so at the beginning of the second act when the Kafkaesque satire on bureaucracy starts to sound like Courteline-become-metaphysical. In addition, every character in the play, when confronted with the Plague, embodies a simple attitude, a commonplace opinion or way of behaving. The most important one, next to the rebellious hero's, is that of Nada, who by his very name represents man at the level of nihilistic despair. Allegorical as it may be, the play does remain "existentialist" in its general philosophy. The hero is he who successfully counters the established order with the refusal of a free being—a refusal which, ironically enough, almost seduces Death, but which the hero finally pays with his life. And actually the play contains symbols of all the necessary stages: *inauthenticité,* rebellion, confidence in life despite everything. A "total" play in its themes, Camus and Barrault wanted also to make it a total play on a scenic level: abstract dialogue, lyrical *tirades,* individual and collective pantomime, spectacular effects, etc. Both totalities are meant to correspond in the alternation between the comments of the real people (lovers, fishermen, etc.) and the speeches of personified abstractions (the Plague, Death). The play's partial failure comes from the fact that the whole is more an intellectual allegory than a living synthesis. Yet it is one of the rare attempts at uniting modern philosophy and modern theatre.

Camus' and Sartre's esthetics are as different as their general ideologies are similar. In Sartre innovations in form are secondary to content. In Camus esthetic consciousness is inseparable from the substance. Yet their intentions are much alike in that both have tried to give French audiences theatre that is neither an agreeable repetition of past masterpieces, even recent ones, nor a purely modernist esthetic thrill. They have also agreed on the idea of an art that is completely concerned with and in terms of our times. Their common purpose has been both to describe the man of today and to write for the man of today. Such is doubtless the intention of all writers, but in Sartre and Camus it takes the form of a conscious rule, affirmed and reaffirmed as a writer's first duty. An acute consciousness of the modern world and a true identification with its problems and demands have determined the themes and esthetics of both. And although Camus had time and again refused to be labeled "existentialist," he *can* be considered committed or *engagé*, if literary *engagement* is taken in its broadest sense as writing for one's time, directly or indirectly about one's time, with man's freedom as an ultimate goal.

In the light of such an attitude many literary positions must be rejected as survivals of a dead past. Psychological analyses in classical terms, reducing man to a determinism which is now thought to be precisely not man; historical and picturesque reconstruction for itself; freezing man in the ice of dead essences; the exclusive cult of beauty; placing the meaning of the world outside man—all are eliminated, not absolutely but relatively: the present and man's tragedy at this moment of history are considered more important and rich enough to take precedence over any other concern.

Thus the central problem of Malraux's novels has been brought to the theatre by Sartre and Camus. They chose their subjects among the most burning issues of our times: wars, oppression, rebellions, revolutions, and through them reached the so-called universal themes—but stated in new terms. Instead of traditional psychologism, the entire human being is called into question.[6]

Camus' allegorization and his refusal to emphasize, as does

6. As if by chance, a whole group of "engaged" plays appeared on Paris stages during the forties and fifties, presenting the point of view of the right as well as the left. Aside from the Anouilh plays that skirt existentialism, the most interesting works, in reaction or in imitation, are Thierry-Maulnier's *la Maison de la nuit* (1953) and Colette Audry's *Soledad* (1956).

Sartre, the topical aspect of his dramas, show that he aimed at a non-historic universality. Yet in his plays today's problems are always in the foreground. His choice of the plague as a symbol was determined less by its timeless universality than by its particularly violent activity at the present time. "Today the technique is perfected," says the Plague in *l'Etat de siège,* after having gone over the plagues of the past "when the idea was there. But not the whole idea. . . ."[7] In other words, although the plague is doubtless continuous and permanent, it is at its height in our times. "Codified" to perfection, it is close to an absolute victory over subjugated man. Yet today is also a time of hope among men who have understood that they are free.

In trying to make this clear in their plays and also in order to reach the largest public possible, Sartre in his works as a whole and Camus in *l'Etat de siège* were often forced, given the difficulty of their philosophies, into simplifications and sometimes even concessions. Sartre gave in and used Boulevard-type details and facile naturalist techniques, especially flagrant in *les Séquestrés d'Altona.* He also spelled out certain of his arguments in easily assimilated formulas, and by seeming intellectually clearer, sacrificed many nuances necessary to a complete understanding of his philosophy, while losing in dramatic reality as well. As for Camus, his often abstract maxims, used as articulations, are often more intellectual than dramatic.

For theirs is a theatre of ideas—exactly the kind Gide had hoped to see created by Giraudoux. Neither Sartre nor Camus are primarily playwrights. Sartre is above all a professional philosopher. Camus is obviously more of an artist and was always active in the world of theatre,[8] but all his works are

7. The term Idea, as an expression of the abstract system that crushes man, can also be found in the Inquisitor's speeches in Anouilh's *l'Alouette.*

8. For example, his collaboration with "le Théâtre du Travail," founded in Algiers in 1935, and his many adaptations.

dominated by intellectual searching and the examination of ideas. Yet what distinguishes their plays from other "philosophical" theatre is the absolutely dramatic and concrete nature of their philosophy itself. The fundamental problem of the definition of man and the world is truly embodied in living acts.

PART III

REVOLUTION CONTINUED

CHAPTER 7

POETRY AND DISCOVERY

Historical perspective has made it relatively easy to pick out the outstanding names among the "elder" playwrights: Giraudoux, Claudel, Cocteau . . . Nor is it difficult to isolate those of more recent date such as Sartre, Camus, Anouilh, Salacrou, Montherlant. But during the 1950s, from one year to another, many new and disparate works—always revolutionary, often promising, sometimes enchanting—have kept French theatre in a constant state of alert. Among the new crop of writers, Eugène Ionesco and Samuel Beckett are the unquestionable masters. But the others?

Those mentioned in the following catalogue will surely be astonished to find themselves put side by side. Brought to the public's attention by directors of little theatres that have been particularly energetic since the war, they have been compared to "rocks lost in the middle of the sea." [1] And in fact, excepting the general movement represented by Beckett, Ionesco, Adamov, and Arrabal, it is impossible to group together worlds as different as those of Ghelderode, Schehadé, and Jean Vauthier, for example.

Yet they are all bound by a systematic refusal to return to naturalism and the consequences of that refusal, an ever increasing poetic freedom. Aside from Schehadé, they all deal in violence, each one in his way and with his own universe, trying to give a hyperbolic image to the spasms of a world being torn apart. Most of them handle their violence with the devices of farce, a genre that has been generally revived during

1. Guy Dumur, "les Poètes au théâtre," *Théâtre de France*, No. 4 (1954).

the last twenty years.[2] From the acts of the Frères Jacques to Ionesco's theatre, truly modern farce has become somewhat Baudelairean. Its humor is sacrilegious, is conscious of being sacrilegious, wants to be sacrilegious. As suffering is at the root of laughter, the modern public, permeated with humanitarianism, necessarily finds it cruel. Its revengeful laughter is now conscious of its profanation and modern humor has become "dark."

Such similarities do exist, but individual temperaments are far stronger. In some, lyricism stifles the farce. In others, an earthy well-being wipes out the pessimism or cruelty. There are also varying degrees of originality. Shades of earlier poets such as Supervielle or Roger Vitrac lurk behind Schehadé's poetry or certain of Ionesco's absurdities. The only justification for grouping the following writers is their impact on French theatre in recent years.

First among the playwrights produced by the little theatres is Michel de Ghelderode, whose case is a special one. He is Belgian, has been writing for the theatre since 1919, has been performed in his own country since 1925, but never really reached French audiences until the performance of *Fastes d'enfer* in 1949. Since that date, young directors have continued to draw upon his plays for their repertoires; in France his complete works have been published by Gallimard; and in the United States David Grossvogel has given him primary importance in his book *The Self-Conscious Stage in Modern French Drama*.

The surface characteristics of Ghelderode's universe are

2. During the forties and fifties, farces of the past (Molière's, the *vaudeville* of Labiche and Feydeau) were seen more and more on the official stages and in avant-garde theatres. Imitations of traditional farce, such as Claude Santelli's *la Famille Arlequin,* have been produced. And at the same time, modern farce has been developing and multiplying, either in the form of more or less contemporary sketches (Guillaume Hanoteau's *la Tour Eiffel qui tue*) or as an Aristophanic magnification of today's political conflicts (Sartre's *Nekrassov*).

dazzling. Masqueraders, grotesque figures, living corpses, gluttonous and lustful men and women frantically move about in a décor of purple shadows, full of strong smells, and throw violent, foul, or mysterious phrases at each other in highly-colored language filled with Belgian idioms, archaisms, and shrieks. There is no rest in Ghelderode's theatre; the shock is permanent. Everything is pushed toward a paroxysm of language and spectacle—a flamboyant theatre, based on Flemish art, its culture, its puppets, its painters, its legends, its humor. But in overstressing Ghelderode's Flemish background, so obvious in itself, one is in danger of losing sight of his works' deeper value and of seeing them only as an overwhelming display of folklore. A joyful or macabre kermess, his theatre brings out the real meaning of the village fair. Its picturesque quality stops being just a curiosity and becomes poetry. Rather than set up a barrier of exoticism, it heightens our own colors.

Some of Ghelderode's plays are devoted to the world of theatre and its mystery (*Sortie d'acteur, Trois Acteurs, un drame*). Many of his characters are clowns, jesters, or masqueraders. As a theatre of theatre, it brings out the reciprocal relations between theatre and life. To more charitable relations of Creation, Ghelderode opposes a vision of life conceived as a parody of Creation, as a painful Farce.

One substance in his enormous Farce is real and felt in all of its frankness and weight: the flesh. It is deformed, obscene, stinking, demanding. It is shown by every possible means and nails the characters to earth. Even in suffering, it is the object of baroque acceptation, not of negative distress, as in Beckett's theatre. On a broader level, Ghelderode's theatre is made up of matter, a stuff that is forced on all the senses. Flesh, crimson velvet, gold, and excrement are an essential part of the spectacle and the language. Ghelderode's poetry consists in constantly harking back to that bath of matter. Lavishly handled, it leads to nothing other than itself and to the appetites of which it is the object: avarice, gluttony, or sexual desire.

Constantly present to all the senses, matter is the stuff of the characters' actions and excitement. Ghelderode used a process of baroque amplification to create a burlesque of man's condition. Each character is kept in a state of indignity by the weight of his body, his physical deformations, his sensual relations with other matter. Where the matter would ordinarily be accepted as a sign of grandeur, Ghelderode shows it in decay or gives it monstrous forms so that the usual symbol is replaced by the recognition of matter as such: In *Hop Signor!* the garden resembles "some old forgotten cemetery," in *Fastes d'enfer* the hangings in the episcopal palace are falling in shreds.

All that would be no more than a savage masquerade and pure farce if every play did not imply a more or less explicit higher appeal. Some of what Ghelderode has to say is fairly simple. For example, in *Christophe Colomb* it was not Columbus' intention to discover America, that material object which satisfied such puppets as the character l'Homme-Foule; he was in fact looking for the "ideal sphere." In *l'Ecole des bouffons,* while rebellion would seem to be the solution that would bring Folial's disciples out of their misery, a reversal of the situation reveals a higher truth: the condition of all great art is cruelty. But more than values like the absolute, love, or art, the pole of dramatic tension as opposed to the massive and weighty presence of matter is principally represented by death and its mysteries. The allegory of *la Ballade du Grand Macabre,* Lazarus with roots growing out of him in *Mademoiselle Jaïre,* all the hangmen, all the corpses are concrete manifestations of death, which haunts Ghelderode's works. Death is in the matter itself: it eats it away, deforms it, tears it apart.

The mystery of death rises up before the evidence of the flesh. Sometimes at the end of the farce, brutal and ironical as in *Magie Rouge,* sometimes the very subject of the play as in *Mademoiselle Jaïre,* the obvious fact of inevitable death gives Ghelderode's theatre its tragic aspect. On the whole, the plays are constructed according to two different patterns: either they are similar to certain types of baroque and classical comedies of intrigue, although the artificial happy endings of traditional comedy are replaced by a necessary death—negation of the life of the flesh and the senses, of indeed the very motivation of the plot (*Hop Signor!, Magie rouge*); or both levels are constantly juxtaposed, and the consciousness of their permanent relationship creates the play's tension (*la Ballade du Grand Macabre, Mademoiselle Jaïre, Fastes d'enfer*). Fundamentally an annihilator of the universe of intrigue and sensual pleasure in which the characters swarm, death is also the bearer of meanings which give tragedy its transcendency and always more or less transform the play into a mystery: the union in death of Purmelende and Sire Halewyn in a frenzied and Gothic transposition of the theme of Judith in *Sire Halewyn*, that of the executioner Larose and Marguerite in *Hop Signor!*, the union of Mademoiselle Jaïre and Lazarus, both risen from the dead, modified by the expectation of a second death and a fusion with God.

Since the conflict is above all one between death and the flesh, it is only natural that Ghelderode often allude to the mystery that best expresses it: the mystery of Lazarus. It is also natural that within that mystery, he choose and develop the theme of *jam putet* in all its horror. The smells of the kermess are comparable to the odors of corpses, which are themselves held up to ridicule in the enormous olfactory confusion at the end of *Fastes d'enfer*. Ghelderode's force lies precisely in that skillful mixture of the greatest horror and the most knockabout farce, a kind of exaggerated Romanticism. One cannot exist without the other, one issues from the other.[3] The mystery of death is so grandiose that it must be enveloped by rite, by ceremonies which of themselves turn to buffoonery.

Ghelderode's theatre indicates a way toward the realization of a "primordial" drama, where tragic horror and the frankest

3. The absence of farce in *Sire Halewyn* almost reduces it to a pompous Romantic-symbolist melodrama.

guffaws are indissolubly mixed. By using local tradition and pushing it to the limit of its possibilities, Ghelderode is not far removed from the Elizabethans and the Spanish dramatists. He touches on the primitive joys of the body, its appetites and their satisfaction, inseparable from the ambiguous fear of individual or collective death, annihilating and revealing at the same time—in other words, an Apocalypse.

A combination of farce and melodramatic horror, blended with outbursts of poetic language, is also at the basis of most of Audiberti's plays. But Audiberti added parody and an accumulation of surprises, thus creating a very special type of adventure-comedy. His effects are sometimes facile: the intrusions of typed characters like the volcanic and revolutionary Mexican woman in *Quoat-Quoat* or disguised characters like La Bequilleuse in *les Naturels du Bordelais,* who is successively a dealer in aphrodisiacs, a fashionable poet, and a police assistant; behavior contrary to the situation or station of the characters, like the Prime Minister's arrogance toward his king in *le Mal court,* the Princess's strip tease in front of the Cardinal in the same play, or the puny son's unexpected success with thirty women in *les Femmes du Boeuf.* But he uses his comic and even farcical elements, borrowed from various traditions, as pretexts for verbal embellishments and displays. Where Ghelderode always pushes in the same direction, Audiberti freely breaks loose. He draws his comedy from the Boulevard, from farce, from melodrama—imaginative fireworks and a burlesque poetry whose boldness goes beyond parody and irony, and reintroduces anxiety, mystery, horror. The scene in *Quoat-Quoat* in which the hero tells his secret to the captain's daughter, the scene in *le Mal court* in which the Princess describes her own body, the transformation of the characters into crickets in *les Naturels* are so many quasi-surrealistic or terrifying extensions of situations otherwise parodic and simple.

The objective of the parodies and an unrestrained, often delirious poetry is to disclose a monstrous reality behind the jesting or the absurdity of the adventures. Audiberti's drama is built on the relations between a surface life, represented by the plot and its absurd reversals, and deeply hidden primitive forces. The surface life is like a repercussion, a reflection which in itself can be treated lightly. The god Quoat-Quoat, the Evil that spreads, the earthly and mythical forces of *l'Ampélour,* the natural forces of *les Femmes du Boeuf* or *Pucelle,* the sensual appetites of *la Logeuse* are all representations of forces that are perhaps hidden but always present and controlling.

Audiberti's originality lies in the play between the language describing the monsters and ambiguous scenic effects. The language creates a state of belief in the supernatural, in its incarnation. And at just the right moment, the spectacle presents a tableau, not of the incarnated supernatural, but of a coalition of concrete phenomena, all characteristic of the monster, and implying that the monster is really within man. The character-poets, as well as Audiberti the poet, are creatures almost equal to God or the Devil, but they are limited. They create belief, they create the effects, but they do not succeed in giving individual and permanent flesh to the forces they have evoked. What remains of their works are but corpses and myths. Unfortunately Audiberti popularized the theme of the creative imagination to such an extent in his last play *l'Effet Glapion* that it lost all its disturbing magic.

Doubtless a good example of *poésie de théâtre,* Audiberti's works are sometimes too complacent with regard to themselves. What constitutes their charm contributes also to their weakness. Although the onslaught of images, springing out of the familiar, and the variations of the variations on a central theme create the plays' poetic atmosphere and give them their savour, they also attract more attention than they should and somehow make the mask opaque instead of contributing to its transparency.

Acutely conscious of evil and the tragic, the poets of today are quick to recognize signs of them in traditions as well as in the most trifling objects. In his now farcical, now melodramatic adventures, Audiberti tries to project the familiar into the unreal so as to achieve an actualization of metaphors. Others use a subtle deviation from the familiar to suggest a system of symbols. Such is the case with Georges Schehadé. Farcical, tragic, or parodic tones are juxtaposed or mixed in Schehadé's works, just as in Audiberti's, but instead of a rich or exuberant language imposing its content as reality, we have an aerated poetry in which every metaphor is a door opened onto a mystery.

George Schehadé's theatre is at first misleading. Each play goes out to meet the spectator on his own ground instead of beginning with a dazzling avant-garde attack: a valet informs the spectator that his master is about to leave (*Monsieur Bob'le*); in a rather ordinary Inn, a gowned magistrate flirts with its proprietor (*la Soirée des proverbes*); a young officer is lost in a sinister forest (*Histoire de Vasco*). Even when the opening scene is intriguing, its strangeness is somewhat familiar. Then the language becomes increasingly metaphorical, the images increasingly obscure, the situations increasingly unreal. Everything happens as if the poet were taking the spectator by the hand and gradually leading him into his universe of enchantment. The separation into scenes or tableaux is traditional; little changes except the poetry, which becomes more and more intensified. Thus the adventures of the poet, the characters, and the spectator are parallel. The spectator is led to leave the beaten paths, just as Argengeorge in *la Soirée des proverbes* abandons Hélène to go and discover the secret of the rendezvous at Les Quatre Diamants.

Characters and spectators wander about in a world of strange and comic antics and wonders, a maze of wrong tracks and enticements, in search of Truth or signs of Truth. A theatre of enigmas, the plays seem like detective or adventure stories. Mysterious rendezvous and secret missions suggest questions but the answers are always delayed. As the Hat-maker Max says in *la Soirée:* "Truth has many faces, falsehood but one."

We get a glimpse of Truth amidst the lies, but Truth appears only to slip even further away. It is somewhere behind the words of Monsieur Bob'le, it is in the snows of Hunter Alexis' "fifth season," it is in the meeting of Marguerite's dream and Vasco's innocent fear. It is so fleeting, so manifold that all the poet's imagery is needed to suggest it. Simple and clear symbols are enough for the lie: Judge Domino's gown or the soldiers' unsubtle disguises in *Vasco*.

Schehadé's theatre is a fireworks of equivalences. In *la Soirée* the fish Marcellus in his jar is one. He is the symbol of silence —"or even worse!" adds Frightful Philippe. In his universe, everything is a sign: words, objects, crows, costumes, names. But at the end of each quest, Schehadé does not lead the spectator back to his own ground. On the contrary, he launches him out into an even vaster mystery, that of death.

The constant tension maintained by the drama lies in the distance between things, people, and familiar words, and all that they permanently symbolize, which is itself impossible to grasp. The characters live in that dangerous zone. Sometimes they refuse the mystery; other times they clumsily search for the key to it—as do the guests in *la Soirée,* who struggle with proverbs that are unsatisfying or visions that terrify them and bring out their bad faith. But each play has at least one hero, endowed with an innocence called Poetry. Monsieur Bob'le, Vasco, Argengeorge are all pure, but their purity has "many faces": wisdom, curiosity, courage, seeming cowardice readily transformed into heroism.

Psychology has little place in such theatre. The characters are less motivated personalities than points in space which attract swarms of images, grouped by affinities. Psychological coherence is replaced by poetic coherence, equally capable of representing passions and bringing out the modulations of their intensities.

Critics have emphasized Schehadé's Eastern origins. His poetry is very close to that of Persian tales, to their enigmas and their charms. And he is about the only poet of the post-war period whose works are almost entirely free of bitterness or anger. Rarely sarcastic in his satire, he attains more of a majestic sadness in tragedy than horror. With great tact, Schehadé firmly and skillfully asserts the rights of poetry.

More violent in that it claims to express the drama of our times, Henri Pichette's theatre attempts to create the equivalent of this century's exasperations and horrors. Ambitious and militant, his two plays, *les Epiphanies* and *Nucléa,* fight against a world judged as unacceptable and set up the Poet (or his substitute, the Lover) as bearer of the only truths.

To the violence of the world, the Poet opposes the violence of his art. It is often verbal, and Pichette's attitude, more Romantic than Rimbaldian, again brings up the question of the distinction between poetry *in* the theatre and poetry *of* the theatre. The verbal deluge in *les Epiphanies* shows the poet's confidence, too great confidence, in words alone. The second part of *Nucléa,* a kind of fresco of love in which different lovers who speak in alexandrines pass through, is a long allegory, a modern *Embarkation for Cythera,* but the variations on a theme have more importance than the drama itself. When lyricism of language obtrudes to that extent, the stage is in danger of again becoming what the poets want precisely to avoid: a platform for the virtuosity of actors, who recite and play out poems.

Pichette's language—in its frenzy, its overabundant imagery, its search for shocks which are meant to result in explanations of the world—is clearly in the surrealist tradition. Surrealistic also is his didacticism in so far as innocence is concerned, the thesis which in a way gives his two plays their general direction: the systematic rejection of the world of conventions and war in order to assert and impose the reinvention of poetry and love.

Here we have the substance of great drama: the drama of

revolt and the demand for an elevation of man amidst modern calamities. One of the poles of that tension, the calamities, is represented by the most spectacular of all—war. With the help of his directors, Pichette succeeded in creating a tableau of modern war that is the best part of his dramatic works. The symphonic sound-effects in *Nucléa,* as skillfully dissonant as contemporary music, transmitted by stereophonic machines (the noise of airplanes, gun shots, bombs) are mixed with shrieks and violent verbal images, while the spectacle itself unfolds in a stage set designed by Alexander Calder. The first part of *Nucléa* is one of the most effective theatricalist syntheses of the last few years. Pichette succeeded in making the spectator-auditor relive the experience of *the* calamity par excellence—seen and heard by the poet and recreated as a staggering allegory.

Whether war-apprenticeship *(les Epiphanies)* or war-nightmare *(Nucléa),* the theme is a means for the hero to react and be thus impelled toward the search for his true destiny: poetry or love. A demoniac character (Monsieur Diable, Gladior) always accompanies the hero on his quest. Cynical, positive, and cold, he tries to restrain the hero and by the same token, represents the obstacle needed by the hero to better define his values. Finally, the poet will continue to sing "to the last pulsation of the world," the lovers are united in glory, while Monsieur Diable shouts out his defeat and Gladior withdraws from the game. This second pole of tension is drowned in lyricism. The imagination is more verbal than dramatic. What is meant to be an *élan*—the poet's or the lover's—is often no more than just imagery marking time. The alternation of voices is not enough to suggest a drama; the succession of themes or tableaux is not enough to create action. Performed poems, Pichette's plays juxtapose a spectacle and a recitation, and constitute a magnificent visual and auditory display around a drama which, itself, is never performed. *Les Epiphanies* is a kind of allegorical *bildungsroman* performed on stage. *Nucléa* is made up of an epic strophe and a lyric antistrophe. The stage here is used more for the actualization of other genres than for theatre itself.

Quite the opposite of Pichette's epic drama is Jean Vauthier's private intimate world. The characters are limited to one, two, or three, closed in a room. Perhaps using great classical tragedy as a model, Vauthier tried, through concentration, to reach a maximum of intensity.

Whereas the poets have created metaphors of action, Vauthier goes back to action itself in all its brutality. By creating a permanent and ever increasing tension, he managed to write what might be called "pure" drama. Moreover he has shown that a play destined for the smallest stages can also be total theatre in frantically combining the exasperation of characters, actors, and audience into a crescendo which reaches a climax of revelation, leaving the three participants liberated, but exhausted, and in making no distinction between the invention of dialogue, staging, his own comments on the drama, and the general impression he tries to communicate. All the elements are integrated into his manuscript by means of special typographical effects. In constructing his plays, Vauthier lives the whole theatrical experience himself—as writer, director, and spectator.

Vauthier's situations could not be simpler: the relationship of a man and woman (*Capitaine Bada*), the relationship of a man, a woman, and an old nurse, who is more an object than a character (*les Prodiges*), a man "found between two texts" and a hotel employee (*le Personnage combattant*). Exaggerated versions of Strindberg's *The Dance of Death* and Sartre's *Huis Clos,* Vauthier's plays communicate the most frightful inner destruction and make the spectator participate in it through a spectacle of desperately strained bodies and shrieks torn from the depths of anguish.

Le Personnage combattant, fortissimo is at the most extreme point of this extreme theatre. When he performed it in 1955, Jean-Louis Barrault accomplished as great a feat as he did in 1935 with Faulkner's *As I Lay Dying*. The play presents a character struggling with himself in a universe of objects and noises. He is the "character found between two texts"—an elegant writer in a hotel room, trying to rewrite a novel that he had begun in the same room many years before when he was still young. The present writer and man is opposed to the writer and young man that he was. There is no allegorical personification of the past to destroy the living synthesis of the present. The world of objects through which the young man had sought to make contact with the real is described such as he had formerly experienced it and as he experiences it in the present. The Character tries desperately to reconstruct the conditions of his past experience, for he believes that his salvation lies in being able to grasp the objects as such.

Originating in Sartre's *la Nausée,* then picked up and transformed by the poet Francis Ponge, the theme of objects, of their being in relation to man in search of being, has most recently been developed in *le Personnage combattant,* just as it has taken a completely new direction in the novel, with Robbe-Grillet and Michel Butor. One of the signs of the Character's drama, obvious from the very beginning, is that the world of objects is no longer the same. The objects have somehow betrayed him. The room has been strangely decorated, it has been contaminated by others. And what happens outside does not correspond to his expectations: the noise from neighboring rooms interrupts his work and his experience; the trains, which pass just outside his window, do not come by at the appointed hours. Besides, the Character himself has changed. He has become rich; mostly, he has matured. From time to time, as a mirror of that growth and aging, the hotel employee appears, shady and brutal, an adult form of the little homosexual boy he had known there in the past.

The Character struggles in a prison made up of time that

has passed, the resistance of objects, absurd and uncontrollable circumstances, and his own "nature." Constantly thrown back on himself, powerless to break the walls of his prison, he experiences a night of agony, in every sense of the word, at the junction of every possible exasperation. He is between two definitions of himself—an exemplary situation. Consequently, his cries and agitation are valid for any anguished struggle.

In *le Personnage combattant* Vauthier has rediscovered the inner torments of French classical theatre. Yet his form of expression is absolutely modern. The monologue expressing the Character's suffering, as well as the dialogue affirming the separation of the protagonists in *Capitaine Bada* and *les Prodiges,* are not turned inward. There is no abstract struggle of a soul suspended in a vacuum. The Character's being is always a "being-in-the-world." Vauthier escapes from traditional systems of psychology, according to which feelings and passions exist and are explained independent of their object, according to which inner life and relations with the world can be conceived and analyzed separately. The Character's being is presented in its concrete totality. He doesn't just suffer; he suffers-with-an-armchair. Solitude is always a state of consciousness and, as such, inseparable from everything of which one is conscious. Vauthier has succeeded in representing on stage the paradox of the combined transcendence and immanence of objects in relation to consciousness, or of one consciousness in relation to another.

Sartre's infernal vision of relations with others and even with oneself strongly colors Jean Genêt's universe as well as Vauthier's. *Les Bonnes* and *Haute Surveillance* pick up the theme from an original point of view. It is also the basis for "collective" plays such as *le Balcon* and *les Nègres.* But what dominates Genêt's theatre is the frenzied anger of his characters, who are prisoners of definitions imposed on them by others, and their escape toward a rebellious heroism which is identified with poetry itself. Theatre then becomes an act of revolt, a "crime."

By way of a preface to the published text of *les Bonnes,* Genêt condemns Western theatre for its exhibitionism and triviality. Following the theories of Antonin Artaud, he believes in the grandeur of a theatre detached from the constraints of our society, a theatre similar to the oriental, in which ceremony would replace the masquerade and symbols replace the characters. For Genêt, there is "nothing more (theatrically) effective than the elevation" during Mass. Religious mystery and communion are the two necessary components of true theatre. Beauty would replace faith, but "that beauty must have at least the power of a poem, that is, of a crime"—a deliberate identification of poet and criminal, characteristic of Genêt, and the desperate appeal for a new mysticism.

His idea of theatre is more precisely expressed in the following: "A performance that does not act on my soul is vain. It is vain if I don't believe what I see, which will stop—which will never have existed—once the curtain falls." Theatre is thus defined as a dream, a dreamed Mass, believable while it lasts. One's whole being is involved in the dream, but on awakening one realizes that nothing has happened. And it is Genêt's dream that unfolds on stage during the performance—a dream that the spectator is invited to share. What psychiatrists often call a directed dream, it is made up of the poet's phantasms, organized according to his own desires and directed toward an accomplishment which is the objective always sought and always dreaded by the poet.

Le Balcon is Genêt's most explicit play, for he has given us phantasms within phantasms. By assuming an imaginary rank (Bishop, General, Judge, etc.), each character, a visitor at Irma's Brothel, achieves his highest aim. Irma's Grand Balcony, the ideal brothel as dreamed of by Jean Genêt, is peopled with characters who dream like Jean Genêt. But the dream must remain a dream: "They all want it to be as real as possible . . . except for some indefinable thing making it all not real." Thus, in the first act each character "plays" the role of his dreams but is afraid of really being what he is imitating. At the beginning of *les Bonnes,* Claire and Solange play at being Madame and Claire. At the beginning of *Haute Surveillance,* the three prisoners play or try to play at being legendary criminals. The psychological position, at once satisfying and tormenting, has two distinct points of interest. It shows the persistence of childish games or adolescent sexual phantasms in the adult; and it is an excellent theme for theatre since it is based on the same ambiguity as theatre itself.[4]

On stage the characters and objects of their phantasms take real shapes, just as they do at Irma's. The dream of a definitive adventure, attaining a wished-for paroxysm and release, is almost realized. The beauty of the prisoners in *Haute Surveillance,* the incarnation of Blood, Tears, and Sperm in three young men in *le Balcon,* and the muscled femininity of Arthur in the same play show that the plays' universe is Jean Genêt's private Hollywood, a universe in which everything becomes possible and dreams are realized. Complete identification with model, hero, or ideal finally takes place. In *les Bonnes* Claire and Solange, who have plotted Madame's death, become Madame and Claire, and Claire poisons herself while playing Madame. The false Bishop and the false General in *le Balcon* really become the Bishop and the General under a new political regime. At the end of *Haute Surveillance,* Yeux-verts and Lefranc finally manage to become the heroes they have dreamed about.

Genêt's characters, completely bewildered by the objects of their love or hate, elevate them to the level of myth. They

4. In *les Nègres* theatre within theatre is used systematically and amplified: masks are superimposed on masks, and the play itself is presented as a ritual masquerade, meant to conceal the true mystery of the Blacks' revolt from the Whites.

invent sacred scenarios in which they wear masks of their adored or hated gods and lead them to a glorious or ignoble death. Comparable to a spell or expiatory rite, the catastrophe that ends a Genêt play is always vicarious. Just as Claire poisons herself masked as Madame in *les Bonnes,* so the young revolutionary in *le Balcon* castrates himself masked as the Chief of Police. In *les Nègres* the Blacks act out a double myth. They identify with the Whites' image of them and, wearing the mask, they act out the image they have of the Whites. At the end, the White masks, magic substitutes for the real Whites, are led to Hell during a "warning" ceremony.

Policemen, criminals, revolutionaries, masters, and slaves are all caught up in the same whirlpool. And their bewilderment is similar to that which the spectator, intoxicated by an overabundance of violent images, is meant to give in to: He is asked to identify, in his repulsion or terror, with what he refuses to be or refuses to recognize within himself, and to indirectly undergo the agonizing ecstacy of a catastrophe-punishment. On the heights of this new Olympus sits the complex figure of the poet-assassin-victim—a kind of total man who pays for his totality by a martyrdom comparable to that of a saint.

Although Genêt's personal mythology may occasionally evoke more universal symbols, it still remains very special, reserved for a few initiates, and only indirectly concerned with the deep forces that should be at the root of any theatre, Western or Eastern. Yet it's all there: a distance from reality, an intense theatricalism, a drama, tensions which are resolved on more mysterious and higher planes. But the exotic quality, the spectator's consciousness of a universe in which he does not participate, outweighs the communion. Although relatively free in his choice of subject matter, Genêt is more imprisoned within himself than any of the contemporary playwrights. It is "amusing" to see what he does with the myth of the Revolution in *le Balcon.* But instead of participating, we are made to feel like spectators of a personal phantasmagoria. The same can be said for the themes of homosexuality and crime which, in Genêt's works, remain very much his own. Even in *les Nègres* the poet's personal obsession often limits the scope of a most ambitious play. Individual phantasms and a constant use of travesty bring the audience into the private universe of the poet with his masks and his demands.

Here again, despite the play's power, the poet wins out over the playwright. And the actor-martyr never completely avoids self-contemplation.

Adamov, too, builds his theatre around personal dreams. He himself explained[5] that a play like *le Professeur Taranne* is hardly more than the transposition a dream he really had, and *les Retrouvailles,* the transposition of a false dream—a dream he as a writer might have had. But Adamov's dreams can be termed realistic, for the framework, objects, and characters belong to the writer's everyday universe. His dreams are merely rearrangements of the elements, a new logic imposed on the relations of people among themselves, an order and a causality sometimes normal and sometimes absurd in the eyes of someone awake. The nonsense appears only in the sequence of events. Beyond the impression of nightmare, yet because of it, the spectator—who has not been enchanted by any great display of fantasy—meets with an impression that reflects on the normal world: that of the instability of the real, the possibility of ordinary things taking unforseeable directions with the same apparent necessity as that we generally accord them— and the resulting terror.

Adamov's dreams concretely represent a possible universe which potentially exists in what we call reality, is on the verge of becoming actualized, and would have as much justification for existing as our world and its order. When at the beginning

5. Arthur Adamov, "Note préliminaire," *Théâtre,* Vol. II.

of *le Professeur Taranne,* the protagonist, accused of exhibitionism in front of children, is not recognized by his friends, the universe of accusation and indifference surrounding him is presented with a feeling of evident and concrete reality. Thus the spectator understands that there is as much reason for a character to say to Taranne: "I don't know you, sir," as the expected formula: "Good morning, Professor Taranne." Once that direction has been taken, the logic according to which Taranne is no longer what he was, nor what he thinks he is, imposes a development on events that is as cold, calm, and convincing as the logic of permanent identity.

In his note to Volume II [6] Adamov says that in *la Grande et la Petite Manoeuvre* he tried to achieve the "inopportune junction" of "intensely experienced feeling . . . and reasoning." The formula could well apply to most of his works. The dream-like quality in *le Professeur Taranne* is no more than a device used to concretize a feeling or combination of feelings, readily experienced in everyday life. If at the outset, a respectable professor feels ashamed at undressing for a swim without taking a bathhouse and feels that such an act is not in accord with the respectability he values, a whole series of fears and evasions follows, resulting in a combination of terror and the desire to be "someone else." The dream actualizes his terrors and desires. Moreover the objectivity of a feeling thus actualized makes the flow of action demonstrative and appears as the explanation of a mechanism which steals an individual's identity from himself.

In the whole of Adamov's theatre, even in his more recent plays *le Ping-Pong* and *Paolo Paoli,* the thesis demonstrated is almost always the same: that of the isolation of the individual at the mercy of a world geared to crush him. According to Adamov himself, *la Grande et la Petite Manoeuvre* "demonstrates" that "whatever one does, one is crushed," resulting in a theatre of fright in which the characters are always threat-

6. *Ibid.*

ened. Whatever the threats (subconscious forces, a Mother's power, the social mechanism), the fear they provoke always throws the individual back on himself and cuts him off from any communication with others.

Since *le Ping-Pong* Adamov has tried to avoid the somewhat timeless nonsense and abstraction of his early plays, in order to return to certain "realities" that might be termed traditional, particularly the so-called social reality. *Le Ping-Pong* is a detailed analysis of the functioning of society—a society based on the lure of profit and the search for prestige. Going still further in his desire to embody the subject of his play in actual history, Adamov precisely dated each tableau of *Paolo Paoli* and described, always in the same detail, the mechanism of frivolity during "la Belle Epoque," showing how man's life and death hinged on it. But here Adamov's rather anonymous style and flat dialogue no longer give the impression of strangeness, as in his more fantastic plays, and thus fall into boring realism. He says that he wanted to avoid "schizophrenic lucubration" but at the same time he lost in shock value and in the poetry of logical delirium.

Yet he kept one of the basic constructions of his early plays: the flow of a long story that moves ahead by reversals of situation (*Tous contre tous*) or by sudden and unexpected changes (*l'Invasion, la Parodie*). The changes and reversals become surprises and express the vision of an unstable world where new situations are brutally imposed from the outside and man's only recourse is to adapt himself as best he can and somehow continue to live. In *Paolo Paoli,* for example, historical and economic circumstances create a new situation every minute, reversing the ruler/beggar relationship among the characters. The device is simple and obvious but draws its power from being repeated during the twelve long tableaux. And the play does not stop of itself; it is stopped by the war of 1914, which interrupts what Lesage would have called a "ricochet of double dealing" and which in itself has no reason to end.

Both later plays escape from traditional naturalism by Adamov's choice of a symbolic object, which provokes the determining passions and is situated at the center of the play: the pinball machine in *le Ping-Pong,* the butterflies in *Paolo Paoli.* Around and apropos of such useless and apparently marginal objects, Adamov constructed a whole mechanism of what might be called serious business. Thus society is seen in its totality but the perspective is unusual. Adamov refuses to remain exclusively on the psychological level and displaces his central point from the human being to the object. When writing about *le Ping-Pong,* he did say that he tried not to give his central object the epic and allegorical proportions of a "machine at the center of the world"; and in fact the pinball machine and the butterfly collection never seem any more than what they are: manufactured or natural objects, inoffensive and insignificant in themselves, passive. But he did make them objects around which the actions of men crystallize.

Here perhaps lies the underlying unity of Adamov's works, despite his renunciation of actually "fantastic" theatre. All his plays are series of adventures seen from one precisely defined perspective. Psychological analysis is replaced by a spectacle of man's behavior, considered from one particular point of view: either from the angle of things, in which case it seems to rejoin objective realism, or through one character's terrified consciousness, and thus subject to the deformations of expressionism. In both instances the play's universe is prisoner of the point of view. Each play is a machine that inexorably turns round its own center. Each individual is a cog that never escapes from its special function. When the protagonist is a victim, the whole machine seems to be organized around him with the object of crushing him. Although certain characters within his universe change their identities, their situations or fates remain the same, for the functions and the play of forces are always controlled by the same determinism.

The vision of a dehumanized universe, Adamov's theatre

emphasizes the horror of losing the human element. By translating the whole into objective terms, he succeeds in giving a powerful image of his vision but at the same time situates his plays outside the spectator. The protagonist's isolation, the lack of real communication that separates the elements of a universe in which individuals mesh with one another like toothed wheels but never interpenetrate, corresponds to a mechanical relation between the spectator and the play. The spectator witnesses the hero's suffering from the outside.

Adamov writes about the imaginary as a naturalist, but his imaginary world is made up of nothing other than situations toward which our real situations seem to tend. The terror we feel is not provoked by the play itself, but rather by the consciousness that it would not take much for reality to go one step further and appear to us in terms of his plays. His theatre is half-way between eighteenth-century philosophical allegory and the works of science-fiction to which Huxley and Orwell have accustomed us.

The so-called avant-garde theatre has its obvious dangers and complacencies. Too great an attempt to reestablish the spell of language can lead to verbalism. Too great a demand for freedom in the theatre can lead to an exuberance or confusion that stifles dramatic tension. Too exclusive a search for "pure" theatre can lead to a kind of inhuman kaleidoscope. And an individual and intransigent search for original means of expression can lead to poetic exhibitionism. In short, the dangers of 1950–60 are no different from those of 1890 or 1930. Yet the avant-garde has always shown a constant vivacity of poetic imagination. The poets have tried to create the myths of today's theatre, poetry being the only communion that has some chance of being universal.

From one year to the next, the avant-garde picture changes. Quite recently Jean Genêt's reputation as a playwright rocketed after productions of le Balcon in Paris and New York and the

Parisian success of *les Nègres*. Adamov proved disappointing with *Paolo Paoli*. Jean Vauthier and Georges Schehadé seem to have disappeared from the scene.[7] Audiberti had fantastic success on the Boulevard with his rather facile and vulgar *l'Effet Glapion* but what he gained in popularity he lost in poetic quality. Pichette has not been heard from since *Nucléa*. On the other hand, Jean Vilar produced an excellent posthumous play of Boris Vian, *les Bâtisseurs d'Empire,* rather Adamovian in tone. And much interest has been shown in a young Spanish-born playwright, Arrabal, certain of whose plays (*Fando et Lis, le Cimetière des voitures*) seem like baroque variations on themes similar to Beckett's.

Yet out of the constantly fluctuating whole, two names stand out as established: Eugène Ionesco and Samuel Beckett.

7. As this book goes to press, J.-L. Barrault announces the opening of Schehadé's new play, *le Voyage,* for February 1961.

CHAPTER 8

A WORLD OUT OF CONTROL: EUGENE IONESCO

Sketchy characters carried away by words, changing identities, having three noses, laying eggs, talking without communicating, preys to organized disorder, murder, the most grotesque cruelty, living out directed dreams, being transformed into rhinoceroses—indeed Ionesco's plays seem rather baffling at first. Despite the direct language and somewhat dreary realism of the settings, his works—sometimes called "characterless theatre," sometimes "tragic farce" or "metaphysical farce" or "anti-theatre"—are above all poetic. They present a concrete realization of metaphors and an immediate experience of existence, grasped in the relations of the individual to his surrounding world.

Like many of the French poet-playwrights, Ionesco brings the intangible elements of his vision of the world to the stage in the concrete form of objects or acts. But by going beyond a representation of his private imagery, he succeeds in giving a metaphysical impression, elementary enough to have universal value, at least in our times, and faces the spectator with a direct metaphor of the horror of the modern world, sending him back to his own anguish instead of drawing him into the mysteries of a privileged imagination.

The revolutionary aspect of his plays, denying the traditional flow of action and traditional concept of characters, plus the often incoherent or disconnected appearance that results makes them seem like parodies of the real world. Here fantasy is not a door opened onto a beyond; it is the source of a farcical universe parallel to traditional reality.

By presenting his inner fantasies with the objectivity of realism, Ionesco creates a dream-like atmosphere reminiscent of both Kafka and Strindberg. Within the worlds of his plays either the insignificant takes on the greatest importance and becomes the object of infinite discussion, or plans are delayed indefinitely and thwarted to the point of frustration and exasperation. In addition, certain Freudian themes recur frequently, especially the image of the Mother. Directed dreams, substitution of characters, changes of identity, abortive acts, all contribute to the general nightmarish quality of the whole. Nor is it difficult to interpret the actualized metaphors in such terms. In *Amédée ou comment s'en débarrasser,* the growing corpse and the mushrooms might be considered as part of an arsenal of dream symbols referring to a guilt complex. And most of the characters themselves can be compared to dreamers who have no idea that they are dreaming. For the spectator, the flow of events is absurd or incoherent, but it is accepted as real by the characters, just as in our dreams, we consider the most delirious wanderings as the only possible logic of the world.

But to consider Ionesco's theatre as merely the actualization of nightmares would be to limit it unjustly. Freudian symbolism may be a part of the playwright's world, but it is not the key to it. The elements of dream are simply given elements of an inner world, used and rearranged, not to define man by his obscure psychology, but to complete a perceptible image of the human condition in its totality.

Most important is the idea of totality. It includes the refusal to limit man's condition to one level, the political level in particular. There is no positive *engagement* in Ionesco's theatre. In fact he vigorously protested against any such attitude. As far as he is concerned, despite its pretensions at demystification, it merely falls back into or sets up new mystifications.[1] Even his last play *Rhinocéros,* in which we see all humanity

1. See *Cahiers des quatre saisons,* No. 15, Winter 1959.

transformed into rhinoceroses and which ends with the hero's refusal to become a rhinoceros like the others, is less an attack on totalitarian regimes (obvious though it may be on one level) than a personal refusal of any political or social involvement.[2]

Not that Ionesco's disengagement excludes a strong position of denunciation. Although his theatre could hardly be considered as belonging to a literature of *praxis,* it does offer a judgement on the world in the name of certain non-esthetic values. On the most superficial level, he has written a ferocious social satire and it constitutes the most obvious element of his "dark" humor. By substituting imaginary behavior patterns for real ones, yet keeping the general logic of the real, Ionesco reveals the ridiculous, absurd, and even monstrous aspects of social habits and customs. The madly delirious conversations in *la Cantatrice chauve* and the fiancée's two or three noses in *Jacques ou la soumission* are not there only to provoke the joys of the absurd or to recreate an atmosphere of nightmare: they are analogous to the facts of real life, and the destructive laughter they provoke reflects on their real correlatives. Ionesco creates a universe parallel to ours which, presented with the greatest objectivity and in the terms of realism, enjoys the same right to exist as our world. By extension, our world is neither more nor less justified than what unfolds on stage and can be considered quite as ridiculous.

Ionesco thus uses nonsense as a counterpart of reality. The spectator bounces back from the play into his own universe with the greater knowledge that one system is worth another on the level of underlying justifications and reasons for being. Indeed Ionesco's satire is total in that it results in the rejection of any belief in the reasonable justification for behavior, institutions, or values. His theatre gives men no opportunity to take themselves seriously. In fact in *l'Impromptu de l'Alma,* after having ridiculed theoreticians of the theatre and philos-

2. See Pierre-Aimé Touchard, "Un Nouveau Fabuliste," *Cahiers Renaud-Barrault,* No. 29, February 1960.

ophers, he ridicules himself when, at the end of the play, he begins to expound his own theories.

In *Tueur sans gages,* Ionesco leads his hero Bérenger toward a final scene in which the process of complete demystification is explicitly developed. Bérenger finds himself alone with a killer and tries to convince him of the criminal and useless nature of murder. In his long monologue, he gives the arguments both for and against, discovering simultaneously that although there is no reason to kill, there is no reason *not* to kill. Happiness, the brotherhood of man, all the good reasons are destroyed even in Bérenger's mind by the Killer's silence or derisive laughter, especially because, getting no response at all, Bérenger himself goes beyond the reasons he presents in order to find more convincing ones, and in fact only ends in confusion:

> I don't know anymore, I don't know anymore. Maybe you're wrong, maybe wrong doesn't exist, maybe it's we who are wrong to want to exist . . . Explain. What do you think? I don't know, I don't know. (The Killer sneers.)

The Killer's "infinite energy of obstinacy" wins over all the values, even over Bérenger's instinct of preservation. For Bérenger drops his pistols and lets himself be knifed, muttering: "What can we do . . . What can we do. . . ."

Tueur sans gages is a perfect example of Ionesco's vision of the world and, by extension, clarifies all his preceding works. Ionesco began in being irreverent with regard to the daily routine of life and gave new form to a hackneyed theme. Actually his irreverence was aimed at all action and all behavior, and the whole of his works is a cluster of metaphors illustrating Bérenger's final idea: "Maybe it's we who are wrong to want to exist." But when he questions the existence of human beings themselves instead of merely that of their behavior, Ionesco's tone changes from farce to pathos and we stop laughing. For here more is at stake than just reasons. A feeling of

A World Out of Control

Grand-Guignol takes the place of humor, and Bérenger's fall is seen not as the well-deserved punishment of a fundamentally grotesque character, but as the result of a frightful revelation within a sympathetic character.

The richness of Ionesco's theatre—and also what makes it confusing—comes from the mixture of the domains he puts under question. All the absurdities are given equal importance, whether they be the presence of things, man's decisions, social disorder, social conventions, psychological impulses, old age, or the problems of city traffic. The world is seen simultaneously on all levels, with the result that the main problem or subject does not exclude the other levels. *La Leçon* is at the same time a quasi-surrealistic use of certain textbooks, a satire on teaching, and a terrifying psycho-drama. In *Tueur sans gages* a tableau of everyday life is mixed with the nightmare of organized disorder in a large modern city, a psychological study, and the tragedy of Bérenger in search of and then faced with the Killer. By juxtaposing themes as disparate as the satire of big city traffic and the failure of Bérenger's reason, a universe is evoked in which any hierarchy of levels is suppressed. Ionesco's theatre is the image of a world where everything is equally important—and, by the same token, unimportant.

All that can be said for this universe is that facts, events, beings, and things exist. And indeed they exist in abundance. One of the authentically dramatic dimensions of Ionesco's theatre lies in the tension between a superabundance of being and the absolute impossibility of justifying the fact of being. It is therefore metaphysical drama to the extent that it reveals existence as having no reason to exist and the unjustified as existing in superabundance. In short, the world is superfluous.

Visually, the feeling is communicated by an overcrowding of the stage, an accumulation of objects or their increase in size. On the most elementary level, *l'Avenir est dans les oeufs* merely has the stage fill up with millions of eggs until it finally col-

182

lapses. In an ironic tone, the protagonist of *le Nouveau Locataire* willingly imprisons himself in the midst of endless pieces of furniture which he has brought to his room. More subtly, the two old people's imaginary world in *les Chaises* is overpopulated, and the crowd is visually suggested by empty chairs which multiply on stage. In addition to things and beings, there is also a superabundance of words themselves. The dialogue is drawn out for no particular reason and filled with repetitions that end by producing a kind of incantation, as in the case of *les Chaises*.

There are doubtless similarities between Ionesco's conception and certain passages of Sartre's *la Nausée*. But where, in Sartre, the impression is qualitative, in Ionesco it is quantitative. The viscous substance of existence is replaced by an accumulation of individual things or beings, a numerical or measurable (as in the case of the corpse in *Amédée*) superabundance.

The quantitative aspect of such devices makes it possible to establish a simple form of comedy, not far from Bergson's definition of the mechanical imposed upon the living. When the mechanism is applied to the phenomena of daily life, to insignificant activity, to the many domains we habitually think of in non-mechanical terms, it touches the essence of both comedy and laughter. When in a conversation about members of a family, their births, marriages, jobs, and deaths, Ionesco gives all the members the name of Bobby Watson, he is certain to get a dual effect: comedy in the contrast between what a family should be and the incongruity of the Watson family, supposedly typical—in other words, the classic device of revealing the truth behind appearances previously considered as the norm; and laughter because the truth behind the accepted conception of the family is found to be rigorously mechanical (*la Cantatrice chauve*).

Not only is a mathematical rigour imposed on human phenomena, but it is completed by a process of geometric progression or acceleration. Machines are slow and regular at first, in the same way as the corpse's growth in *Amédée,* the production of eggs in *l'Avenir est dans les oeufs,* the arrival of the furniture in *le Nouveau Locataire,* the repetition of dialogue in *les Chaises,* the professor's nervous irritation and confusion in *la Leçon,* and the multiplication of rhinoceroses in *Rhinocéros.* Then the growth or accumulation gathers speed until it reaches a mad precipitation. Here, in addition to the influence of gags such as those of the Marx Brothers, we feel that of the technical acceleration of the motion picture image itself.

The general impression, dominating certain plays and constituting their rhythm, is that of a machine out of control. The variations of speed lead to some pauses, but as in *le Nouveau Locataire* or *Rhinocéros,* they are more comparable to a shifting of gears than to the slowing down of a machine or the return to a more human perspective. As the acceleration is always cumulative and applied to both the speed and the object's increase in number, the loss of control finally applies to the very phenomenon of *being.* Ionesco's theatre is the comedy, both laughable and terrifying, of man transcended by being itself.

According to the so-called existentialist theatre, man has the freedom and indefeasible power to make himself and make the world. Ionesco's theatre is one of disenchantment. His vision is somewhat similar to the existentialists' but only in certain themes relevant to early phases of the philosophy: the isolation of the individual consciousness in our absurd universe, the unjustified presence of the being of things, the unbearable fact of existence itself—such as they appear in Sartre's *la Nausée* and Camus' *l'Etranger.* But where both writers developed their themes toward reasons for action, Ionesco—one literary generation younger—marks the failure of any such ambition.

Ionesco's theatre then is in many ways a return to the well-known nihilism of which existentialism, and in fact any exercise of lucidity, has so often been accused. Ionesco went deep into the immediate experience of the metaphysical absurd by isolating and objectifying it. No magic, no divinity with impenetrable ways is held responsible. Nor are any psychological or sociological explanations given. Ionesco quite simply communicates the bewildering paradox of man's life and the complete absurdity of the mechanism of being.

Those who have termed such theatre a "theatre of the atomic age" are right in that any hope in an efficacious *praxis* has been considerably shaken by a consciousness of the possibility of total destruction. Faced with total destruction, not only do the problems of modern naturalism (homosexuality, drugs, conflicts limited to the levels of family and society) have little weight, but the theme of political revolution loses its acuity and is leveled to the rank of the others. Sartre and Camus needed great exemplary acts to describe the human condition more effectively in their plays. But in the perspective of absolute annihilation, all acts are equalized, in Ionesco as in Beckett.

Not that the end-of-the-world atmosphere is always explicit. Although it is easy to interpret the setting of Beckett's *Fin de partie* as a symbol of the world after the H-bomb, in Ionesco there is but one precise suggestion of it in *les Chaises:*

> The Old Lady: Paris never existed, my dear.
> The Old Man: It must have existed, since it collapsed. It was the city of light, since the light has been out, out, for 4,000 years. . . .

Even if the image is a product of the Old Man's delirium, it still reveals the psychosis of A.D. 1000, an obsession with universal catastrophe—but this time there is no Last Judgement and therefore no hope of redemption in a beatific beyond.

Ionesco never conceptualized the feeling or philosophized on it. He translated it directly into concrete images which the spectator must accept without argument. The "stories" he tells on stage, often parallel to reality, are meant to make the spectator feel it in a particularly vivid and one might say pure way.

Both he and Beckett succeeded in recreating a metaphysical atmosphere through intensification. They also succeeded in making that atmosphere the source of two contrary reactions: laughter and pathos.

Ionesco's "tragic farce" is often funny, not only because of its mechanical elements, but because of the application of those elements to apparently trivial situations: the boredom of bourgeois life, the fiancée's three noses, the arrangement of a room. The entire universe may be questioned, but on the individual level, there is no danger of any serious catastrophe. In other situations, when the danger of death becomes evident, all laughter stops and pathos takes over. And the laughter stops —which is not the case even during murder in a play like Jarry's *Ubu Roi*—because the characters are endowed with enough density and humanity to cause an identification with the general vision of the world and individual suffering.

Indeed in this universe, where individuals never communicate among themselves and acts are ineffectual, there is often a desire for communication, an appeal for tenderness expressed in normal terms. The Old Man's whining in *les Chaises* and Bérenger's awkward good will in *Tueur sans gages* and *Rhinocéros* are of that order. From minute to minute the characters' psychological makeups are revealed and, without taking the center of the play, bring the spectator closer to them. Ionesco keeps that one traditional element which enables him to work on both levels (farcical exteriorization and inner psychology) at the same time.

Ionesco claims to have written plays that exclude any traditional psychology:

> We will give up the principle of identity and unity of character for the benefit of movement, a dynamic psychology . . . We are not ourselves . . . Personality doesn't exist. Within us, we have merely contradictory and non-contradictory forces.

So declares Nicolas d'Eu in *Victimes du devoir*. He adds further on: "We have Ionesco, and Ionesco is enough!" Here Ionesco presents himself as inventor of the new theatre. But Nicolas' comments are parodic and through them Ionesco simultaneously theorizes about his own works and destroys his theories by ridiculing them. In any case, neither the comments nor the plays eliminate *all* psychology. The psychology he works with is simply new, corresponding to that found in many contemporary French novels. The characters are defined both by their function in the mechanism that surrounds them and by the inner play of their "contradictory and non-contradictory forces." In *Amédée* the cancer of guilt is represented objectively by the ever-growing corpse and the mushrooms that grow in the parlor, and also expressed in psychological terms through the dialogue. In *Tueur sans gages* Bérenger's desires are represented both by the real existence of a modern sun-lit city and the analysis of his inner necessity, and both are combined in the remark:

> In short, inner and outer world are bad expressions; there are no boundaries between those so-called two worlds. There is a fundamental impulse, obviously, which comes from us, and when it can't be exteriorized, when it can't be objectively realized, when there is no complete accord between my inner me and my outer me, the result is catastrophe, universal contradiction, the final break.

Bérenger never succeeds in communicating his analysis to the Architect, and there we have a first drama or conflict. But on a deeper level, his comments potentially contain an adventure to come and one he has already gone through within himself, the abrupt transition from joy to melancholy, a "kind of tumultuous vacuum—like at the moment of a tragic separation, intolerable." Just as the new city is the hyperbolic realization of the force of joy within him, so the presence of the Killer and the final murder will be the amplified and extreme realization of the opposite force. Bérenger's inner struggle, given in terms of psychological analysis, is represented in concrete and objective acts and objects. The play is complete and rich because of Ionesco's skill in playing with the four elements of the drama: inner joy, inner vacuum, City of the Sun, Killer— inserting "breaks," as Bérenger calls them, at given points between the subjective and the objective, not relating them symbolically but concomitantly.

A meeting point of contradictory forces, each character carries his universe about with him and goes on with his series of metamorphoses independent of the others. The agonizing drama comes when the character becomes conscious of his solitude and tries to cling to others, like the old people in *les Chaises* or Bérenger in *Tueur sans gages* and *Rhinocéros*. But whether the character be unaware or anguished, he is always a moving and incoherent being without any real communication with others. In rejecting conventional psychology, which has been transcended by modern science and no longer corresponds to living experience, Ionesco once again presents the chaos and mystery of the individual.

Absence of communication in the actual farces is expressed by all types of puns, long automatic speeches, meaningless dialogue in which the characters answer *as if* they were communicating. In the more serious plays, the drama is based in part on the hero's desperate attempts to communicate. In *Tueur sans gages* Bérenger confides in the Architect but his words fall on deaf ears, and his long final monologue never gets through to the Killer and ends destroyed by its own logic. The same Bérenger in *Rhinocéros* watches his friend Jean and the woman he loves gradually escape from him, moving further and further away as they are transformed into rhinoceroses. In addition to the many themes it symbolizes, the herd of rhinoceroses at the end represents the vague mass of the *Others,* with whom the hero can no longer communicate.

Ionesco does no more than portray the situation. But his

portrayal has a special meaning. As Rosette Lamont notes with regard to *les Chaises:* [3] "It is a twentieth century morality play which does not preach. The message of the play is an anti-message: speech, art, communication of any sort, are the illusions man needs while there is breath." At the end of *les Chaises* the Orator entrusted with communicating the Old Man's message is able only to emit "the gutteral sounds of a mute" and writes an obscure word on the blackboard, disconnected letters from which the word "Adieu" is finally made out. Ionesco thus emphasizes the vanity or vacuity of what everyone is trying to communicate.

This point of view has led Ionesco to a special attitude with regard to his own works. Having produced a meaningless mirror of a meaningless world, it would be impossible for him to take the first any more seriously than the second. Whence a general indifference to what the director does or could do to the text of his plays. As his aim is to represent the absence of gravity and justification as effectively as possible, only the effect counts, and the playwright himself shows no great respect for his own text. One has only to read Ionesco's ironic notes on Nicolas Bataille's changes for the staging of *la Cantatrice chauve,* or his "indications" for the staging of *Tueur sans gages,* in which he authorizes "all the cuts needed" in the second act, or the different possibilities of ending *l'Avenir est dans les oeufs.* When he carefully gives details on how to stage his plays, on the rhythm to follow, etc., he does so either to make the director's job easier or to make certain of a particular effect on the spectator, and not in the name of his sovereignty as a poet or the esthetic perfection of his play.

As Ionesco's message is that there is no message, he would never think of transforming his feelings into dogma. What he tries to do is reproduce on stage the tension between the individual's activities and fantasies and the vacuum in which

3. Rosette C. Lamont, "The Metaphysical Farce: Beckett and Ionesco."

they are suspended. The elements he embodies them in *directly* —that is, without arguments, theories, or abstractions—come from his inner imagery.

> Theatre for me is the projection on stage of the inner world. I reserve the right to take this theatrical material from my dreams, my obscure desires, my inner contradictions.

Such are Ionesco's words in *l'Impromptu de l'Alma* before he mocks his own serious and academic tone. The "material" itself is held up to ridicule, exploded by its own contradictions, or shown as absurd. What remains is a brutal and simple image, objective and concrete, which shows either a return to his original anguish (the sneers of an invisible mob in the empty décor of *les Chaises*), or annihilation (the final collapse in *l'Avenir,* Bérenger on his knees before the Killer in *Tueur sans gages*), or the stabilization of an inexorable and unjustified mechanism (end of *Victimes du devoir, la Leçon,* and in a comic vein, *la Cantatrice chauve*), or in grotesque and spectacular fantasy (end of *Amédée*).

Ionesco's conclusions, usually theatrical, are a kind of negation of everything that went before, with either the tragic situation held up to ridicule or "annihilated," or its adventurous quality negated by the idea of beginning again, making it an interchangeable link in an undefined chain which relates to nothing. However the end of *Rhinocéros* is somewhat ambiguous. As all humanity is transformed into rhinoceroses, Bérenger, the only remaining man, surrounded by the rhinoceroses, and after having gone through the temptation of also becoming transformed, cries out: "I am the last man, I will remain so to the end! I will not surrender!" His refusal could be compared to the "no" of Anouilh's heroes—Antigone, Joan of Arc. And indeed instead of accepting defeat as in *Tueur sans gages,* Bérenger protests. His protest might be seen as Ionesco's first positive "message." But could it not also be interpreted as a standstill more than a victory? The curtain goes down on an immobilization and not a solution of the conflict between the desperate resistance of an individual to the superabundance of massive and mechanical being, presented in an extreme form.

A new psychology, absence of communication, the anti-message, unresolvable agony—such elements of seriousness and pathos do not keep Ionesco's theatre from being closely related to farce. For whether they be considered "tragic" or "metaphysical," Ionesco's plays present characters that are not on the same level as the spectator, that is, their existence is inferior to what the spectator considers his own. Whereas serious theatre stylizes man, traditional farce partly humanizes objects. The spectator's laughter and satisfaction come from the humanized object's failure to imitate life. The clown imitating a man of the world, the marionette aping a lover, the puppet Ubu imitating Macbeth or Richard III, are so many silhouettes, inferior forms that never succeed in being equal to their own ambitions and never reach the consistency and weight of their human objective's existence. The puppet is constantly called to order by a continual resurgence of mechanical forces that limit his imitation, thus provoking laughter.

And so it is in the works of Ionesco. Yet his true farcical moments have a very special flavor in that, while the mechanism, object, or puppet is given in advance, the human element is given as a *real* dimension—however stifled and impossible, or almost impossible, to bring out. Where the hero of traditional farce is satisfied with himself and believes in his own success, the hero of modern farce is conscious of his failure. At that level, the laughter stops and the farce becomes "dark." In a Romantic world, the laughter stops when the clown starts to cry; but Ionesco has replaced sentimentality by an anguish which excludes self-pity through protest. Using the mechanism of objects, expressionistic masks, and schematic and fantastic worlds, he has created a farce in which an embryonic humanity is unsuccessful in transcending the anguished consciousness of an inferior existence.

Even "darker" is the implication that Creation itself is nothing other than the mechanical ballet of sorrowful and grotesque masks, continuing on its own momentum, without justification and without control. Called anti-theatre by many critics, despite the fact that all the theatrical elements are included, such farce might be better termed *Théâtre en liberté* or liberated theatre, the mirror of the world as a nonsensical mechanism, mad in its ways, and thus giving the playwright complete freedom to indulge his fantasies.

CHAPTER 9

EXISTENCE ON STAGE:
SAMUEL BECKETT

Despite the success of Genêt, Adamov, and Ionesco, despite the recent interest in Jean Vauthier and Arrabal, Samuel Beckett is still considered the unquestionable originator of a new conception of theatre. Since the 1952–53 season, during which he was in danger of being eclipsed by more established names, critics and a great majority of the public have almost unanimously recognized the importance of his first play *En Attendant Godot*.

Today there is little point in defending Beckett's play. The play is "important," it is new, it lives, it represents a true insight into a way of feeling typical of our times, it goes even further and formulates a definition of man that transcends our times. It invents a new form of dramatic expression; in fact it would seem like the end result of a long search—through the bitterness of naturalistic plays, the mysticism of Catholic drama, the transcendency of poetic theatre—in the attempt to express man's fundamental drama. With *Godot* theatre avoids anecdote and established ideology without falling into abstraction.

Certain critics have described *Godot* as an "allegorical play," whereas *Godot* is in fact totally symbolic without being traditionally allegorical. Allegory consists of an analysis, an exteriorization, and a concrete representation of the elements of the analysis. And this is surely not the case in *Godot*. The elements of waiting (psychological, symbolic, or metaphysical) remain within the characters. They are not even individually thought out; they are continuously and synthetically experienced by the characters. In *Godot* there are no personifications of the abstract or the imaginary. Vladimir is not the personification of the soul or the thirst for God; Estragon is not the personification of material Hunger. Both characters are miserable. They wait and they suffer. They carry within themselves meanings which transcend the story they are living, but only because they are participating in a vaster meaning and a vaster story. Characters and objects (tree, hats, shoes, carrots, turnips) may have a symbolic value—just as Phèdre symbolizes love or Thésée's helmet and beard symbolize royalty-paternity. Although the subject of *Godot* is the waiting for what never comes, and although the play, from beginning to end, evokes that gaping emptiness within each of us which, according to the play, is our very condition, it does not contain the intermediary that is characteristic of allegory: the reduction to abstract elements.

The play also avoids the traps of expressionism and the dangers of the "play of ideas," as there is no question of abstract qualities or analyses of intelligence. Although Vladimir and Estragon sometimes "philosophize," they are in no way like those profound and lucid tramps occasionally found in theatre or films. *Godot* does not imply that wisdom comes from the mouths of tramps. What they say is not explicit and is immediately transposed into poetry. We witness an effort toward ideas, toward memories, toward a rough intellectualization of feelings or impressions—so that our interest is not in their reasoning, but in the effort they make to reason. The vague ideas they express are not there for themselves. They have a purely dramatic function; they are one of the poles toward which the characters desperately strain. There is neither debate nor confrontation, as in Giraudoux, Anouilh, or Sartre; there is merely the representation of the vacuum that separates the characters from what they want to attain.

The absence of any intellectual debate and the representation of a constant state of tension sets *Godot* radically apart from the "play of ideas" and recalls symbolist drama. The intellectual content is there but does not take a logical and discursive form of expression, unsuitable for treating a reality which in itself is experienced. The late nineteenth-century symbolist playwrights were concerned with reaffirming the reality of the Idea as against ideas, that is, the totality of an Essence grasped by intuition as against analytic categories. By the same token, Mood (*état d'âme*) was opposed to Discourse. Whereas Discourse gradually develops in time, advances through the moments of an action, Mood is immobilized in order to evoke an eternity. To the naturalistic discourse, to the sequence of events linked together by the relation of a cause and effect, in a time comparable to that of an office worker, a physicist, or even Darwin, symbolist drama opposed "moments, minutes that are eternal." [1] By its almost Bergsonian intentions, it became "static drama"—a drama which does not move forward, in which nothing happens, similar to a "ball that seems inert" but is "charged with electricity." [2] In extreme cases it has been reduced to the presentation of a painting on stage (see Introduction).

Rémy de Gourmont's description of symbolist drama would seem to anticipate *Godot:*

> Hidden in mist somewhere there is an island, and on that island there is a castle, and in that castle there is a great room lit by a little lamp. And in that room people are waiting. Waiting for what? They don't know! They're waiting for somebody to knock at their door, waiting for their lamp to go out, waiting for Fear and Death. They talk. Yes, they speak words that shatter the silence of the moment. And then they listen again, leaving their sentences unfinished, their gesture uncompleted. They are listening. They are waiting. Will she come perhaps, or

1. Rémy de Gourmont, *le Livre des masques* (article on Maeterlinck)
2. *Ibid.*

won't she? Yes, she will come; she always comes. But it is late, and she will not come perhaps until the morrow. The people collected under that little lamp in that great room have, nevertheless, begun to smile; they still have hope. Then there is a knock—a *knock,* and that is all there is: And it is Life Complete, All of Life.[3]

The play itself must flow; its time is that of the performance. But within the play time is neither that of the scientist nor that of the watch-wearing spectator; it is in the synthesis of the time of the anecdote that is played out and the time of "All of Life." Since waiting contains all of its dimensions at every moment, it is the same whether it lasts for one hour or for fifty years. Here the similarity is obvious. In each act of *Godot* there is an anecdote that takes place in the evening and continues for a few hours. The two evenings are consecutive, yet they are situated in different seasons and "one day we are born, one day we die, the same day, the same second." [4] Moreover the inaction, characteristic of static drama, is closely related to that of *Godot.* Gestures or words—taking place in the flow of normal time—lose their inherent finality when considered in the light of eternity. They are all leveled off by the waiting, by the consciousness of a missing transcendency. Experiencing great love or eating a carrot are two "adventures" which dissolve in the same greyness, the same hollow.

A transcendency can color the world in two contrary ways. It can enrich it: two pieces of wood become the Cross; a red rag embodies the liberation of man. Or it can throw it into insignificance—which is exactly what happens in Rémy de Gourmont's description, as in *Godot.* The transcendency that strips the meaning or ordinary value from an action and substitutes no glorification on any other level can be found in

3. *Ibid.* As quoted by John Gassner in *Form and Idea in Modern Theatre.*

4. *En Attendant Godot,* Act II.

another form in Shakespeare. The fury and sound of Macbeth's adventures dissolve into a final nothingness, and life becomes no more than a tumultuous story "told by an idiot." Didi's and Gogo's clownish tricks and screams, like Macbeth's machinations, would not be insignificant were they given for themselves, but their meanings are reduced to zero by the waiting for Godot. In *Macbeth* that zero is reached at the end of a long trajectory, a long evolution, whereas in *Godot* the zero is not revealed progressively; it is given in advance. Whence the play's apparent inaction, despite innumerable happenings; whence the fact that it marks time; whence the impeccable constancy with which the basic tension is maintained.

En Attendant Godot is a new form of static drama in which three levels are constantly interwoven: (1) the level of words and actions (poetry, clownish tricks, embryonic scenes); (2) that of the direct significance of those words and actions (love, misery, hunger, the role of the intellectual, the dialectic of master and slave, the dimness and confusion of memories, fear, bad faith, even a certain "miserabilism"); (3) that of the waiting which levels everything off. As raw material, Beckett used comedy and the drama of the bum, similar to Chaplin's art or to Fellini's film *la Strada:* a farce about poverty or solitude, based on realistic observation, in which the spectator is asked to recognize an image of his own condition. Although *Godot* has a more universal and deeper meaning, Beckett used the same foundation, the same background of observation.

As the minutes pass by, Vladimir and Estragon produce an unpretentious mixture of "sound and fury"; they live, they eat, they suffer, they dance, they move about. Their activities are the stylization of a kind of tramp's slice of life. They make use of the objects they find; they eat the bones left by a rich picknicker; they are cold; they are beaten by the "others." On a psychological level, Vladimir and Estragon are much more coherent and individualized than Ionesco's "characterless" characters. They are characters in the traditional sense of the word. Each has a coherent and original personality, a body, a past. Yet they are often treated anonymously. They are called Vladimir and Estragon but only in the program: the young boy calls Vladimir "Monsieur Albert"; Estragon introduces himself as Adam (Catulle in the French version); between themselves they resort to childish nicknames, Gogo and Didi. According to Edith Kern, they are as anonymous as A and B in *Molloy*.[5] Yet such anonymity would seem more comparable to that conferred on characters in farce or in Molièresque comedy through the use of conventional theatricalist names, than to the abstractions A and B or the numbered characters in certain expressionistic plays. Didi and Gogo are not interchangeable either between themselves or with the members of a collectivity. They are not far from the colorful, turbulent, diversified fauna that desperately peoples the works of the Irish.

In his radio play *All That Fall*, Beckett showed his gifts as an observer in the traditional style. The setting in *Godot* is less precise: an Irish landscape could hardly be evoked from that vague platform with one lonely tree. Nor are Gogo and Didi as localized as Mrs. Rooney, Mr. Tyler, Tommy, and Jerry of *All That Fall*. But Gogo and Didi are tramps. They have cut off all attachments to their places of origin; they come from different backgrounds; they met somewhere a long time ago. Indeed it seems as if each one's absolute uprootedness was part of his individual definition—an uprootedness accompanied by partial amnesia, and perhaps even explained by it.

Their partial amnesia is not gratuitous. It helps create the atmosphere of doubt, hesitation, the almost dreamlike haze that clouds the waiting for Godot. But on the level of characterization, the play presents a portrait of two tramps, separated from their pasts, rather vague about their memories, incapable

5. Edith Kern, "Drama Stripped from Inaction: Beckett's *Godot*."

of retracing their own lives or even understanding the ins and outs of their present situation. Yet the fact that they only dimly recall their pasts does not mean that they have none. They are suggested through passing illuminations of flashes. We know, for example, that their youths were more promising than their presents. "In the nineties," says Vladimir, "hand in hand from the top of the Eiffel Tower, among the first. We were respectable in those days. Now it's too late. They wouldn't even let us up." We also know that Estragon was a poet, that they harvested grapes together, that Estragon threw himself into the Durance and Vladimir fished him out—unconnected memories in a state of uncertainty which is in keeping with the characters' general psychological confusion.

The realism of Vladimir and Estragon is increased still more by their differences. The lines of one could not be spoken by the other. Vladimir thinks more; he is more cultured; his anguish is more intellectualized; he is more hesitant and more demanding in his choice of words. Estragon is more spontaneous and more lethargic; he is more childish; he sulks more; he is more eager for protection; he is more egotistical and more obstinate; he holds to his own vocabulary and refuses Vladimir's nuances. Vladimir is more restless, more active; Estragon, more inert. Vladimir has the responsibility; he is in charge of the carrots, radishes, and turnips which make up their meals. Estragon is more the victim; he is the one kicked by Lucky. It is Vladimir who tries to make conversation with Pozzo and who tries to seem "well-bred"; Estragon listens only because he is threatened or ordered to, otherwise he independently follows the flow of his own thoughts. Didi and Gogo clearly recall traditional couples in vaudeville. In fact their ancestors come directly from farce: the yokel and his sly partner, transformed in the modern world into the two soldiers of the nineties in French military vaudeville, the comic teams in American movies, Lemmy and George in Steinbeck's *Of Mice and Men*.

On the level of anecdote, the difference between the two characters creates a dramatic tension. Vladimir and Estragon are bound by a relationship that subsists on their dissimilarities. Their dialogue is not only a kind of antiphonal chant of misery; it is also a theatrical dialogue in which the two characters attract and repel, possess or elude one another. Basically they need each other like an old married couple. Vladimir needs someone to talk to, a sound board for his verbal digressions, and tension is created the moment Estragon refuses to "return the ball." Estragon wants protection and in that respect he is the feminine half. He actually demands protection, reproaches Vladimir with singing in his absence, gets angry, leaves, then is afraid and comes back—a kind of coquettish friendship. This study of two tramps would be merely grotesque or clinical were their friendship not profound. It provokes emotion and recognition in that its basic element, independent of needs or habits, is tenderness. They talk about a common past, they help each other, they kiss each other, and even when their actions are tinged with farce they are steeped in compassion. Once again we are reminded of Charlie Chaplin and the film *la Strada,* although Beckett's works are infinitely less tearful.

Obviously the play's ultimate objective transcends the anecdote and characterization. But despite its originality as a whole, *Godot* is made up of traditional elements. In the first production of the play in Paris, those elements were stressed. The acting was similar to the inner realism of the Stanislavsky method. As a result, the spectator's participation was increased, the misery of the characters made more striking, the tension between a life similar to ours and an indifferent and forgetful universe made more convincing and more poignant.

On another level, the spectator participates because that slice of a tramp's life is charged with human suffering; and even if he does not identify with the characters, he is bound to be sensitive to the spectacle of misery in general. For although *Godot*'s "miserabilism"—similar to Chaplin's—is one of the least important aspects of the play and the virtues of the poor are not naïvely glorified, it is constantly present.

In a broader sense Vladimir and Estragon symbolize man in general, and, on that level, the play presents a commentary on life and a definition of man. Edith Kern points out that Vladimir and Estragon are outside of society, that they are not what the existentialists would call *en situation*.[6] Actually they are *en situation* in that they are beaten, they beg, etc. But they are detached from the machinery of society, in which they no longer have any function, and also from the historical situation, which the play ignores. Therefore they have the time to be men. They play at the kind of purity that the classics have bestowed upon certain tragic heroes.

The tramp then is the modern metaphor for universal man. The King in tragedy—risen above men, conducting his politics for himself, closed within his own glory, in direct contact with Fate and Values—represented man's condition in its pure state, without intermediaries and freed from bondage. When Voltaire and the Encyclopedists defined man by his function in and relation to the world of objects (manufacture, commerce), the Bourgeois became representative of humanity. He was Sedaine's citizen of the world. By comparison, the royal hero, who did not transform either economy or materials, would seem like an abstraction. Now that the bourgeois society has begun to doubt its own definitions, we have returned to the metaphor of man in the form of a detached character: the Proustian hero, for example, that bourgeois who does nothing. Leftist ideologies continue to define man by his relation to transformable materials but consider the bourgeois relation as abstract and take the proletariat as the symbol of humanity—a humanity *en situation,* defined both by its work and by the conquest of its freedom. But if one believes in the permanence of universal man it is difficult to accept the proletariat as a satisfying metaphor, for at this particular moment in history, the proletarian

6. *Ibid.*

is no more than a "half-man" (Sartre). Beside him, we have the tramp—a symbol of humanity considered as residue, stripped of its functions and plans for transformations, and left face to face with itself. The tramp has become the image of our condition laid bare, with everything else a mere secondary quality or anecdote. He is an image of humanity reduced to zero, about to start again from nothing. Here there are possibilities for a new classicism: A. J. Leventhal, for example, established a strict parallel between man according to Beckett and man according to Pascal.[7]

The tramp represents man as such, as detached from society. He is in some ways the symbol of the inalienable part of every man, the irreducible element which transcends particularities and remains aloof from social, political, civic, or ideological brigades. He marks the renunciation of bourgeois participation in common values, as well as the idea of humanitarian *engagement* or commitment. Man now seems better defined by his solitude and his estrangement than by his participation.

All existence is solitary, and one of the signs of solitude is physical suffering. Where sympathy is possible in the case of moral suffering, physical pain seems to throw the individual into isolation. When Vladimir suffers, he is no more than a spectacle for Estragon. From the very beginning of the play, each tramp remains outside the other's pain:

> *Estragon:* Help me!
> *Vladimir:* It hurts?
> *Estragon:* Hurts! He wants to know if it hurts!
> *Vladimir:* . . . I'd like to hear what you'd say if you had what I have.
> *Estragon:* It hurts?
> *Vladimir:* Hurts! He wants to know if it hurts!

7. A. J. Leventhal, "Mr. Beckett's *En Attendant Godot.*"

No one feels physical suffering *with* another. Here again a comparison can be made with man according to Pascal—the "Man without God," who cannot even use his suffering as a means to salvation. The idea of solitude as unbearable is Pascalian also. The friendship/of the two tramps shows the incapacity of man to remain alone with himself. The drama of the human condition thus lies in the uncertainty of each man's relationship to others. The Sartrian analysis of the "others" gives the existentialist theatre its basic drama. The vision of man in *Godot* is similar to it: a perpetual series of rebounds, in which man is constantly thrown back into his solitude. At one extreme there is the idea of a kind of "togetherness" in common action, thanks to which emptiness and solitude seem to be filled:

> *Estragon:* We don't manage too badly, eh Didi, between
> the two of us?
> . . . . . .
> We always find something, eh Didi, to give us
> the impression we exist?

In contrast to Estragon's "we" is the other extreme: a total absence of communication, even an absolute rejection of the other as when Estragon, in a moment of brief but cruel betrayal, closes his eyes and in the depths of solitude, calls to another, infinitely more powerful than Vladimir:

> *Estragon:* (*Stopping, brandishing his fists, at the top of
> his voice*). God have pity on me!
> *Vladimir:* (*Vexed*). And me?
> *Estragon:* On me! On me! Pity! On me!

Man's situation cannot be defined by his communion with others, nor by an absolute absence of relations with others, but by a fluctuation between the two extremes, by *élans* toward communion that are perpetually broken off, by a mobile synthesis between permanent solitude and the effort made to come out of it. The fluctuation is characteristic of our activities and brands them as futile. Vladimir and Estragon do not act; they try to act. They invent games and then quickly tire of them. Their agitation is a kind of Pascalian diversion practiced by characters who know that they are only amusing themselves. What Beckett's man has that Pascal's free-thinker lacks is lucidity, the consciousness of his own condition. Pascal's King who hunts continues to hunt because he does not know why he hunts. Vladimir and Estragon know that they act in order to avoid thinking about their condition. They act merely to fill up a vacuum, a fact of which the King was unaware. The tragedy of their condition takes the form of a circle: man's condition is unbearable, but the only apparent means of escape are illusory.

Suicide was twice considered as a possible solution. In the first act, presented as a sinister form of amusement on the same plane as the others, it is attractive only momentarily (for the sexual consequences of hanging) and then rejected because it may separate the two tramps should one of them fail to die. The idea is renounced merely because it means complications. At the very end of the play they come back to the same idea. But they still do not commit suicide, this time because of a technical accident: the cord breaks. Yet they never give up the idea and the dialogue shows that suicide might be a solution when, at the end, Estragon declares that he "can't go on like this," suggests to Vladimir that they separate, and Vladimir answers that they will hang themselves next day. However there is no suicide, only two attempts. There again, even in the case of suicide as a last possibility, the true condition of man is not in the realization but in the effort made. Since the attempt miscarried, it made suicide an action like any other. Moreover it represents what is most theatrical in any action— the moment when the character tries to act and seems immobilized between two modes of being: this time, the being he is and the non-being he envisions. The drama is neither in the "to be" nor in the "not to be," but in the "or" which links them together. Thus another tension in *Godot* is that which is established between the importance we ordinarily attach to the "or" and the character's apathy in regard to it. "Why don't we hang ourselves?" is a proposition that has neither more nor less importance than: "We could do our exercises." Although actions take on meaning when thought of as actions-in-the-world, in *Godot*, just as in Camus' *l'Etranger*, the character, thrown into solitude or estrangement, considers his own actions and the actions of others equally meaningless.

Suicide is parodied in a way by the characters' inactivity or desire for inactivity in the scene in Act II in which, once they fall down, they remain lying down. That kind of "Oblomovitis" —the lethargic irresponsibility of man lying down—is made impossible by Pozzo's agitation. The world of the others, who beat Estragon, also condemns him to getting up and acting.

An intrusion into the monotonous flow of the tramps' gestures and comments is provided by the entrance of the couple Pozzo and Lucky. That type of intrusion, so frequent in theatre, the arrival or passing through of an apparently different kind of person, makes the spectator wonder whether the intruder will succeed in transforming the play's universe, or whether his difference will prove to be no more than illusory. For the two tramps, Pozzo and Lucky constitute a fantastic spectacle offered by the society of men from which they are excluded. By the same token, they are treated less realistically than the two heroes, for they are a sort of metaphor of what the tramps see in the society that is foreign to them.

Their nature and the nature of their relationship are immediately clear to the spectator. Pozzo, dressed like a country gentleman, carries a whip and holds, at the end of a rope, a pale and thin creature wearing a valet's vest and heavily burdened down. One is the master, the other the slave. They enter shortly after the following exchange of words:

Estragon:	(*His mouth full, vacuously*). We're not tied?
Vladimir:	I don't hear a word you're saying.
Estragon:	(*Chews, swallows*). I'm asking you if we're tied.
Vladimir:	Tied?
Estragon:	Ti-ed.
Vladimir:	How do you mean tied?
Estragon:	Down.
Vladimir:	But to whom? By whom?
Estragon:	To your man.
Vladimir:	To Godot? Tied to Godot? What an idea! No question of it. (*Pause*). For the moment.

Almost directly, Pozzo appears on stage holding the rope to which Lucky is *tied*. Is Lucky's rope similar to the bond that might possibly unite the tramps to Godot? Are they not in fact waiting for the opportunity to give themselves up to bondage? They are waiting to be taken over by Godot, they hope to be, but they never explain what they want of him. All that Vladimir and Estragon say is that they are waiting to be "saved." The idea of salvation without any concrete content is suddenly actualized by the rope that ties Lucky to Pozzo. If salvation consists in being possessed by Godot, the desire to meet Godot and the repulsion provoked by the rope would be the two poles of a fundamental hesitation, a movement back and forth comparable to that which attracts the two tramps to one another and then separates them. Here again is the tragic circle, similar to that in existentialist drama: the vacuum of freedom calls for something to fill it, for the nothingness is unbearable; but when the total commitment or possession is realized, the resulting state is just as agonizing. Man is caught between the vacuum of waiting for Godot and the bondage of a Lucky (Lucky: the lucky one who has found his Godot).

Neither possession nor bondage would seem to be solutions.

The friendship between the two tramps and Pozzo's and Lucky's rope are only sketches or parodies of a true union—both desired and feared, yet never realized. They seem to imply that we never arrive at more than a pitiful or grotesque approximation of a union, just as, through action, we arrive at no more than the "impression we exist."

Our lives are farces of Life. The master-slave relationship and Pozzo's acts represent one aspect of the farce, the most ordinary and the least lucid. The rope is meant to reassure Pozzo, just as through his comments, Estragon reassures himself in stressing the friendship that ties him to Vladimir. But where Vladimir and Estragon make a pretense at acting, fighting, or playing, Pozzo takes his actions seriously and the least of his gestures becomes a whole spectacle, glorified by noble language. In exaggerating the simple processes of life—having Lucky serve him his lunch, sitting down again after having got up, describing the sky, lighting his pipe—Pozzo tries to drown his life in a general atmosphere of ceremony so as to cover up its insignificance. Either man waits for Godot, or he clutters up his life with all the outer signs of importance.

In the second act Pozzo is blind. For Edith Kern, Pozzo's blindness and Lucky's muteness are signs of the inevitable degradation of the master-slave couple. Actually Pozzo's blindness leads to a partial reversal of the relationship. He no longer drives Lucky, he follows him, and the rope has become shorter —a kind of parodic and concrete sketch of the master-slave dialectic. Besides, although the rope is shorter, Pozzo's blindness throws him into the shadows of his solitude. He thus grasps more accurately the horror of his condition, which has now become an amplification of Vladimir's and Estragon's. For even more than having doubts about time and his situation in space, Pozzo is in complete ignorance or total confusion.

Indeed it would seem that truth lies in the depths of the confusion. Pozzo's definition of life, implied by the play as a whole, is drawn from his darkness: "One day we were born, one day we shall die, the same day, the same second. . . ." Since the days are all alike, they merge into one indefinite day. There is no flow, only a state. Yet the words were spoken by a character who is in perpetual motion. Beckett plays with contrasts and creates a whole network of subtle tensions between the *state* and the *effort*. Pozzo, who passes by, clings to his state. The tramps, who remain, are always making an effort to get up and do something. When Estragon almost reaches a state (the death-like state of man lying down), it is Pozzo who, also fallen down, makes an effort to get up. That scene, in which Vladimir and Estragon call themselves "men" and Pozzo "all humanity," with all the characters who have fallen down, now trying to get up, now refusing, going from immobility to effort and vice versa, is the most developed metaphor of the human condition. It has an echo in *All That Fall,* when Mr. and Mrs. Rooney, he blind, she lamed by her obesity, try not to fall.

Pozzo tried to give his life a structure by his possession of Lucky and the visible sign of his possession, the rope. By the same token, Lucky is "saved" by that bond, by his function and his state of servitude. But servitude leads to a mechanization which crushes the individual. Lucky is reduced to basic reactions: he trembles, he cries, he kicks. He has a past: he had been a better dancer; he had been Pozzo's "thinker"; he had been, and still is his valet and his jester. Lucky is more than a servant in the ordinary sense of the word. He represents other servitudes, principally that of the intellectual and the artist. He thinks *for* Pozzo; he dances *for* Pozzo. Vladimir and Estragon think and play, or try to think and play, for themselves. Their efforts are perhaps ridiculous. But Lucky's are inhuman and abstract—at least they have become so in Pozzo's service. When independence (analogous with solitude) is opposed to service (analogous with union), the two situations result in grotesque failures. Moreover the complexity and incoherence of Lucky's long speech [8] make it possible to see his situation at that moment as a farcical satire on the condition of professional intellectuals. Supported by a society for whom they are all valets, they "produce" thought, as they are asked to do, but exasperate their masters by their verbal delirium. The result of such deteriorization is silence. In the second act Lucky has become mute.

Their new state introduces a usual notion of time. We are born and die the same day, but still the change indicates that we are born *before* we die (in *All That Fall* there is mention made of a little girl who dies because she has not been born). Pozzo and Lucky have changed from one act to the other, from one day to the next from winter to spring. The amount of time is undetermined but the direction of time is preserved. In the compressible but irreversible time that Vladimir and Estragon fill up in their monotonous way, the Pozzos and the Luckys "evolve":

Vladimir: How they've changed!

Estragon: Who?

Vladimir: Those two.

Estragon: That's the idea, let's make a little conversation.

Vladimir: Haven't they?

Estragon: What?

Vladimir: Changed.

Estragon: Very likely. They all change. Only we can't.

Where the two tramps are immobilized by their waiting for Godot, the couple Pozzo-Lucky, who are not waiting for anything, deteriorate in time. If they were meant to represent a society entirely concerned with itself, a kind of prophecy can be seen at that level. Desperately clinging to its present struc-

8. Lucky's speech recalls that of the Doctor in ancient farce and the Pedant's in classical comedy, both represented as buffoons of a given society.

ture (the master-slave relationship) and its rites, amused by an abstract and anguished art (Lucky, who formerly danced the jig and the fandango, breaks out into a symbolic pantomime of "the net") and by means of an intellectual delirium that no longer has meaning, society will evolve into a world of blind Pozzos and mute Luckys—or toward the world of Hamm and Clov in *Fin de partie*.

The scenes including Pozzo and Lucky show the meeting of two living durations in different modes that merge: the perpetuation of waiting, a monotonous flow experienced by men who ask for happenings and change (*Estragon:* Nothing happens, nobody comes, nobody goes, it's awful!); and the transition, change, and deterioration experienced by men who cling to their state, although conscious of the speed of destruction and the unexpectedness of events (*Pozzo:* . . . night is charging and will burst upon us—pop! like that!). In contrast to social and historic man, who is in a hurry to be something or thinks he is, in the brief decrescendo that makes up the duration of a life or civilization, the play offers a portrait of man as withdrawn from history and society, left to his existence, and continuously yawning in the indefinite flow of monotonous time.

In both cases, the activities and effort are in vain and serve only to fill in time. What maintains and reinforces this particular meaning of the play, what keeps the spectator from attributing an inherent finality to any one activity are the constantly repeated references to Godot, who is awaited but never comes. Pozzo and Lucky come up to us like the person who stops and tells us the story of his life while we are impatiently awaiting a friend. The fact that we are waiting takes away all real finality from his words and relegates them to a negative universe marked by the absence of the friend we are awaiting. In the same situation, the drink we are having is not drunk for itself; it is drunk-while-waiting. And it is the *waiting* that permeates all of the tramps' gestures and comments and relegates their acts to a background of non-being such as Sartre analyzed in *l'Etre et le néant*.

And yet besides the agitation invented to pass the time, the moments of life marked by hunger, blows, fear, or physical suffering are real. They are experienced in horror. But even that reality is finally reduced to insignificance. It, also, becomes the negative background marked by the absence of Godot. The transcendency by which suffering is negated is itself no more than an absence. In the symbolist drama, the Idea—as mysterious, obscure, or chaotic as it may be—is reality. In *Godot* the real remains at the level of what is directly experienced, and Godot is systematically absent; his very existence is uncertain; he is the phantasm that is satisfying because it gives content to man's desire for a frame of reference. Man is unable to accept insignificance, unable to understand that his misery and his existence are themselves devoid of meaning. Godot is that by which man both justifies and confirms the insignificance of existence. He is the Hypothesis that explains a negative phenomenon. He is the Yes dialectically necessary for life to be the No that it is. The question is not to justify being, but to justify non-being. The development in *En Attendant Godot* consists in three movements: consciousness of insignificance; the assertion of a meaning (Godot) in relation to which it is possible to conceive of an absence of meaning; and the strengthening of insignificance through a consciousness of and the waiting for something that *has* meaning.

On the level of anecdote Godot is a character just like the others. His absence makes him more blurred and more uncertain, but enough details are given to form a sketchy but concrete image. He has shepherds, agents, a family, a bank account. He even has a beard. He is distant, capricious, and powerful, like the Masters in Kafka's world. Exactly who is he and whom does he represent? Edith Kern suggests God plus the ending "ot" of Charlot, the name given to Chaplin's Little Man by the French. In fact the meaning of the play does not lie in explanations of what Godot symbolizes. Whether he signifies God or any other belief or illusion is of secondary importance.[9] The subject of the play and its drama is not the identity of Godot but the waiting itself.

Therefore the play does not fall into any established categories of religion or ideology, which in themselves would suggest a definition of Godot. It represents a reversal of the Romantic attitude—that of Chateaubriand, for example, for whom God came first and then the *vague à l'âme,* a rather indefinite anguish and melancholy, as a sign of our desire for God. Here the desire for Godot to arrive comes first. Godot is the positive element created to correspond to the feeling of emptiness and insignificance, which alone is real and experienced.

The universe revealed by the play is one of insignificance. The drama that gives it tension is the conflict between insignificance and man's effort to have meaning despite everything. The metaphor of waiting is the best form of expression for that conflict, in which lies Beckett's final definition of man. *En Attendant Godot* is not an allegory, an incompleted *Pilgrim's Progress.* It is a concrete and synthetic equivalent of our existence in the world and our consciousness of it.

En Attendant Godot is Beckett's most important work to date. His later works *Fin de partie,* the pantomime *Acte sans paroles,* the radio play *All That Fall,* and the monodrama *Krapp's Last Tape* pick up certain of *Godot*'s themes and express them in different metaphors, without ever quite reaching the plenitude and immediacy of his first play.

Yet all have one quality in common: their intense theatricalism. Besides the value of his vision of life, besides his drama,

9. Beckett sometimes does use Christian symbolism as a literary device. The tramps, for example, compare themselves to the two thieves crucified with Christ, implying that one might be saved and not the other. The tree then might be interpreted as an empty Cross and Godot as the absence of God.

Beckett is acutely conscious of the essence of theatre itself. He writes for the Italian-type or picture-frame stage. His characters live within a stage frame; they must be seen from the same angle by the entire audience at the same moment. This is particularly noticeable when he tries to produce a "full-face" effect. In *Fin de partie* Hamm in his armchair must be seen from the front, just as Giacometti's figures, looming out of a space enclosed on three sides, are prisoners of their frames, or like one of Francis Bacon's horrifying apparitions. The play can only be performed in a box set, strictly limited by its frame. *Krapp's Last Tape* must also be played on the picture-frame stage if Krapp is to disappear into the background to drink in obscurity.

Using the traditional stage, Beckett is free to respect the convention of the fourth wall or break it at will. In *Godot,* by unexpectedly destroying the conventional illusions, he produces unoriginal but surprising effects. In the first act the audience is taken for a "bog" or is ironically considered as "inspiring prospects." The background itself suddenly stops being the space alongside a road and again becomes a stage set when Estragon, in a moment of panic (Act II, French version), rushes headlong "toward the backdrop, gets entangled in it, and falls." Certain lines are both a direct expression of the character's thoughts, and comments addressed to the spectator by the playwright:

> *Vladimir:* This is becoming really insignificant.
> *Estragon:* Not enough.

In *Fin de partie* the asides to the audience are more obvious. The play begins like a late nineteenth-century bourgeois comedy: the servant's pantomime of his domestic duties, followed by several remarks which explain the situation. Comments on the meaning of the play are more frequent. Clov's last declamatory speech, for example, is addressed directly to the audience.

Beckett's theatre goes even further and presents life as an

imitation of theatre. The master in *Fin de partie* is called Hamm, implying a ham actor. Hamm tries to perform certain numbers, like Pozzo and Mr. Rooney. All of them feel they are giving a structure to their lives by choosing particular events and telling about them in an affected style with rhetorical effects, and conscious, not of reliving, but of replaying them. "How did you find me?" asks Pozzo after his description of nightfall. Hamm demands an audience and constantly interrupts to comment on his own style: "Nicely put, that . . . A bit feeble, that. . . ." And Mr. Rooney asks, after an interruption: "Where was I in my composition?" Such "composed" narratives are part of a system of rites by which Beckett's characters try to give form to life by fitting it into a framework of beautiful language or deliberately masking its horror. In *Krapp's Last Tape* the hero records the narrative of his life as it unfolds and listens to himself. Proust's hero set about saving his past by making it eternal through art; Beckett's heroes try to save their lives from insignificance through narrative. But for Beckett, literature is not salvation: Pozzo and, particularly, Hamm are conscious of the vanity of their attempts; Krapp's tape turns silently at the end of the act. Literature then is not necessarily salvation; it is an effort made to save oneself, perhaps as futile as any other. Yet Beckett himself makes the effort.

Presented as theatrical numbers, the "narratives" and, by extension, literature and theatre, are games. Conscious of the esthetic quality of their monologues, Pozzo, Hamm, Mr. Rooney, and Krapp (who found a tape recorder the best means for listening to himself) play and watch themselves play. By the same token, Vladimir and Estragon never succeed in taking their own actions seriously. They rapidly become aware of the fact that their actions are theatrical numbers and that they are actors and spectators at the same time. Life consists in pretending to live—like children pretend that they fly or are animals—and yet we have nothing more than our lives. Thus there is a correspondence between our lives in the world and the essence of theatre, in which, paradoxically, what is performed is both reality and a game, and requires both participation and detachment. Beckett's vision of life is made for the stage.

Life is no more than the comedy of life, no more than an attempt to play at living, no more than an embryonic farce. The often childish or capricious "games" that represent life on stage must necessarily be borrowed from genres in which failure, stumbling, and the resistance of objects make up the spectacle: circus and vaudeville sketches and their outgrowth, the motion picture farce. Among others, the hat number in *Godot* and Mrs. Rooney's difficulties with Mr. Slocum's car in *All That Fall* clearly establish the equivalence between daily life, made up of obstacles, repetitions, and failures, and the most elementary and grossest forms of theatrical comedy. Farce of that kind is grating, precisely because the equivalence is made so obvious and because our lives are directly concerned. The characters in Beckett's theatre are constantly caught between their own clumsiness and the resistance of objects, including their own bodies: shoes that are too narrow, hats too small, car doors too low, windows too high, prostate conditions, hemorrhages, itching. Moreover they forget necessary objects or misplace them, especially in *Fin de partie* and *Krapp's Last Tape*. Beckett's universe is one of perpetual irritation. Nothing in it works: a universe of imperfections in which things would seem to have been created, not for man, nor actually against him, but merely in order to exist in a state of passive resistance to his efforts. In *Acte sans paroles* Beckett is both more explicit and less convincing. Objects literally slip away from the character, and the remarkable atmosphere of concrete uneasiness that pervades his spoken plays is replaced by an abstract notion of frustration.

All the small obstacles of daily life cause man to make a series of efforts that represents, in a way, the more general attempt of giving a structure and meaning to life. The various attempts made are given a theatrical quality through techniques borrowed from the art of clowns and resulting in pure theatricalism. In *Godot* Beckett uses a twentieth-century myth—the one that best expresses man's attempt to live decently in a world of hostile objects and social groups: Charlie Chaplin's Tramp. In the second act of *Godot* the curtain rises on Estragon's boots placed "front center, heels together, toes splayed," and Lucky's bowler hat thrown somewhere in the background. Chaplin's cane is missing, as if the tramps, relatives of Chaplin's Little Man, had not managed to achieve his elegance.

Chaplin's Little Man is a modern myth and, apart from Hitler, the only modern myth sufficiently distant and individualized. Hollywood, the Party, the middle-class American and Frenchman, the Capitalist, are all institutions, collectivities, or abstractions raised to the level of myth. Chaplin's Little Man emerged directly as a myth, with his own individuality and his own past. His universality is guaranteed in part by his generality. He is known, recognized, and loved by about everyone. When Beckett suggests Charlie Chaplin, he is using a contemporary tradition in order to give a visible sign of the play's universality and also to show that the universal is in the present.

In *Godot* Beckett managed to multiply the Little Man's family. The character closest to the source is Vladimir, with his attempts at playing a certain worldly game: "Never neglect the little things in life," he says as he buttons his fly; or when he is asked his opinion on Lucky's dance: "There's something about it . . . ," he says "squirming like an esthete." On the other hand, Estragon's shoes most clearly recall the Little Man's classic attributes, and it is Estragon who kicks like him in order to have his revenge. All the characters wear bowler hats as a sign of their participation in the myth. For Chaplin's Tramp is the myth of man who, despite everything, *plays* at being a man.

Although Beckett's other dramatic works are not concerned with the myth, the idea of life as a game and man's attempt to play it remains a central theme. The myth is replaced by "explanations" that might be considered a weakness in Beckett's later works. In *Fin de partie* the theme is stressed in the title itself (*End Game*) and by passing remarks ("Me—to play," says Hamm). The attempt to play is opposed, as in *Godot,* to the desire for release through annihilation. The characters in *Fin de partie* waver between the two attitudes; Mrs. Rooney, in *All That Fall,* wants to be transformed into a "big fat jelly" or disappear into her comfortable bed. The struggle between an attempt at playing and the wish for self-destruction is always accompanied by a consciousness of life's absurdity and brevity: "The same day . . . ," as Pozzo said; and Mrs. Rooney's: "Just one great squawk and then . . . peace. They would have slit her weasand in any case," after Mr. Slocum had squashed a hen with his car; and Hamm's: "Moments for nothing, now as always, time was never and time is over, reckoning closed and story ended," at the end of *Fin de partie.* *Krapp's Last Tape* ends in a kind of stupor and the tape recorder turns silently after Krapp's last words concerning the best years of his life: "I wouldn't want them back." Beckett's great feat is to make the spectator experience simultaneously the interminable series of minutes that make up his life, a game which never stops ending, in which he exists in a state of permanent tension, perpetually headed for defeat, and the somewhat objective consciousness of life's absurd brevity. "The end is in the beginning and yet you go on," says Hamm parodying T. S. Eliot. Life is a bad play, performed for nothing, yet it is the only one we have. Mrs. Rooney dreams of annihilation, but continues nonetheless to appreciate the landscape and makes every effort to walk without falling. Hamm and Clov call out for the end to come, but continue to play the hateful game of the man who can't sit down and the man who can't get up.

Beckett's characters are never alone in their efforts. They are bound two by two in differing forms of solidarity: Vladimir and Estragon, Pozzo and Lucky, Hamm and Clov, Nagg and Nell, Mr. and Mrs. Rooney, even Krapp and his recorded voice. The character of *Acte sans paroles* is in contact with a kind of invisible and superior being who plays with his desires just as Pozzo plays with Estragon when he is about to give him the chicken bones. Beckett's theatre is a theatre of couples. Each character rebounds against another. Each one acts now with, now against that other. The relationship with another seems necessary to the effort of playing at living, dialogue being one of the forms of the tension that is our existence. Tenderness, need, and hate are the psychological constituents of the bond, always treated with an irony in which sarcasm is mixed with emotion—emotion because the characters are bound by the recognition of a common misery; sarcasm because the bond remains unworkable and never transforms the misery, and because each one uses the other, pretending to communicate with him. When Nell and Nagg reminisce about a boat outing on Lake Como, they realize that, for different reasons, they had experienced the happy moments each alone, and their so-called common past had not saved them from final agony in separate garbage cans. The master-slave relationship is the most frequent and clearest sign of an absence of equality between people. Any relationship with others must needs be that of conqueror and conquered, executioner and victim, possessor and possessed—and theatre feeds on the contradictory efforts made by the characters to solidify the relationship or burst it wide open.

Although the themes and theatrical devices can be found over and again from play to play, and although Beckett's general vision of life and definition of man remain the same, each play is nonetheless situated in a different universe. *All That Fall* takes place in the peopled and known world of realism. Mrs. Rooney has gone out. She regrets it because of the dangers of the outside world, but persists in following the road to the station amidst people, animals, and flowers. The point of view is always Mrs. Rooney's, but the people she meets are treated with an objectivity à la Maupassant. *Godot's* universe is also that of the outside world, but its space is interpreted by the subjectivity of the characters, a kind of desert shot through with rare and unjustified happenings. In *Fin de partie* Beckett's characters no longer go out. They are voluntary prisoners of their own private dramas, just as the characters in *Huis Clos* refuse to leave their room in Hell when the door opens. The outside world, which continues to interest them, can only be seen through a telescope. It is an end-of-the-world landscape in which life has almost disappeared and the sea itself has become immobilized. "To hell with the universe," says Hamm, as he plunges back into the interminable quarrel that binds him to his servant, Clov. The indefinite space of *Godot* has been replaced by a closed room. The open image of waiting for salvation has been replaced by the closed image of waiting for annihilation. Finally, in *Krapp's Last Tape,* the room itself is a shadowy hole, in the center of which the character talks to himself, telling the story of his own life.

The silence of Krapp and his tape recorder is the last image to date of Beckett's man. Language has become powerless to express the dialogue of man with himself, and man remains suspended for an indefinite time between two states of consciousness: the interminable effort of living and the vanity of life. In Beckett's theatre, man is again put face to face with himself. After the successive demystifications represented by the works of post-war playwrights, Beckett has tried the supreme demystification. He attacks life itself. He does it without long speeches, without contradictory debates. He merely places existence on stage. His works cannot be called existentialist, although they can be explained through the use of existentialist categories. His is a *theatre of existence* which, in itself, is outside any one school of thought.

To exist, for Beckett, means to watch oneself trying to exist and, by the same token, to be either fully aware of the effort it takes or to attempt to blind oneself to it. The dogmatism of the Cartesian *cogito* is transformed into a skepticism tinged with Eastern philosophy: "I see myself trying to exist; therefore I exist." And as Pozzo says: "Sometimes I wonder if I'm not still asleep." In point of fact, the drama that makes up the substance of Beckett's theatre is the ironic duality of demystified man.

Beckett's characters silently struggle toward forms of being or structures that are suddenly disclosed by a gesture or in words. Lyricism, eloquence, invectives, and clichés are like fixatives which make existence intelligible and temporarily "save" it. The words hesitatingly move on from image to image toward the greatest possible precision or toward an enrichment or transformation of reality. Screams and swearing are often meant to "fix" a gesture or an impression. The poetry of the language is not in its profuse imagery but in its precision, in the music of intersecting voices, in the calculated alternation of pauses and transparent words. But the fixatives are ephemeral and the words fall back into silence, just as water subsides to form a new wave. The pulsation of effort, forever repeated and forever vain, gives Beckett's works their rhythm, their balance, their form. When all of life is a game, theatre, the game par excellence, has the last word.

THE GAPING MASK

In the sixty theatres of Paris, with an average of five openings a week from September to July, an impressive number of really original plays have reflected certain trends of thinking over the past thirty years: nihilism as opposed to political or religious optimism, an earnest approach to great problems as opposed to the victory of irony and humor, a world of fixed essences as against a free or absurd world, estheticism as against *praxis*. Such diversity has given free rein to the individualism of writers. For although representative, outstanding playwrights have remained unique. Each has his signature, a mark that can be recognized at every level of his work, from surface effects to a fundamental vision of man and the world.

Each work presents a veritably different universe. The following lines from the prologue of Apollinaire's *les Mamelles de Tirésias* might apply to each playwright:

> His universe is his play
> Within which he is the god creator
> Who disposes as he will
> Sounds gestures gait masses colors
> Not with the sole objective
> Of photographing what is called a slice of life
> But to bring forth life itself in all its truth
> For a play should be a complete universe
> With its creator
> In other words nature itself
> And not only
> The representation of a small fragment
> Of what surrounds us or what once took place.

Conclusion

Because of the variety, the modern spectator is led, more than ever in the history of theatre, to consider each play as a possible metaphor, an objectivized hypothesis of man's and the world's condition. Not only is each adventure exemplary, as in all theatre, but the play's universe itself is a metaphor of a hidden structure of the proposed universe. Writers of the past simplified, discovered, or poeticized the real universe. Modern writers invent their own systems. Although an occasional playwright, such as Claudel, considers his own universe as the only truth for all eternity, the spectator must think of each as a *possible* system. In other words the modern spectator must regard his playwrights as poets, as makers of metaphors, tangible symbols of a truth that is always transcendent.

One basic feeling or basic abstraction is common to all the playwrights, each work being an illustration and a concrete explanation of it. It can be expressed in the most general terms and is the condition *sine qua non* of all truly dramatic works: the very nature of man is to be torn apart within himself and it is an irrecusable fact. In the past the dramatic hero was seen in contrast to a world of unified individuals, at peace with themselves or at least without conflicts. In today's theatre the inner struggle is not considered to be exceptional or caused by circumstances, but constitutes the very definition of man.

The scenic metaphors expressing man's dramatic nature are doubtless part of a general evolution. And although a lack of historical perspective makes any clear development impossible to define, certain aspects are evident enough today to be isolated.

The transition we indicated from the supernatural to man does not exactly correspond to a chronological evolution of French theatre. Claudel's definitive acceptance by the public at large and the success of Bernanos' *Dialogue des Carmélites* more or less coincided with the rise and renown of Sartre and Camus. Yet while both tendencies are somewhat parallel in time, the new plays since the war show a definite return to man in his isolation. The idea of the divine may sometimes be apparent in Montherlant or in Beckett but never the divine itself. Such plays express the conflict between man and his own idea of the supernatural, not the conflict between men and the gods. And although the return to man has occasionally led to forms somewhat similar to the old naturalism (Salacrou, Sartre, Anouilh), more recent playwrights have avoided the danger by exteriorizing and concretely representing elements of their inner worlds and reintroducing scenic fantasy in more or less allegorical form.

There is no doubt that the current two-fold movement extends, in modern times, the continual debate in French thinking, following the dialectic line Montaigne-Pascal-Voltaire-Rousseau-etc., from humanism to Jansenism, Jansenism to rationalism, rationalism to vague Romantic mysticism, Romanticism to positivism, positivism to Baudelairian and Rimbaldian symbolism, and continued on into modern dialogues such as that of Gide and Claudel. What characterizes the present state of the debate is the fact that it is generally no longer between forms of rationalism and a Christian vision, but that both factions claim the notion of transcendency, one as residing in an outer reality (God, cosmic forces, a possible "kingdom"), the other as residing in man alone.

Thus it is sometimes difficult to distinguish between the symbol of an element or dimension of an inner world and the tangible symbol of an outer reality or another order. While there is no doubt as to the meaning of Claudel's symbolism, there may be some concerning certain of Giraudoux's fantasies. And while it is obvious that Sartre's Jupiter represents no more than a satirical allegory of the idea of God, Audiberti's monsters are ambiguous, as is Beckett's Godot.

Despite the productions of plays like André Obey's *Une Fille pour du vent* (an adaptation of the myth of Iphigenia), another movement today would seem to be the progressive

Conclusion

indifference to the traditional material of professors and diplomats. Although Giraudoux and Cocteau drew freely from ancient mythology, Sartre used it in only one play, Camus touched on it only through a historical character, and the poets either turn toward national and regional folklore or invent new myths and legends. Ionesco, Adamov, and Beckett deliberately move away from traditions of culture, and their myths are rather the modern ones, such as Charlie Chaplin and the Marx Brothers. The gods of Olympus have been gradually replaced by clowns in modern dress. The fact that the process had become a convention can be seen from Anouilh's *Antigone,* in which the use of certain of Cocteau's and Giraudoux's devices is particularly obvious, despite the play's style and power. And Sartre's choice of Greek myth for *les Mouches* is quite clearly a deliberate and topical answer to Giraudoux's *Electre.* Moreover the new playwrights prefer to start from zero, or rather to base their theatre primarily on a direct experience of life and not on bookish culture. In considering only the front line of important discoveries or contributions, the movement of humanization without recourse to academic humanism is one important characteristic of the French theatre's evolution in the past thirty years.

Even more essential in regard to an *idea* of theatre is the influence of Antonin Artaud, which has become increasingly vigorous during the last years. Although in general Jacques Copeau was the main artisan of the return to integrity on the French stage, Artaud's spirit has progressively restored theatre's disrupting power.

Artaud is "an influence more than a presence, a presence more than a work."[1] He belongs to that breed of seers who leave trails of fire behind them as they pass through the world. Artaud might be said to have been part of the surrealist movement, to which he belonged from 1924 to 1927. But after a

1. André Frank, *Encyclopédie du théâtre contemporain,* Vol. II.

great row, he gave up the surrealist experiment and his works clearly transcend it. In fact he was a unique phenomenon of the French literary world of the thirties. In the realm of theatre alone, he was an actor of both stage and screen, the founder of the Alfred Jarry Theatre in 1927 (with Roger Vitrac) and the "Théâtre de la cruauté" in 1933, the author of a group of essays, begun in 1931 and published in 1938 as *le Théâtre et son double*.[2] When he died in 1948, the poetry review *K* published a testimonial issue including articles by Charles Dullin, Arthur Adamov, Henri Pichette, Audiberti, and Roger Blin. It seems today that his influence on the French theatre extends, with varying intensity, beyond the contributors to that issue of *K* to the whole movement of theatrical evolution.

Artaud tried to totally redefine theatre. By using the now well-known metaphor of *le Théâtre et la peste,* he claimed that theatre is very much the same as the plague in that both provoke liberating and revealing "frenzies." During the plagues of the Western world, men were rid of their Western character (order, reason, morality) and restored to their true powers. Great theatre not only presents the spectacle of individuals restored to their true powers, but reveals those powers within the spectator. The acts committed on stage, just as those committed by the inhabitants of a plague-ridden city, are both monstrous and gratuitous. True theatre, like the plague, rids life of its "utility" and brings back the pre-logical, non-civilized world that has been suppressed by the Western "conspiracy."

> Like the plague, theatre is the time of evil, the triumph of dark powers that are fed by a power even more profound, until extinction.
>
> . . . and if these powers and possibilities are dark, it is the fault, not of the plague, nor of the theatre, but of life.[3]

2. See bibliography.

3. Antonin Artaud, "le Théâtre et la peste," *le Théâtre et son double.*

Conclusion

Moreover:

> Theatre, like the plague, is a crisis which is resolved by
> death or recovery. And the plague is a superior disease
> because it is a total crisis, after which nothing remains
> but death or an extreme purification. . . .
>
> The action of theatre, like that of the plague, is bene-
> ficial for, pushing men into seeing themselves as they are,
> it causes the mask to fall, reveals the lie, the moral inertia,
> baseness, and hypocrisy of our world.
>
> . . . and in revealing to collectivities their dark power
> and hidden force, it invites them to take, in the face of
> destiny, a heroic and superior attitude they never have had
> without it.[4]

Artaud thus goes back to a definition of what tragedy actually
is—but a definition that is non-rational, stripped of Aristotelian
concepts, and restored to the feeling of magic found in the
works themselves, not in the theorists. For Artaud was concerned with a magical operation and not with the resolution
of "conflicts of a human and passionate nature" through ra-
tional ethics or psychology.

Theatre is a delirium—not far from Rimbaud's *dérèglement*
—which restores man to the inhuman. Artaud, who believed
that he himself was "really not in the world," [5] refused what
is "human," to the extent that such humanity is merely the
artificial creation of Western thought. Before leaving for
Mexico in search of the secrets of the Indian tribes, he wrote
to Barrault: "Stop looking for human characters, Man is what
annoys us the most, and come back to the subterranean gods,
that is, to the enemy forces which become embodied as soon
as we want to grasp them." [6] There is no contradiction between

4. *Ibid.*
5. Antonin Artaud, "Correspondance avec Jacques Rivière," *Oeuvres
complètes,* Vol. I, Gallimard, Paris, 1956.
6. *Lettres d'Antonin Artaud à Jean-Louis Barrault.*

his rejection of man and the idea of a theatre which reveals man to himself, since according to him, man's true destiny lies in that which is beyond him.

Among his concrete examples, Artaud chose, as a play to his taste, John Ford's *'Tis Pity She's a Whore*. And indeed it does express and provoke "the exteriorization of the underlying and latent cruelty by which all the perverse possibilities of the mind are localized in an individual or in a people." [7] The "cruelty" in question here is not seen as a psychological phenomenon but as a method. In the name of that method, Artaud founded his "Théâtre de la cruauté" and wrote his own play *les Cenci,* performed in 1935, based on the tragedy by Shelley and Stendhal's *Chroniques italiennes.* The anecdote, made up of incest, parricide, and execution, was performed at a frantic pace, with moments of pantomime, accompanied by a kind of concrete music, and played in a setting by Balthus. The production was greeted with much reserve on the part of the critics and lasted only fifteen days. As a first experiment in "total theatre," as Barrault understands it today, it seemed hardly to have any future at all. Artaud's draft for another play, *Montezuma ou la conquête du Mexique,* exists only in outline form.

Artaud's actual dramatic works are few: one play, a scenario, several essays, some ideas for stage sets. Yet his concept of theatre seems to have penetrated today and colored a good many works. The powers that break loose and become embodied in Audiberti's plays; Adamov's characters, considered as the playthings of forces; Jean Genêt's fantasies; the attempts in Sartre, Camus, Pichette, Vauthier, and Ionesco to produce theatrical shocks—all indicate a close relationship with Artaud's theories. In a more general way, an atmosphere of the whole helped create a shattering theatre which not only deeply moves the spectator but disturbs his very being. Almost all the great playwrights of today try to prevent the spectator

7. "le Théâtre et la peste," *op. cit.*

from drowsing in a peaceful definition of man. Few of course go as far as Artaud in rejecting Western thought as a whole, but all question the basic values of our world, the conceptions of Good and Evil, the satisfactions of rationalism. Although, except for certain poets, they do not invoke the return to a totally magical and mystical vision of the world, they do use violence, cruelty, derangement, and crime as *methods* for awakening in the spectator a consciousness of his possibilities and for trying to bring out, beyond the falsifications of civilization, what is truly man—man being situated at a level that would traditionally be called inhuman.

In his preface to *les Lettres d'Antonin Artaud à Jean-Louis Barrault*, André Frank mentions, in connection with Artaud's conceptions, *le Partage de midi*, *le Procès* (Kafka/Gide), *l'Etat de siège*, and *Malatesta*—all plays directed by Barrault. Although the instance of *Malatesta*, where the portrait of an individual dominates the symbol, is questionable, all the works show a common use of passion, violence, and horror as a means for shaking the spectator out of his own complacency, and the same presentation of destiny as a battle among forces which transcend the individual. Even far from the hotbed of Artaudian activity represented by Barrault, the same spirit can be found in various forms and with increasing frequency.

In many cases the influence is obvious and direct: in Audiberti, Genêt, Pichette, Adamov, Camus. In others, such as Ghelderode, the general character of certain works just happens to coincide with Artaud's theories. Influences independent of Artaud are of course at work, but they have become part of the same movement: the influence of Aeschylus, the Elizabethans, Büchner, and Strindberg, as much through his intense naturalism as through his dream-like quality. While Artaud is not the only influence, he is the center of an increasingly generalized movement toward creating a theatre intended, more than ever, to shatter the spectator.

In order to reach his objective, Artaud, influenced by the

oriental theatre, suggested the use of a theatrical sign language, in which language itself would play but a secondary part. In that way a real metaphysics would be directly experienced in the symbolism of gestures, postures, lights, bodily rhythms, and sound patterns. Giraudoux reacted strongly against that type of spectacle, assimilating it to a German conception of drama. And actually French theatre has remained a theatre of language. Even in the Barrault-Claudel idea of "total theatre," the Word is on the same level with the Gesture. On the whole, the language of the French stage has remained literary, all the great playwrights are great stylists, and despite its incantatory quality, language has kept to its normal functions.

In fact as André Frank points out in his preface to the correspondence of Artaud and Barrault, "Anouilh, Sartre, Achard, Aymé, and many others have consolidated the position of that Western theatre 'of a human and passionate nature' against which Artaud rose up in revolt." And indeed Artaud's dream was not of a sentimental theatre, a satiric theatre, an intellectual theatre, or an elegantly theatrical theatre, intended to amuse or satisfy "the intellectual's exasperated sensibility." Neither Marcel Achard's Boulevard type sentimentality nor Marcel Aymé's violent, fantastic, or humorous satire questions the definition of man in any disconcerting way. And the role of language and the appeal to Western intelligence found in Anouilh and Sartre remain traditional.[8] Neither Anouilh nor Sartre are mystics; both believe that everything comes from man and men: there are no Mexican gods, no powers in the Tarot cards, no magic spells, only attitudes of consciousness. The return to man, as a dominant tendency of the theatre in the 1940s, is obviously against Artaud's belief in a *real* presence of

8. Audiberti's Joan of Arc is probably closer to Artaud's intentions than Anouilh's, one being the creation of obscure powers within man and outside men, the other considered as free will, an individual negating power.

spiritual or subterranean powers, possessive or destructive.

Artaud's major contribution, then, would seem to lie not so much in form itself, but in a basic intention: a theatre of shock intended, not to awaken the public to current problems, but to use them or go beyond them in revealing man's metaphysical reality, hard as it may be to take. The modern French theatre wants to be metaphysical and such metaphysics can only be brought out through an extreme bewilderment of shocking violence.

When Sartre and Camus use traditional or "Western" forms of thought and structure, their idea is to transcend them in an attempt to emphasize both the topical value of the subject or problem *and* the terrifying metaphysics it implies. Anouilh's plots are resolved in human terms, but the fundamental question transcending the plots is stated. Although any suggested attitude to action (social, political, moral) is meant for the present, the opening onto a metaphysical substructure is never closed and the terror of existing is powerfully brought out.

While continuing the trend of a return to man, Jean Genêt and the trio Adamov (first period)-Ionesco-Beckett are even closer to Artaud. Sartre's anecdotic demonstration is replaced by the shock of direct images and the elimination of "utilitarian" elements. And their characteristic dream-like quality escapes from traditional psychologism as well as surrealism. In fact they would seem to comply with Artaud's statement:

> I propose to renounce that empiricism of images, which the unconscious produces at random and which we throw out also at random, calling them poetic images . . .
> I propose to return, through theatre, to an idea of the physical knowledge of images and the means of inducing trances.[9]

9. Antonin Artaud, "Plus de chef-d'oeuvres," *le Théâtre et son double.*

For their imagery is always more physical than verbal, and although taken from the depths of dream or the subconscious, it is always planned with an eye to a shock effect, or organized into a series of impressions more tangible than intellectual and comparable to the punctures of Chinese medicine, as Artaud had suggested.

The resemblance stops at that level. Yet the shattering violence and shock-images taken "from an inner world," at the same time personal and "an ancestral legacy . . . the universal language," [10] a psychology based on the play of inner and outer forces, and a science of the effects produced by the very rhythms of the general structure and scenic movements make such plays part of a "theatre of cruelty." However they lack the gigantic or epic dimensions, the collective intent, the mysticism and true ritual aspects of Artaud's ideal.

All through the first half of the century, and with an intensity due in great part to Artaud, the French theatre has managed to "cause the masks to fall"—the masks behind which man was hiding the fact that he is a metaphysical and tragic being. Whether man is, from a mystical perspective, always elsewhere, or from a purely existential perspective, always in a state of transcending himself, whether such contradiction or absurdity is expressed in actualized metaphors or in intellectual debates, his situation in the French theatre of today is always that of a being, if not without hope (for there is Claudel's salvation and Sartre's action), at least without illusion. The time of what Artaud called "human conflicts," with the meaning he gave to the adjective, is over in true theatre.

And yet man has been thrown back more and more upon himself. The rebound has ended by provoking a burst of laughter—that of modern farce. It is special laughter which has nothing to do with the detachment of the past. For the climate

10. Eugène Ionesco, *l'Impromptu de l'Alma.*

created by Artaud, as well as by the times themselves, hardly authorizes frivolity.

The new laughter sprang from the consciousness of the old idea that life is a farce. The mask worn on stage is symbolic of another mask. To that cliché, modern theatre has added a terrifying qualification: the farce is acted out for nothing and for no one. Where Claudel's comic characters dance about under the eye of God and act out scenarios which have meaning, Beckett's and Ionesco's are only seen by themselves. Artaud's vision of a dual universe of dark powers and spiritual redemption [11] is replaced by the dizzying emptiness of unjustified existence. Artaud's method drives the spectator out of himself as it should, but toward nothingness. More than a failure of metaphysics, the new trend might be seen rather as a metaphysics of failure. The irony goes to work on itself and Satan dominates: Satan falls because he laughs and laughs because he falls. When we laugh at the farces of today, we are toppling over into the chasms of our own mouths.

> We sail over a vast sphere, always uncertain and floating, pushed from one end toward the other. Whatever point we think we can fasten onto and steady ourselves breaks loose and leaves us; and if we follow it, it eludes our grasp, slips away from us, and flees in eternal flight. Nothing stops for us. It is our natural state, and yet most contrary to our inclination; we burn with the desire of finding a firm foundation and a last and unchanging base to build a tower reaching to Infinity; but our whole foundation cracks, and the earth opens up to unfathomable depths.[12]

So Pascal tried to evoke reason's failure to explain man's situation in the universe. Today, after the bankruptcy of all great ideologies, including rationalism, the anxiety of an "earth

11. Although after his conversion in Ireland in 1937, he denied ever having been Manichaeist.

12. Pascal, *Pensées,* Ed. Brunschvicg, Section II, Frag. 72.

open(ing) up to unfathomable depths" is at the central point of modern consciousness. The multiplicity of theatrical worlds proposed by various thinkers and writers make up a group of poetic hypotheses. The idea of an "answer" is replaced by the dual idea of lucidity and creative power. We are perhaps now ready for the great Tragedy Camus dreamed of. One can hope that today's "dark" theatre, having furnished perfect metaphors of the metaphysical abyss and modern tragic terror, will go on to complete the tragedy by adding the necessary dimension, not of happiness and facile solutions, but of that higher exaltation Yeats called "tragic joy."

APPENDICES

I. DIRECTORS AND PRODUCTIONS

II. FIRST PERFORMANCES AND IMPORTANT REVIVALS

APPENDIX I

DIRECTORS AND PRODUCTIONS

1. *Before Jacques Copeau*

The theories of André Antoine were influenced by a general climate of naturalism and the discovery, in 1884, of foreign stagings (Henry Irving, the Meiningen Players). Antoine did not invent scenic realism; he pushed it to an extreme. As early as Romantic theatre, emphasis was put on a search for exactitude in painted décor, combined with the use of real props. But even when the décor was scrupulously detailed, it was used for every play of the same period, and the attempt at illusion was paradoxical in the juxtaposition of painted canvas and the real volume of objects. In his Théâtre Libre, founded in 1887, Antoine's first objective was to do away with the paradox and establish a consistency in the décor by placing the real objects within a real construction. His second objective was to create a unity between the décor and the play's content—in other words, its psycho-sociological implications. Décor "is the milieu which from now on varies with the movement." But most important of all, he revolutionized acting. He replaced the stylized declamation and conventional posture with a direct copy of man's speech and behavior.

Acting, décor, lighting effects, and text were all subordinated to the whole, which is life as we perceive it. Only at that price would theatre correspond to Stendhal's wish and Ibsen's formula: a removal of the fourth wall. And only at that price would a play stop being a pretext for the recitations of well-known actors and become a living work, whatever its limitations.

237

The dangers of scenic verism have often been pointed out: the audience is transformed into a group of Peeping Toms, the general interest is in surface effects, the suggestion of what cannot be perceived is either eliminated or reduced to a minimum. Antoine brought Ibsen to the French but saw and emphasized only the naturalistic dimension of his plays.

After his Théâtre Libre closed, Antoine developed his theories. He never betrayed the principles of scenic verism, of a unity of the whole; but he went from an overloaded realism to a simplified realism and, in décor, with his productions at the Odéon, to a reinvention of the real rather than an imitation of it. In his productions of Shakespeare, he tried to solve the problem of quick changes of décor by use of curtains and mobile sets.

On the whole, the French naturalist experiment had a lasting influence on the basic principles of theatrical production, but it was immediately transcended—both because of an absence of great naturalist playwrights and because of the violent symbolist reaction.

ANDRÉ ANTOINE (*1858–1943*): Outstanding Productions

At the Théâtre Libre:
Tolstoy's *The Power of Darkness* (1888)
Ibsen's *Ghosts* (1890)
Ibsen's *The Wild Duck* (1891)
Courteline's *Boubouroche* (1893)
Strindberg's *Miss Julie* (1893)
Gerhart Hauptmann's *The Weavers* (1893)
At the Théâtre Antoine:
Jules Renard's *Poil de Carotte* (1900)
Shakespeare's *King Lear* (1904)
At the Odéon:
Shakespeare's *Julius Caesar* (1907)
Molière's *Tartuffe* (1908)
Shakespeare's *Coriolanus* (1910)
Shakespeare's *Romeo and Juliet* (1911)

The history of theatre reproduced the general intellectual conflict of those years: positivism, psychologism, a deterministic, naturalistic vision of man and his universe in opposition to a certain Protean idealism, partially inspired by German idealism, but particularly indicative of the impatience of minds faced with the limitations of positivism as a vision of the world. In France the reaction was successfully expressed in the realm of literature and the arts by a form of Wagnerism and by symbolism. Barely three years after the foundation of the Théâtre Libre, an anti-naturalistic theatre appeared: in 1891, after the experiments of the Théâtre Mixte and the Théâtre Idéaliste, Paul Fort, aged seventeen, founded the Théâtre d'Art. It was inspired by Verlaine, Mallarmé, and Maurice Denis, just as the Théâtre Libre had been by Emile Zola and Paul Alexis. Stage sets became "ornamental fictions." The unity and consistency of the spectacle, imposed by Antoine, was kept, but in the sense of a suggestion, an opening onto "poetic truth," which was in fact never really defined. Symbolist poems were produced, as well as Marlowe's *Doctor Faustus*, Shelley's *The Cenci*, Maeterlinck's *l'Intruse*. The Théâtre d'Art was more literary and decorative than theatrical. Taken over by Lugné-Poe in 1893, it became the Théâtre de l'Œuvre, and continued the same type of productions but with greater scope.

A member of Antoine's company, but also a friend of young painters and poets, Lugné-Poe tried to formulate a theatrical program of anti-naturalism. But it remained vague: a theatre of ideas, with everything subordinated to the idea. With Lugné-Poe, who began during the period of Antoine's overloaded realism, décor became simplified and the painted backdrop took back its rights, not to create an illusion of the perceived real but to eliminate it and rather to suggest a hidden idea or bring out the "soul" of a place. Some of his innovations have been picked up by today's theatre: the elimination of footlights, a sloped stage, actors performing behind a transparent curtain, extras playing the parts of doors, etc. He also replaced realistic

239

acting by a kind of chanted diction which was to be suggestive of the "inhuman" sources of language.

Lugné-Poe opened the door to anti-realism which from then on dominated the French stage. He was the first to present Jarry, Claudel, Crommelynck, and Salacrou to the French public. He made possible the victory of painters—Maurice Denis, Pierre Bonnard, Odilon Redon, Edouard Vuillard —over set designers, that is, the victory of plastic imagination in direct relation to the text over the indifferent routine of specialists.

Yet Lugné-Poe's attitude was not rigid. He often went back to more realistic devices. Ibsen's theatre was a case in point. Antoine saw it as pure naturalism, whereas Lugné-Poe began by seeing it only in terms of symbol and produced *An Enemy of the People* in the same way as he had produced *Pelléas et Mélisande*. A visit of the Danish director, Bang, followed by a meeting with Ibsen himself, convinced him that less fantastic techniques and acting were in order. After having been the champion of symbolism in the theatre, Lugné-Poe remained audacious and original, but very eclectic.

AURÉLIEN LUGNÉ-POE (*1869–1940*): Outstanding Productions

Maeterlinck's *Pelléas et Mélisande* (1893)
Ibsen's *Rosmersholm* and *An Enemy of the People* (1893)
Ibsen's *The Master Builder* (1894)
Oscar Wilde's *Salome* (1896)
Ibsen's *Peer Gynt* (1896)
Jarry's *Ubu Roi* (1896)
Shakespeare's *Measure for Measure* (1898)
Gide's *le Roi Candaule* (1901)
d'Annunzio's *The Daughter of Jorio* (1905)
Gorky's *The Lower Depths* (1905)
Claudel's *l'Annonce faite à Marie* (1912)
Shakespeare's *Hamlet* (1913)

Claudel's *l'Otage* (1914)
Crommelynck's *le Cocu magnifique* (1921)
Jean Sarment's *le Pêcheur d'ombres* (1922)
Salacrou's *Tour à terre* (1925)
Stève Passeur's *l'Acheteuse* (1930)
Anouilh's *l'Hermine* (1932)
Salacrou's *l'Inconnue d'Arras* (1935)

2. Foreign Influences

During the 1880s and '90s, the scenic reform was not restricted to France. In Germany, Russia, and England directors, writers, and theorists were raising their voices, founding theatres, and publishing manifestoes—first in order to fight against outdated traditions and commercialization, and then either to carry on the realist·experiment or to create a new poetry of the theatre. Several important events might be mentioned: the reform of the *mise en scène* of historical dramas by the Meiningen Players and their stage manager, Ludwig Chronegk; the reform of acting by Henry Irving (whom Antoine saw in London in 1888); George Bernard Shaw's articles in *The Saturday Review* in favor of Ibsenian realism (1895–1898); the first essays of Adolphe Appia (*Die Musik und die Inszenierung*, Munich, 1899); the founding of the Moscow Art Theatre by Stanislavsky and Dantchenko in 1898; the beginning of Gordon Craig as director for the Purcell Society in 1899; the beginning of the Irish Dramatic Company and Max Reinhardt's Kleines Theatre in Munich in 1902. The first years of the twentieth century are essentially marked by the rise of Stanislavsky and the development of Adolphe Appia's and Gordon Craig's theories.

The importance of Stanislavsky's contribution lies in the breadth and flexibility of his conception of realism. Forsaking surface realism, he used Chekhov's plays to bring out, by scenic means but mostly through acting, the "underlying text" of a play. His symbolist experiments (Maeterlinck's *l'Oiseau bleu*) made it possible for him to complete his "inner realism" by a rediscovery of theatricality. Stanislavsky transcended the conflict between realism and anti-realism. He created a totally human theatre, keeping the naturalistic surface but making it more and more transparent.

For Gordon Craig (*The Art of Theatre*, 1905), if theatre was to be an art, it had to be absolutely controlled by esthetic intelligence. Everything accidental and unexpected had to be eliminated. The actor was to be replaced by a "super-marionette," whose acting had to correspond absolutely to the most precise orders of the "author." Décor was to be an intellectual construction, in which lines, colors, and lighting effects contribute, with uncompromising precision, not to a representation but to a revelation. Where Stanislavsky stressed the actor, Craig stressed the design of the production. Theatre became a movement in itself, independent of the other arts, one whose true "author" is the director.

At the same time in Switzerland, Adolphe Appia developed closely related theories, starting with a reform of the Wagnerian *mise en scène*. His objective was to "express a thought plastically," in space and in time. Although acting remained the vital element, it was only effective when rigorously subordinated to a rhythm of the whole, based on the text (spoken or musical). His most important idea was the conception of a three-dimensional architectural décor, set up in free space.

A fourth influence, bearing primarily on décor, was that of Diaghilev's Ballets Russes, first produced in Paris in 1909: a triumph of color. Then, gradually, they developed in the direction of constructivist techniques, with emphasis on the depth of space and vertical planes made visible by a succession of structures on several levels. And just as the Théâtre de l'Œuvre used certain Impressionist painters, the Ballets Russes worked with the Fauves and the Cubists: Picasso, Matisse, Braque. Although their décors were reproached with crushing the ballet itself, they did show the possibilities of color and construction.

The major foreign discoveries were assimilated by Jacques Rouché in his book *l'Art théâtral moderne*, published in 1910. Short but clear and synthetic, the book was equivalent to a manifesto—the first really coherent and revolutionary work on the subject published in France.

3. *Jacques Copeau*

In 1913 a second manifesto was published and served as a basis for almost all of French theatre today: Jacques Copeau's article, "Un Essai de rénovation dramatique: le Théâtre du Vieux Colombier" in the September issue of the *Nouvelle Revue Française.*

The intransigent critic of *l'Ermitage,* then of *la Grande Revue,* Copeau kept a careful watch on Parisian theatre, judged it severely, and demolished Hervieu, Bernstein, Bataille, Rostand, and the commercial spirit, which had remained a sore spot. In 1911 he gave Jacques Rouché, for the Théâtre des Arts, an adaptation of *The Brothers Karamazov* and it was performed in the spirit of an "imaginary Russia."

From 1909 to 1913, he was literary director of the *NRF,* which he had founded with André Gide and Jean Schlumberger. In 1913 he founded the Théâtre du Vieux Colombier. Although he recognized and praised the foreign anti-realist experiments, he was on his guard against pedantry and any "extravagant systematization." A suggestive art can become vulgar and naïve through a too obvious use of material symbols. Overemphasizing them means sidestepping theatre:

Being in favor of such or such decorative formula always means being interested in theatre by way of its side-issues. Being enthusiastic about the inventions of engineers or electricians always means giving usurped importance to

> canvas, painted cardboard, lighting arrangements, always
> means falling somehow or another into tricks. Old or new,
> we repudiate them all. Good or bad, rudimentary or per-
> fected, artificial or realistic, we intend to deny the im-
> portance of all machinery. (*NRF,* Sept. 1913)

Copeau refused to believe that "the future of our theatre is
bound to a question of machinery." What he wanted was in
some way, a return to the very essence of the stage:

> The tyranny of the stage and its gross artificiality will act
> on us like a discipline in forcing us to concentrate all of
> truth in the feelings and actions of our characters. May
> the other marvels vanish and, for the new works, leave
> us with a bare stage. (*Ibid.*)

His principle of absolute simplicity, after the experiments of
preceding reformers, was justified both by the continued existence of commercialism ("the monopolizing of most theatres
by a handful of entertainers in the pay of shameless merchants")
and by the confusion that reigned among the different schools,
misleading the public and often resulting in no more than
surface effects.

To reform theatre, Copeau wanted to reinvent it, starting
from the most elementary principles. He had his "bare stage"
correspond to what might be called "bare actors." As early as
1913, he tried to strip down his actors and discipline them by
what he called "exorcisms":

> If I have the patience and the strength, in two or three
> years these actors will have almost become men.
>
> (Letter to André Suarez, July 14, 1913, quoted by
> Georges Lerminier; see bibliography.)

Copeau knew about the attempts of Stanislavsky, Appia, and
Craig. On many questions, his work was parallel to theirs, at
least in spirit. Like Stanislavsky, he stressed the actor and an

inner realism, leading quite naturally to a transposition. Like Appia, he wanted a stripped and functional décor:

> [Appia] sacrificed attractiveness to rigor, virtuosity to an inner law. [He replaced *trompe l'oeil* décor] by a three dimensional architectual décor, purely practicable, in other words, purely dramatic or dynamic. The major reforms of the contemporary stage stemmed from there.
>
> (*Encyclopédie Française,* Tome XVII, 1936.)

And from there, in great part, also stemmed "le dispositif fixe" or permanent set—a concrete architectural whole, with several levels, a projecting apron, and an arch at the back, framed by two stairways, all very Elizabethan in feeling, invented by Jacques Copeau and Louis Jouvet and built in the Vieux Colombier in 1920, after having been tried out in the Garrick Theatre in New York. From Gordon Craig, Copeau took the idea of an independent theatre, completely devoted to its own unity and its power of suggestion in space and in time. All his life Copeau was suspicious of theorists' "systems," but he acknowledged his agreement on basic principles with Appia and Craig, whom he met in 1916, as well as with Stanislavsky, whom he entertained in Paris in 1922.

From the very beginning, Copeau's art was marked by the greatest simplicity. His bare stage remained almost bare, and when the "dispositif" was built, he used it for all plays and it was almost sufficient unto itself. Of course the lighting was skillful, the costumes and decorative elements were calculated with care, and the taste for spectacle of his stage manager, Louis Jouvet, sometimes dressed up the bareness. But the text always came first. All the theatre arts were subordinated to it with a maximum of discipline and a minimum of means. Copeau wanted to bring out all the direct reality and poetry contained in the text without misrepresenting or stifling it. All the interest was to be in the play, rather than that the play be used merely as a pretext for exhibitionists. Critics occasionally reproached Copeau for his too great austerity, but they always acknowledged the value of his work.

For Copeau was more than just another theorist or just another audacious director. He represented a philosophical position in France which involved not only the dramatic arts, but all of man. He was close to Charles Péguy (whom he knew well) in his refusal of a world in which the relation of man to what he makes was becoming more and more abstract. He felt that mass production and gaudy luxury should be replaced by craftsmanship, with man giving himself completely to the one object he makes with his own hands, starting from zero. Similar to Péguy also was the mystical atmosphere surrounding his work. Jacques Copeau was the first in France to conceive of the director-actor as a priest, a conception currently embodied by Jean-Louis Barrault.

That conviction required a total reeducation of both the public and men of the theatre. And it was on the theatrical world in particular that Copeau left his mark. He was the leader of a whole generation of directors and actors. In 1913 Copeau took his entire company to La Ferté-sous-Jouarre:

> There, every day, for five hours, they studied the plays of the repertory. In addition, two hours were devoted to reading aloud out of doors, as an exercise in intellectual flexibility and vocal articulation, also to analyses of texts and to physical exercises. ("L'Ecole du Vieux Colombier," *NRF*, Nov. 1921)

In 1921 he founded the Ecole du Vieux Colombier, where he trained actors to be as good singers as reciters, as good dancers as improvisers. A sculptor taught them to make masks, the Fratellini clowns taught them mime and acrobatics. In 1924 Copeau retired to Burgundy, disgusted by the compromises he was forced to make in Paris. His students followed him. There were gymnastics, acrobatics, and exercises in mime every morning; sewing, modelling, painting, then improvisation and rehearsals every afternoon. The objective: "The renewal of theatre . . . which seems to me essentially to be a renewal of man in the theatre." Gymnastics were meant to create "an obedient body"; dance and mime, "the idea of inner rhythm." At first the instruction was the same for all, then specialized. So that poet, dancer, mime, and actor all emerged "from the same tree," "not artificially regrouped and polished, but inspired from within, organically united." And actually Copeau finally replaced the idea of the *vedette* or star, plus just any group of actors casually brought together, by an "organic" conception of the theatrical company. In 1929 Copeau closed his school but it continued on its own as "La Compagnie des Quinze."

Since the 1930s the French stage has been dominated by men who were more or less trained by Copeau, as collaborators or students: Charles Dullin, Louis Jouvet, Jean Dasté, Michel Saint Denis, Jean Vilar, the mime Decroux, the actress Valentine Tessier, and, indirectly, André Barsacq and Jean-Louis Barrault. In the United States the post-war little theatres and the Theatre Guild owed much to Copeau's stay in New York from 1917 to 1919; in Belgium the Théâtre du Marais was based on the spirit of the Vieux Colombier and trained the director Raymond Rouleau; in Italy, where Copeau worked for the 1933 and 1935 Maggio Fiorentino, the Piccolo Theatro di Milano was founded in 1947 according to his principles.

Copeau's own career was difficult. The Vieux Colombier grew in reputation from 1913 to 1914 but was closed by the war. During the seasons of 1917–18 and 1918–19 in New York, Copeau was overwhelmed with work and often humiliated, having been forced into rush jobs and made to produce plays he despised. Despite the Vieux Colombier's success from 1920 to 1924, Dullin and Jouvet left him and financial difficulties piled up. Disgust, illness, and religious fervor led to his retirement in 1924. From then on, besides his teaching, lecturing, and some directing in Paris and outside France, he spent his time meditating on the theatre and on his past. He dreamed of a great outdoor theatre and admitted that the Vieux Colombier experiment was necessarily limited to the "little theatre." From 1936 to 1940 he had the opportunity of directing a few productions at the Comédie Française. He died in 1949.

Copeau never succeeded in creating the great modern poets he dreamed about. With a few exceptions, he was forced to draw either from naturalistic (Renard, Becque) or poetic (François Porché) works whose scope fell short of his ambitions. Nor did he manage to create an ideal public. The Vieux Colombier, in its day, was an avant-garde theatre, reserved for an elite. So that his students and successors were the ones who finally made greater contact with the public.

They invented their own styles, were influenced by others, and even repudiated certain of his principles. But Copeau's experiment was situated beyond styles and schools and therefore more far-reaching. It gave the French stage its spirit, in other words, a *mystique* and an ethics.

JACQUES COPEAU (*1878–1949*): Outstanding Productions

At the Vieux Colombier:
Heywood's *A Woman Killed with Kindness* (1913)
Molière's *l'Amour médecin* and *l'Avare* (1913)
Claudel's *l'Echange* (1914)
Roger Martin du Gard's *le Testament du Père Leleu* (1914)
Dostoyevsky's *The Brothers Karamazov* (1914)
Shakespeare's *Twelfth Night* (1914)
At the Garrick Theatre in New York (out of more than forty plays in two seasons):
Molière's *les Fourberies de Scapin* (1917)
Mérimée's *le Carrosse du Saint Sacrement* (1917)
Corneille's *le Menteur* (1919)
Maeterlinck's *Pelléas et Mélisande* (1919)
Molière's *le Misanthrope* (1919)
At the Vieux Colombier:
Shakespeare's *Winter's Tale* (1920)

Vildrac's *le Paquebot Tenacity* (1920)
Mérimée's *le Carrosse du Saint Sacrement* (1920)
Molière's *les Fourberies de Scapin* (1920)
Jules Romains' *Cromedeyre-le-Vieil* (1920)
Jean Schlumberger's *la Mort de Sparte* (1921)
Musset's *Un Caprice* (1921)
Beaumarchais' *le Mariage de Figaro* (1921)
Molière's *le Misanthrope* (1922)
Gide's *Saül* (1922)
Goldoni's *la Locandiera* (1923)

At the Comédie Française:
Molière's *le Misanthrope* (1936)
Racine's *Bajazet* (1937)
Mauriac's *Asmodée* (1937)
Corneille's *le Cid* (1940)
Shakespeare's *Twelfth Night* (1940)

4. *Copeau's Contemporaries and Successors. The Cartel*

At the same time that Copeau was working in austerity and for an elite, one of Antoine's collaborators, Firmin Gémier, launched the great spectacle of the masses, for the masses.

Gémier, whose career was somewhat confused and ambitious, went from the Théâtre Libre to Lugné-Poe's production of *Ubu Roi,* from melodrama to *vaudeville,* from the play of ideas to *Grand-Guignol.* But his major contribution lay in his attempt to set up a people's theatre, and one appropriate for performing national epics. As against those who particularly tried to manipulate souls, Gémier tried to manipulate crowds. Outdoor theatres, theatres in tents, theatres in amphitheatres —any great space was to his taste. After 1916 he eliminated footlights and had extras performing in with the audience, all in a frenzy of great collective movements. Gémier's experiments, picked up more coherently today, have given rise to both the dramatic decentralization in France and the basic principle of the Théâtre National Populaire, such as we know it.

Another name stands out in the years following the war: Georges Pitoëff. Trained in Russia at the time of Stanislavsky, director of plays by Molière, Musset, and Becque, which he performed all the way to Siberia, Pitoëff settled in Geneva in 1915, came to Paris for the first time with Lenormand's *le Temps est un songe,* and settled there permanently in 1922. He produced Pirandello, Shaw, O'Neill, Molnar, Chekhov, Lenormand, Cocteau, Anouilh on various stages and with often very reduced means. His contemporaries were especially struck by his acting, despite a rather frail physique, even more by that of his wife Ludmilla, a combination of infallible skill and inspired amateurism, and by the ingenuity of his *mises en scène.* He designed his sets himself with a particular bias for modernism: three-dimensional structures on several levels, tinged with expressionism or cubism, with special emphasis on color and the succession of planes in depth. His objective was to reach a strange and inner poetry that would touch the modern soul, and he tried to bring out "a reflection of our thinking" and "the stirring questions of our times." The coherence of the spectacle and its power was to stem from the rhythmic construction of the whole, a harmony in the rhythm of text, movement, and décor.

What Pitoëff brought to French theatre more than any other theorist was a consciousness of the fact that theatre is part of an evolution similar to that of the other arts. Form, content, and spirit had to be contemporary. He therefore produced Pirandello, who posed the problem of truth in modern terms, and Lenormand, who posed that of the subconscious. Yet like Copeau at the end of his career, he was disappointed by writers and admitted that he had not found "the writer who could express the modern soul."

GEORGES PITOËFF (*1887-1939*): Outstanding Productions

In Geneva:
Tolstoy's *The Power of Darkness* (1917)
Claudel's *l'Echange* (1917)
  In Geneva, then in Paris:
Lenormand's *le Temps est un songe* (1919)
Lenormand's *les Ratés* (1920)
  In Paris:
Lenormand's *Mangeur de rêves* (1922)
Chekhov's *The Sea Gull* (1922)
Pirandello's *Six Characters in Search of an Author* (1923)
Ramuz and Stravinsky's *Histoire du soldat* (1924)
Pirandello's *Henry IV* (1925)
Shaw's *Saint Joan* (1925)
Cocteau's *Orphée* (1926)
Chekhov's *Three Sisters* (1929)
Gide's *Oedipe* (1932)
Schnitzler's *la Ronde* (1932)
Ibsen's *The Wild Duck* (1934)
Pirandello's *Tonight We Improvise* (1935)
Anouilh's *le Voyageur sans bagage* (1937)
Shakespeare's *Romeo and Juliet* (1937)
Claudel's *l'Echange* (1937)
Anouilh's *la Sauvage* (1938)

In 1927 Pitoëff, an independent, founded the "Cartel des Quatre" along with Louis Jouvet and Charles Dullin, Copeau's prodigal sons, and Gaston Baty, one of Firmin Gémier's disciples. Despite their differences, although all anti-naturalists, the members of the Cartel set up an organization for the defense of theatre and for mutual aid, on a financial level and an ethical level: defense against newspaper boycotts, such as the boycott of Dullin in 1929, and against commercial pressures. The four directors were the unquestionable leaders of the French stage in the 1930's.

Charles Dullin, a friend of Antonin Artaud, left the Vieux Colombier in 1919. He founded his first "Atelier" in 1921, and

Appendix I

with Copeau's help, opened a second in 1922, where he remained until World War II. A great actor in spite of his rather puny appearance and weak voice, Dullin emphasized the sincerity of a theatrical vocation and scrupulously careful work on diction, vocal expression, and breathing. His construction of a character from the inside, the deep honesty of his work, his rejection of naturalism, and his conviction that the play comes first and that without a great text, all scenic inventions are merely "music-hall" techniques, were a continuation of the Copeau tradition. With all that in mind, he felt that the mission of actor and director was to clarify the text itself and bring out its essence.

CHARLES DULLIN (*1885–1949*): Outstanding Productions

At the Atelier:

Calderón's *Such Stuff as Dreams are Made of* (1922)
Pirandello's *The Pleasure of Honesty* (1922)
Cocteau's adaptation of Sophocles' *Antigone* (1922)
Achard's *Voulez-vous jouer avec moâ?* (1923)
Achard's *le Joueur d'échecs* (1927)
Aristophanes' *Birds* (1927)
Ben Jonson's *Volpone* (1928)
Salacrou's *Patchouli* (1930)
Salacrou's *Atlas Hôtel* (1931)
Aristophanes' *Peace* (1933)
Shakespeare's *Richard III* (1933)
Calderón's *Physician of His Own Honor* (1935)
Balzac's *le Faiseur* (1936)
Salacrou's *la Terre est ronde* (1938)
   At the Comédie Française: Pirandello's *Right You Are If You Think You Are* (1937)
   At the Théâtre de Paris: Molière's *l'Avare* (1941)
   At the Théâtre de la Cité-Sarah Bernhardt:
Sartre's *les Mouches* (1943)
Corneille's *Cinna* (1946)

Louis Jouvet, stage manager and actor at the Vieux Colombier, left Copeau in 1922 to act as director at the Comédie des

Champs Elysées and then changed to the Théâtre de l'Athénée in 1934. Jouvet's success with a much greater public than his friends of the Cartel was due largely to a less revolutionary attitude. His demands for acting were much the same as Copeau's, but the ground had already been broken by his predecessors and to their discoveries he added a spectacular theatricalism in good taste. The elegance of his great sets in perspective and Christian Bérard's fantasy was hardly avant-garde, and machines filled up the "bare stage." Still, his elegant theatricalism was perfectly suited to Cocteau's *la Machine infernale* and Giraudoux's plays. Jouvet may have been less revolutionary than others, but he was the symbol of the victory of modern theatre, now at ease in the midst of its discoveries.

LOUIS JOUVET (*1887–1951*): Outstanding Productions

At the Comédie des Champs Elysées:

Jules Romains' *Monsieur Le Trouhadec saisi par la débauche* and *Knock* (1923)

Crommelynck's *Tripes* d'or (1925)

Vildrac's *Madame Béliard* (1925)

Gogol's *The Inspector General* (1927)

Giraudoux's *Siegfried* (1928)

Achard's *Jean de la lune* (1929)

Giraudoux's *Amphitryon 38* (1929)

At the Théâtre Pigalle:

Giraudoux's *Judith* (1930)

Romains' *Donogoo* (1930)

At the Comédie des Champs Elysées:

Giraudoux's *Intermezzo* (1933)

Cocteau's *la Machine infernale* (1934)

At the Athénée:

Giraudoux's *Tessa* (1934)

Giraudoux's *la Guerre de Troie n'aura pas lieu* and *Supplément au Voyage de Cook* (1935)

Molière's *l'Ecole des femmes* (1936)

Giraudoux's *Electre* and *l'Impromptu de Paris* (1937)

Achard's *le Corsaire* (1938)

Giraudoux's *Ondine* (1939)

At the Comédie Française:

Corneille's *l'Illusion comique* (1936)

Giraudoux's *Cantique des cantiques* (1937)

At the Athénée:

Giraudoux's *la Folle de Chaillot* (1945)

Claudel's *l'Annonce faite à Marie* (1946)

Giraudoux's *l'Apollon de Bellac* (1947)

Genêt's *les Bonnes* (1947)

Molière's *Don Juan* (1947)

Molière's *Tartuffe* (1950)

At the Théâtre Marigny: Molière's *les Fourberies de Scapin* (1949)

At the Théâtre Antoine: Sartre's *le Diable et le Bon Dieu* (1951)

Gaston Baty was given a theatre by Gémier in 1920, founded a group called "La Chimère" in 1921, and finally took over the Théâtre Montparnasse in 1930. Right from the beginning, and with Gémier's help, he opposed Copeau. Although he denied having contempt for the text of a play, Baty nevertheless made statements against what he considered useless chatter and never hesitated to cut or rewrite texts in order to subject them to his *mise en scène*. Strongly influenced by German theorists and set designers, his productions always came before the acting itself. Décor, machinery, lighting were in the foreground, for he considered the play essentially as a poetic atmosphere to be imposed by material means. At the end of his career, Baty foresook real actors and devoted himself mainly to marionettes.

GASTON BATY (*1885–1952*): Outstanding Productions

Lenormand's *le Simoun* (1920)

Claudel's *l'Annonce faite à Marie* (1921)

Pellerin's *Intimité* (1922)

Jean-Jacques Bernard's *Martine* (1922)

Eugene O'Neill's *Emperor Jones* (1923)

Gantillon's *Maya* (1924)

Strindberg's *Miss Julie* (1925)
Pellerin's *Têtes de rechange* (1926)
Elmer Rice's *The Adding Machine* (1927)
Shalom Anski's *The Dybbuk* (1927)
Pellerin's *Cri des coeurs* (1928)
Molière's *le Malade imaginaire* (1929)
    At the Théâtre Montparnasse:
Brecht's *Three-Penny Opera* (1930)
Pellerin's *Terrain vague* (1931)
Baty's adaptation of Dostoyevsky's *Crime and Punishment* (1933)
Musset's *les Caprices de Marianne* (1935)
Baty's adaptation of Flaubert's *Madame Bovary* (1936)
Racine's *Phèdre* (1940)
Shakespeare's *Macbeth* (1942)
    At the Comédie Française:
Labiche's *Un Chapeau de paille d'Italie* (1938)
Musset's *le Chandelier* (1937)
Racine's *Bérénice* (1946)
Salacrou's *l'Inconnue d'Arras* (1949)

Copeau, Jouvet, Baty, and Dullin were officially consecrated in 1936, when the administrator of the Comédie Française, Edouard Bourdet, called upon them to stage both the classical and modern plays in the repertory. In 1940 Copeau himself became administrator.

5. *After the Cartel*

Pitoëff died in 1939, Lugné-Poe in 1940, Copeau and Dullin in 1949, Jouvet in 1951, Baty in 1952. But new directors, always more or less connected with Copeau, have ensured their succession. The most eminent among them today are Jean-Louis Barrault and Jean Vilar.

An extra in Pitoëff's company, then one of Dullin's students

(1931) and an actor in his company, Barrault rapidly reflected all the most active influences: that of Dullin and Copeau, Gordon Craig, and most particularly the mime Decroux and Antonin Artaud. His first independent production was *Autour d'une Mère,* a pantomime of William Faulkner's *As I Lay Dying.* Then through a synthesis of theatrical symbols, in which bodily expression played a primary role, Barrault tried to recreate the fundamental Drama by means of plays like Cervantes' *Numance* and Knut Hamsum's *la Faim.* During Barrault's career, including his years with the Comédie Française, his direction of the Théâtre Marigny from 1946 to 1956, and of the Théâtre de France since 1959, his style has changed with his subject matter: epico-lyrical symbolism for Claudel's works, expressionism for Gide's adaptation of Kafka's *The Trial,* sophisticated pantomime for Marivaux's comedies, etc. Such surface eclecticism often irritated the critics. But beyond the diversity of styles there is a common basis and objective. Barrault's major contribution, an extension of the theories of Artaud and Claudel, has been an attempt to establish a vocabulary and grammar of theatrical symbols, based on the actor's vocal intonation and rhythms, and on the gestures and relative positions of the body—in some ways a Western equivalent of oriental theatre. He thus tries to express the very mystery of Life, beyond the psychologism to which too many actors are still attached. A carefully calculated symbolic performance and the technical means offered by the modern stage combine to make up "total theatre."

JEAN-LOUIS BARRAULT (*1910–*): Outstanding Productions

At the Comédie Française:
Racine's *Phèdre* (1942)
Claudel's *le Soulier de satin* (1943)
Shakespeare's *Antony and Cleopatra* (1945)
At the Théâtre Marigny:
Shakespeare's *Hamlet* (1946)
Marivaux's *les Fausses Confidences* (1946)

Prévert's *Baptiste* (1946)
Salacrou's *les Nuits de la colère* (1946)
Gide's adaptation of Kafka's *The Trial* (1947)
Molière's *Amphitryon* (1947)
Feydeau's *Occupe-toi d'Amélie* (1948)
Camus' *l'Etat de siège* (1948)
Claudel's *Partage de midi* (1948)
Anouilh's *la Répétition* (1950)
Montherlant's *Malatesta* (1950)
Claudel's *l'Echange* (1951)
Cocteau's *Bacchus* (1951)
Claudel's *Christophe Colomb* (1953)
Giraudoux's *Pour Lucrèce* (1953)
Molière's *le Misanthrope* (1954)
Chekhov's *The Cherry Orchard* (1954)
Racine's *Bérénice* (1955)
Giraudoux's *Intermezzo* (1955)
Aeschylus' *Oresteia* (1955)
   At the Petit Théâtre Marigny:
Schehadé's *la Soirée des proverbes* (1954)
Lope de Vega's *The Gardener's Dog* (1955)
Jean Vauthier's *le Personnage combattant* (1956)
   At the Théâtre Sarah Bernhardt: Schehadé's *Histoire de Vasco* (1957)
   At the Théâtre du Palais Royal:
Meilhac and Halévy's *la Vie parisienne* (1958)
   At the Théâtre de France:
Claudel's *Tête d'or* (1959)
Anouilh's *la Petite Molière* (1959)
Ionesco's *Rhinocéros* (1960)

Also a disciple of Dullin, Jean Vilar's beginnings were less dazzling than Barrault's. A member of an itinerant company ("La Roulotte"), between 1940 and 1942, then the director of two Strindberg plays in small Paris theatres, Jean Vilar had his first great success in 1945 with Eliot's *Murder in the Cathedral* at the Vieux Colombier and was definitively established in 1947 with the Avignon Festival. As his first experiment with an outdoor theatre, it led him to a type of theatre freed from the Italianate stage, set up in great open spaces, and presented to vast audiences. Rather than the outer spectacle, Vilar stressed the character—magnified or masked according to the needs of the space in which the play was performed. He considered the actor as a creator, hence the severity of the training and discipline he thought necessary. However once the actor is really in a part, he is free to improvise or at least vary his interpretation. Out on the large stage, his mission is to provoke the most intimate contact possible between the character and the thousands of spectators. Vilar, director of the Théâtre National Populaire since 1950, sees theatre as a collective ceremony. What Copeau had achieved for an elite, he attempted "for all," with often similar principles and simplicity. And, like Copeau, he is disappointed, but his reasons are of a political and social nature. For Vilar claims that great theatre is unattainable because of the present state of society.

JEAN VILAR (*1912–*) : Outstanding Productions

Strindberg's *The Dance of Death* (1943)
T. S. Eliot's *Murder in the Cathedral* (1945)
In Avignon and at the TNP:
Shakespeare's *Richard II* (1947)
Büchner's *Danton's Death* (1948)
Corneille's *le Cid* (1949)
Montherlant's *Pasiphaé* (1949)
Gide's *Oedipe* (1949)
Shakespeare's *Henry IV* (1950)
Kleist's *The Prince of Homburg* (1951)
Brecht's *Mother Courage* (1951)
Molière's *l'Avare* (1952)
Molière's *Dom Juan* (1953)
Shakespeare's *Macbeth* (1954)

Corneille's *Cinna* (1954)
Hugo's *Ruy Blas* (1954)
Hugo's *Marie Tudor* (1955)
Pirandello's *Henry IV* (1957)
Racine's *Phèdre* (1958)
Jarry's *Ubu Roi* (1958)
Musset's *les Caprices de Marianne* (1958)
Shakespeare's *A Midsummer-Night's Dream* (1959)
   In collaboration, with Gérard Philipe:
Musset's *Lorenzaccio* (1952)
Pichette's *Nucléa* (1952)
Vauthier's *la Nouvelle Mandragore* (1952)
   with Maurice Cazeneuve:
Claudel's *l'Histoire de Tobie et de Sara* (1947)
   with Daniel Sorano:
Molière's *le Malade imaginaire* (1957)
Molière's *l'Etourdi* (1959)

In addition to their productions on the great stages, Jean-Louis
Barrault and Jean Vilar have continued to work in the spirit
of the "little theatre" initiated by Copeau. During the 1950s,
at the Petit Théâtre Marigny, Barrault produced Schehadé
and Vauthier; and in 1959 the French government made Vilar
director of a small experimental theatre, the Théâtre Récamier.
In fact most experimental activity is now taking place on small
stages and is led by a whole new generation of directors:
Georges Vitaly (Audiberti), Jean-Marie Serreau (Adamov and
Ionesco), Roger Blin (Beckett), André Reybaz (Vauthier and
Ghelderode), Sylvain Dhomme (Ionesco).
   Between the great masters and the young revolutionaries, the
quality of directing is kept up by a group of non-theorists who
remain faithful to the principles of the reform and the lessons
of Copeau: André Barsacq—Charles Dullin's set designer and
his successor at the Vieux Colombier, the late Marcel Herrand
—founder of the company "Le Rideau de Paris," Raymond

Rouleau, Maurice Jacquemont, Pierre Valde. Even the Comédie Française has been carried away by the reform: from the modern *mise en scène* of Shakespeare's *Coriolanus* with André Boll's symbolic sets in 1933, the Cartel directors from 1936 to 1939, Barrault's stagings from 1940 to 1946, to the current *mises en scène,* now turbulent, now static, of Jean Meyer.

Since the war there has also been a dramatic decentralization which is responsible both for the diffusion of theatre outside of Paris and for further experimentation. Every summer there are dramatic festivals in Avignon, Angers, and Lyon. In addition new companies have been set up as "Centres Dramatiques" in the provinces: the Centre Dramatique de l'Ouest, the Centre Dramatique de l'Est, the Grenier de Toulouse, the Comédie de Saint-Etienne, the Comédie de Provence—where older directors continue to work (Jean Dasté, a student of Copeau, with the Comédie de Saint-Etienne) and new talents are discovered (Roger Planchon, considered a disciple of Brecht, with the Théâtre de la Cité de Villeurbanne).

Government aid has been instrumental in ensuring a theatre of quality and experimentation by subsidizing the national theatres and provincial companies and giving financial help to young companies and producers of first plays. Also, since 1959 and under the direction of André Malraux, governmental measures have been taken to develop, modernize, and discipline the national theatres: the Comédie Française, the Théâtre National Populaire, the Théâtre de France, the TNP-Récamier.

From 1890 to 1960, the French stage has been more and more strongly marked by the following characteristics—sometimes merely attempts rather than accomplished facts:

1. A coordination of all the arts of a production in order to obtain a unity of the whole on all levels.
2. An assimilation of realism in acting, evolving toward an art of suggestion.

3. An attempt to establish a theatre without stars.
4. The rigorous training of actors.
5. A rejection of the naturalistic stage and often the Italianate stage.
6. The use of modern painters, but a rejection of decorative sets in favor of functional three-dimensional décor, sometimes reduced to its simplest elements.
7. A frequent attempt to establish companies and repertories.
8. An attempt at establishing writer-director teams (Giraudoux-Jouvet, Anouilh-Barsacq, Claudel-Barrault, Audiberti-Vitaly, Beckett-Blin).
9. An attempt to free theatre from commercialism.

While many of the problems remain the same, new ones have developed. For instance, the importance given to staging raises the question of the rights and limits of a director. Copeau, by affirming "the identity of any theatrical composition and the means for expressing it in space and in time," made the director as much a "creator" as the playwright. At the time of its production, where does the "creation" of a play stop and a betrayal of the text begin? Directors are often tyrannical and nothing is helped by the attitude of those who override the plays and consider themselves great priests of a humanity whose church is the theatre.

The somewhat religious view also suggests a second question: If it is true that the objective of theatre is a kind of communion through artifice, has that communion been achieved? Artifice, whether it be the conscious use of the Italianate stage or of new inventions, has made it possible to retheatricalize theatre, making it both more unreal and closer to the spectator, and restoring its aspect of a ceremonious feast in which the spectator is invited to participate from the depths of his being. But have the scenic reform and the consciousness of what theatre must be led to communion? And is true communion possible in the world such as it is today?

The answer to that question is doubtless outside of theatre

itself. But although the reform has not reached all its objectives, it already has an impressive record. And the results are dual: New life has been infused into the great works of the past and authentic playwrights have appeared on the scene.

Consequently theatre is once again being taken seriously. Philosophers and theorists have revived theatre's contact with its origins, Greek and medieval, with the great moments in its history, the Elizabethan period and French classicism, and with the forms it has taken from other civilizations, such as the Balinese and Japanese. Mostly it has once again become an art which draws upon other arts but uses them for its own purposes and transcends them. As such, it is the object of independent studies, the most important of which, outside purely technical works, are those of Henri Gouhier and André Veinstein (see bibliography).

FIRST PERFORMANCES AND IMPORTANT REVIVALS

JEAN GIRAUDOUX (1882–1944)

Siegfried:
May 3, 1928, Comédie des Champs Elysées, directed by Louis Jouvet, sets by Camille Cipra.

Amphitryon 38:
November 8, 1929, Comédie des Champs Elysées, directed by Louis Jouvet, sets by Camille Cipra.

Judith:
November 5, 1931, Théâtre Pigalle, directed by Louis Jouvet, sets by Jouvet and René Moulaert.

Intermezzo:
February 27, 1933, Comédie des Champs Elysées, directed by Louis Jouvet, sets by L. Leyritz.
March 17, 1955, Théâtre Marigny, directed by Jean-Louis Barrault, sets by Maurice Brianchon.

Tessa (adaptation of M. Kennedy):
November 14, 1934, théâtre de l'Athénée, directed by Louis Jouvet, sets by René Moulaert.

La Guerre de Troie n'aura pas lieu:
November 21, 1935, Théâtre de l'Athénée, directed by Louis Jouvet, set by Mariano Andreu.

Supplément au Voyage de Cook:
November 21, 1935, Théâtre de l'Athénée, directed by Louis Jouvet, set by Mariano Andreu.

Electre:
May 13, 1937, Théâtre de l'Athénée, directed by Louis Jouvet, set by G. Monin.
October 28, 1959, Comédie Française, directed by Pierre Dux, set by Wakhévitch.

L'Impromptu de Paris:
December 4, 1937, Théâtre de l'Athénée, directed by Louis Jouvet, set by Vuillard.

Cantique des cantiques:
October 12, 1938, Comédie Française, directed by Louis Jouvet, set by G. Monin.

Ondine:
May 3, 1939, Théâtre de l'Athénée, directed by Louis Jouvet, sets by Pavel Tchelitchev.

L'Apollon de Marsac:
June 16, 1942, Rio de Janeiro, directed by Louis Jouvet, set by E. Anahory.
April 19, 1947, Théâtre de l'Athénée, directed by Louis Jouvet, set by E. Anahory.

Sodome et Gomorrhe:
October 11, 1943, Théâtre Hébertot, directed by Douking, sets by Christian Bérard.

La Folle de Chaillot:
December 21, 1945, Théâtre de l'Athénée, directed by Louis Jouvet, sets by Christian Bérard.

Pour Lucrèce:
November 4, 1953, Théâtre Marigny, directed by Jean-Louis Barrault, sets by A. M. Cassandre.

JEAN COCTEAU (1889–   )

Parade:
1916, Rome; 1917, Théâtre du Châtelet, choreography by

Léonide Massine, music by Erik Satie, sets and costumes by Picasso.

Les Mariés de la Tour Eiffel:
June 18, 1921, Théâtre des Champs Elysées, choreography by Jean Cocteau, set by Irène Lagut, costumes and masks by Jean Hugo, music by "les Six."

Antigone (adaptation of Sophocles):
December 20, 1922, Théâtre de l'Atelier, directed by Charles Dullin, set by Picasso.

Roméo et Juliette (adaptation of Shakespeare):
June 2, 1924, Théâtre de la Cigale, directed by Jean Cocteau, sets by Jean Hugo.

Orphée:
June 17, 1926, Théâtre des Arts, directed by Georges Pitoëff, set by Jean Hugo.

La Voix humaine:
February 17, 1930, Comédie Française, set by Christian Bérard.

La Machine infernale:
April 10, 1934, Comédie des Champs Elysées, directed by Louis Jouvet, sets by Christian Bérard.
September, 1954, Théâtre des Bouffes Parisiens, directed by Jean Cocteau, sets by Christian Bérard.

Oedipe-Roi (adaptation of Sophocles):
June, 1937, Théâtre Antoine, directed by Jean Cocteau, set by G. Monin.

Les Chevaliers de la Table Ronde:
October 14, 1937, Théâtre de l'Oeuvre, directed by Jean Cocteau, sets by Jean Cocteau.

Les Parents terribles:
November 14, 1938, Théâtre des Ambassadeurs, directed by Alice Cocéa, sets by G. Monin.

Appendix II

Les Monstres sacrés:
February 17, 1940, Théâtre Michel, directed by André Brulé, sets by Christian Bérard.

Le Bel Indifférent:
1940, Théâtre des Bouffes Parisiens, set by Christian Bérard.

La Machine à écrire:
April 29, 1941, Théâtre Hébertot, sets by Jean Marais.
March 11, 1956, Comédie Française, directed by Jean Meyer, sets by Suzanne Lalique.

Renaud et Armide:
April, 1943, Comédie Française, directed by Jean Cocteau, set by Christian Bérard.

L'Aigle à deux têtes:
November, 1946, Théâtre Hébertot, sets by André Beaurepaire.

Un Tramway nommé Désir (adaptation of Tennessee Williams' *A Streetcar Named Desire*):
October 17, 1949, Théâtre Edouard VII, directed by Raymond Rouleau, set by Lila de Nobili.

Bacchus:
November 20, 1951, Théâtre Marigny, directed by Jean Cocteau, sets by Jean Cocteau.

Major Films:

Le Sang d'un poète, 1932, directed by Jean Cocteau.

L'Eternel Retour, 1944, directed by Jean Delannoy.

Les Parents terribles, 1948, directed by Jean Cocteau.

Orphée, 1950, directed by Jean Cocteau.

Le Testament d'Orphée, 1960, directed by Jean Cocteau.

PAUL CLAUDEL (1868–1955)

L'Annonce faite à Marie:
December 22, 1912, Théâtre de l'Oeuvre, directed by Lugné-Poe, sets by Jean Variot.
June 10, 1946, Théâtre de l'Athénée, directed by Louis Jouvet, sets by E. Anahory.
March 12, 1948, Théâtre Hébertot, directed by J. Vernier.
February 18, 1954, Comédie Française, directed by Julien Bertheau, sets by Wakhévitch.

L'Echange:
January 22, 1914, Théâtre du Vieux Colombier, directed by Jacques Copeau, sets by Doucet.
November 17, 1937, Théâtre des Mathurins, directed by Georges Pitoëff, sets by Georges Pitoëff.
December 12, 1951, Théâtre Marigny, directed by Jean-Louis Barrault, sets by Wakhévitch.

L'Otage:
June 5, 1914, Théâtre de l'Oeuvre, directed by Lugné-Poe, sets by Jean Variot.
October, 1934, Comédie Française, directed by Emile Fabre, sets by Charlemagne.

Partage de midi:
November 12, 1916, Groupe Art et Action, sets by Autant-Lara, Autant, and Girard.
December 16, 1948, Théâtre Marigny, directed by Jean-Louis Barrault, sets by Félix Labisse.

Tête d'or:
April 25, 1924, Groupe Art et Action, directed by Mme. Lara, sets by Georges Valmier.
October 21, 1959, Théâtre de France, directed by Jean-Louis Barrault, sets by André Masson.

Le Pain dur:
October, 1926, Landestheater, Oldenburg, directed by Hans Pretz.

March 12, 1949, Théâtre de l'Atelier, directed by André Barsacq, sets by André Barsacq.

Le Père humilié:
November 26, 1928, Schauspielhaus, Dresden, directed by Joseph Gielen, sets by Malinke.
May 10, 1946, Théâtre des Champs Elysées, directed by Jean Valcourt, sets by Tahard.

Le Repos du septième jour:
December 10, 1928, Narodowy Theatre, Warsaw, directed by Radulski, sets by Drabik.

Le Livre de Christophe Colomb:
May 5, 1930, Staatsoper unter den Linden, Berlin, music by Darius Milhaud, directed by M. Hort, sets by M. Araventinos.
October 1, 1953, Théâtre Marigny, directed by Jean-Louis Barrault, sets by Marc Ingrand.

La Ville:
February, 1931, Salle Patria, Brussels, directed by A. van de Velde.
December 2, 1955, Palais de Chaillot, directed by Jean Vilar, set by Léon Gischia.

Protée:
April 4, 1933, Municipal Theatre, Amsterdam, Students' Dramatic Association.
May, 1957, Théâtre du Tertre, directed by Serge Ligier, set by Camurati.

Les Choéphores (translation of Aeschylus):
March 27, 1935, Brussels.

Jeanne au bûcher:
May 6, 1939, Théâtre Municipal d'Orléans, music by Honegger, sets by Alexandre Benois.
December 18, 1950, Opéra, directed by Jan Doat, set by Yves Bonnat.

Le Soulier de satin:
November 27, 1943, Comédie Française, directed by Jean-Louis Barrault, sets by Lucien Coutaud.

La Jeune Fille Violaine:
March, 1944, Salle Iéna, directed by Maurice Leroy, sets by Maurice Leroy.

L'Histoire de Tobie et de Sara:
September 5, 1947, Avignon, directed by Maurice Cazeneuve.

HENRY DE MONTHERLANT (1893–   )

Pasiphaé:
December 6, 1938, Théâtre Pigalle, directed by Sylvain Itkine.
Summer, 1949, Avignon, directed by Jean Vilar.

La Reine morte:
December 8, 1942, Comédie Française, directed by Pierre Dux, sets by Roland Oudot.

Fils de personne:
December 18, 1943, Théâtre Saint-Georges, directed by Pierre Dux, sets by L. Leyritz.

Le Maître de Santiago:
January 26, 1948, Théâtre Hébertot, directed by Paul Oettly, sets by Mariano Andreu.
February, 1958, Comédie Française, directed by Henri Rollan.

Demain il fera jour:
May 9, 1949, Théâtre Hébertot, directed by Paul Oettly.

Celles qu'on prend dans ses bras:
October 20, 1950, Théâtre de la Madeleine, directed by Claude Sainval, set by Wakhévitch.

Malatesta:
December 19, 1950, Théâtre Marigny, directed by Jean-Louis Barrault, sets by Mariano Andreu.

La Ville dont le Prince est un enfant:
1952, one scene, Casino de Biarritz.

Port-Royal:
December 8, 1954, Comédie Française, directed by Jean Meyer, set by Suzanne Lalique.

Brocéliande:
October 24, 1956, Comédie Française, directed by Jean Meyer, set by Suzanne Lalique.

Don Juan:
November 8, 1958, Théâtre de l'Athénée, directed by Georges Vitaly, sets by Mariano Andreu.

ARMAND SALACROU (1900–   )

Tour à terre:
December 24, 1925, Théâtre de l'Oeuvre, directed by Lugné-Poe.

Le Pont de l'Europe:
December 24, 1925, Théâtre de l'Oeuvre, directed by Lugné-Poe.

Patchouli:
January 22, 1930, Théâtre de l'Atelier, directed by Charles Dullin, sets by Michel Duran.

Atlas Hôtel:
April 15, 1931, Théâtre de l'Atelier, directed by Charles Dullin, sets by G. Valako.

Les Frénétiques:
December 5, 1934, Théâtre Daunou, directed by Raymond Rouleau.

Une Femme libre:
October 4, 1934, Théâtre de l'Oeuvre, directed by Paulette Pax, sets by Paulette Pax.

L'Inconnue d'Arras:
November 22, 1935, Comédie des Champs Elysées, directed by Lugné-Poe, set by René Moulaert.
January 13, 1949, Comédie Française, directed by Gaston Baty

Un Homme comme les autres:
November 23, 1936, Théâtre de l'Oeuvre, directed by Paulette Pax, sets by Paulette Pax.

La Terre est ronde:
November 7, 1938, Théâtre de l'Atelier, directed by Charles Dullin, sets by André Masson.

Histoire de rire:
December 22, 1939, Théâtre de la Madeleine, directed by Alice Cocéa.

La Marguerite:
October 28, 1944, Théâtre Pigalle, directed by Julien Bertheau.

Les Fiancés du Havre:
December 10, 1944, Comédie Française, directed by Pierre Dux, sets by Raoul Dufy.

Le Soldat et la sorcière:
December 5, 1945, Théâtre Sarah Bernhardt, directed by Charles Dullin, sets by Chapelain-Midy.

Les Nuits de la colère:
December 12, 1946, Théâtre Marigny, directed by Jean-Louis Barrault, sets by Félix Labisse.

L'Archipel Lenoir:
November 8, 1947, Théâtre Montparnasse, directed by Charles Dullin, set by A. M. Rodicq.

Poof:
October 26, 1950, Théâtre Edouard VII, directed by Yves Robert, set by Serge Creuz.

Pourquoi pas moi?:
October 26, 1950, Théâtre Edouard VII, directed by J. Dumesnil, set by Serge Creuz.

Dieu le savait!:
December 2, 1950, Théâtre Saint-Georges, directed by Jean Mercure, set by Wakhévitch.

Sens interdit:
1952, Théâtre du Quartier Latin, directed by Michel de Ré, set by Francine Gaillard-Risler.

Les Invités du Bon Dieu:
1953, Théâtre Saint-Georges, directed by Yves Robert, set by Francine Gaillard-Risler.

Le Miroir:
September 22, 1956, Théâtre des Ambassadeurs, directed by Henri Rollan, set by Jean-Denis Malclès.

Une Femme trop honnête:
December, 1956, Théâtre Edouard VII.

JEAN ANOUILH (1910–   )

L'Hermine:
April 26, 1932, Théâtre de l'Oeuvre, directed by P. Paȝ

Y'Avait un Prisonnier:
March 21, 1935, Théâtre des Ambassadeurs, set by René Moulaert.

Le Voyageur sans bagage:
February 16, 1937, Théâtre des Mathurins, directed by Georges Pitoëff, set by Georges Pitoëff.
April 6, 1950, Théâtre Montparnasse, directed by André Barsacq.

La Sauvage:
January 10, 1938, Théâtre des Mathurins, directed by Georges Pitoëff, sets by Georges Pitoëff.

Le Bal des voleurs:
September 17, 1938, Théâtre des Arts, directed by André Barsacq, sets by André Barsacq.

Léocadia:
November, 1940, Théâtre de la Michodière.

Le Rendez-vous de Senlis:
February 30, 1941, Théâtre de l'Atelier, directed by André Barsacq, sets by André Barsacq.

Eurydice:
December 18, 1942, Théâtre de l'Atelier, directed by André Barsacq, sets by André Barsacq.

Antigone:
February 4, 1944, Théâtre de l'Atelier, directed by André Barsacq, set by André Barsacq.

Roméo et Jeannette:
December 3, 1946, Théâtre de l'Atelier, directed by André Barsacq, sets by André Barsacq.

L'Invitation au château:
November 4, 1947, Théâtre de l'Atelier, directed by André Barsacq, sets by André Barsacq.

Ardèle ou la Marguerite:
November 3, 1948, Comédie des Champs Elysées, directed by Roland Pietri, set by Jean-Denis Malclès.

La Répétition ou l'amour puni:
October 26, 1950, Théâtre Marigny, directed by Jean-Louis Barrault, sets by Jean-Denis Malclès.

Colombe:
February 11, 1951, Théâtre de l'Atelier, directed by André Barsacq, sets by André Barsacq.

La Valse des Toréadors:
January 9, 1952, Comédie des Champs Elysées, directed by Roland Pietri, sets by Jean-Denis Malclès.

Médée:
March 26, 1953, Théâtre de l'Atelier, directed by André Barsacq, sets by André Bakst.

L'Alouette:
October 14, 1953, Théâtre Montparnasse, directed by Jean Anouilh, sets by Jean-Denis Malclès.

Ornifle ou le courant d'air:
November 7, 1955, Comédie des Champs Elysées, sets by Jean-Denis Malclès.

Pauvre Bitos ou le diner de têtes:
October 11, 1956, Théâtre Montparnasse, directed by Roland Pietri, sets by Jean-Denis Malclès.

L'Hurluberlu ou le réactionnaire amoureux:
February 5, 1959, Comédie des Champs Elysées, directed by Roland Pietri, sets by Jean-Denis Malclès.

La Petite Molière:
June 14, 1959, Bordeaux. November 12, 1959, Théâtre de France, directed by Jean-Louis Barrault, sets by Jacques Noël.

Becket ou l'honneur de Dieu:
October 1, 1959, Théâtre Montparnasse, directed by Jean Anouilh and Roland Pietri, sets by Jean-Denis Malclès.

JEAN-PAUL SARTRE (1905–   )

Les Mouches:
April, 1943, Théâtre de la Cité-Sarah Bernhardt, directed by Charles Dullin, sets by Adam.

Huis Clos:
May, 1944, Théâtre du Vieux Colombier, directed by Raymond Rouleau.

Morts sans sépulture:
November 8, 1946, Théâtre Antoine.

La Putain respectueuse:
November 8, 1946, Théâtre Antoine.

Les Mains sales:
April 2, 1948, Théâtre Antoine, directed by Pierre Valde, sets by Emile and Jean Bertin.

Le Diable et le Bon Dieu:
June 7, 1951, Théâtre Antoine, directed by Louis Jouvet, sets by Félix Labisse.

Kean (adaptation of Dumas père):
November 17, 1953, Théâtre Sarah Bernhardt, directed by Pierre Brasseur, sets by Alexandre Trauner.

Nekrassov:
June 8, 1955, Théâtre Antoine, directed by Jean Meyer, sets by Jean-Denis Malclès.

Les Séquestrés d'Altona:
September 23, 1959, Théâtre de la Renaissance, directed by François Darbon, sets by Yvon Henri.

ALBERT CAMUS (1913–1960)

Le Malentendu:
1944, Théâtre des Mathurins, directed by Marcel Herrand.

Caligula:
1945, Théâtre Hébertot. February, 1958, Nouveau Théâtre.

Les Justes:
December 15, 1949, Théâtre Hébertot, directed by Paul Oettly, sets by Rosnay.

L'Etat de siège:
October 27, 1948, Théâtre Marigny, directed by Jean-Louis Barrault, sets by Balthus.

Appendix II

Les Esprits (adaptation of Larivey): June 16, 1953, Château d'Angers, directed by Marcel Herrand, sets by Philippe Bonnet.

La Dévotion à la Croix (translation of Calderón):
June, 1953, Château d'Angers, directed by Marcel Herrand.

Requiem pour une nonne (adaptation of Faulkner):
1956, Théâtre des Mathurins, directed by Albert Camus.

Les Possédés (adaptation of Dostoyevsky):
January 30, 1959, Théâtre Antoine, directed by Albert Camus, sets by Mayo.

MICHEL DE GHELDERODE (1898–   )

(First performances in France. For first performances in Belgium, see David Grossvogel, *The Self-Conscious Stage*.)

La Mort du Docteur Faust:
January 27, 1928, Groupe Art et Action.

Christophe Colomb:
October 25, 1929, Groupe Art et Action.

Escurial:
January 17, 1949, Studio des Champs Elysées, directed by René Dupuy and Michel Vitold.

Mademoiselle Jaïre:
June, 1949, Théâtre de l'Atelier, directed by P. Iglésis.

Fastes d'enfer:
November 22, 1949, Théâtre des Noctambules, directed by André Reybaz.

Hop Signor!:
November 22, 1949, Théâtre des Noctambules, directed by André Reybaz.

Sire Halewyn:
February 17, 1950, Théâtre des Noctambules, directed by Catherine Toth.

Barabbas:
February 21, 1950, Théâtre de l'Oeuvre.

Ballade du Grand Macabre:
1953–1954, Studio des Champs Elysées, directed by René Dupuy, sets by Jacques Marillier.

L'Ecole des bouffons:
1953–1954, Théâtre de l'Oeuvre, directed by Marcel Lupovici, sets by Raymond Raynal.

Magie rouge:
April, 1956, Théâtre du Quartier Latin, directed by Gilles Chancrin.

Trois Acteurs, un drame:
July, 1958, Théâtre de Poche, directed by Gilles Chancrin.

Les Aveugles:
July, 1958, Théâtre de Poche, directed by Gilles Chancrin.

JACQUES AUDIBERTI (1899–   )

Quoat-Quoat:
January 28, 1946, Gaîté-Montparnasse, directed by André Reybaz.

Le Mal court:
June 25, 1947, Théâtre de Poche, directed by Georges Vitaly, sets by Marie Viton. December 15, 1955, Théâtre La Bruyère, directed by Georges Vitaly, sets by Léonor Fini.

Les Femmes du Boeuf:
November 23, 1948, Comédie Française, directed by Jean Debucourt, set by Peynet.

La Fête noire:
December 3, 1948, Théâtre de la Huchette, directed by Georges Vitaly, sets by André Marchand.

L'Ampélour:
February 17, 1950, Théâtre des Noctambules.

Pucelle:
June 1, 1950, Théâtre de la Huchette, directed by Georges Vitaly, sets by André Marchand.

Les Naturels du Bordelais:
1953–1954, Théâtre La Bruyère, directed by Georges Vitaly, sets by Roger Chancel.

La Mégère apprivoisée (adaptation of Shakespeare):
October 10, 1957, Théâtre de l'Athénée, directed by Georges Vitaly, sets by Léonor Fini.

La Hobereaute:
September 20, 1958, Théâtre du Vieux Colombier, directed by Jean Le Poulain, sets by Jacques Noël.

L'Effet Glapion:
September 9, 1959, Théâtre La Bruyère, directed by Georges Vitaly.

GEORGE SCHEHADÉ (1910–   )

Monsieur Bob'le:
January 30, 1951, Théâtre de la Huchette, directed by Georges Vitaly, sets by Dora Maar.

La Soirée des proverbes:
January 30, 1954, Petit Théâtre Marigny, directed by Jean-Louis Barrault, sets by Félix Labisse.

Histoire de Vasco:
October 15, 1956, Shauspielhaus, Zurich; September, 1957, Théâtre Sarah Bernhardt, directed by Jean-Louis Barrault, sets by Jack Youngerman.

HENRI PICHETTE (1924–   )

Les Epiphanies:
December 3, 1947, Théâtre des Noctambules, directed by Georges Vitaly, sets by Matta.

Nucléa:
May 3, 1952, Palais de Chaillot, directed by Gérard Philipe, sets by Alexander Calder.

JEAN VAUTHIER (1910–   )

La Nouvelle Mandragore:
December 20, 1952, Palais de Chaillot, directed by Gérard Philipe, set by Pignon.

Capitaine Bada:
January 10, 1952, Théâtre de Poche, directed by André Reybaz, set by René Allio.

Le Personnage combattant:
February 6, 1956, Petit Théâtre Marigny, directed by Jean-Louis Barrault.

JEAN GENÊT (1909–   )

Les Bonnes:
April 19, 1947, Théâtre de l'Athénée, directed by Louis Jouvet, sets by Christian Bérard. 1953–1954, Théâtre de la Huchette, directed by Tania Balachova, sets by Michel Sarkin.

Haute Surveillance:
January 26, 1949, Théâtre des Mathurins, directed by Jean Genêt, set by André Beaurepaire.

Les Nègres:
October 28, 1959, Théâtre de Lutèce, directed by Roger Blin.

Le Balcon:
May 18, 1960, Théâtre du Gymnase, directed by Peter Brook.

ARTHUR ADAMOV (1908–   )

L'Invasion:
November 14, 1950, Studio des Champs Elysées, directed by Jean Vilar, set by Coussonneau.

La Grande et la Petite Manoeuvre:
November 11, 1950, Théâtre des Noctambules, directed by Jean-Marie Serreau, set by Jacques Noël.

La Parodie:
June 5, 1952, Théâtre Lancry, directed by Roger Blin, set by Vieira da Silva.

Le Professeur Taranne:
March 18, 1953, Théâtre de la Comédie, Lyon, directed by Roger Planchon.

Le Sens de la marche:
March 18, 1953, Théâtre de la Comédie, Lyon, directed by Roger Planchon.

Tous contre tous:
April 14, 1953, Théâtre de l'Oeuvre, directed by Jean-Marie Serreau.

Le Ping-Pong:
March 2, 1955, Théâtre des Noctambules, directed by Jacques Mauclair, sets by Jacques Noël.

Paolo Paoli:
May 17, 1957, Théâtre de la Comédie, Lyon, directed by Roger Planchon, sets by René Allio.

Les Petits Bourgeois (translation of Gorky):
September 29, 1959, Théâtre de l'Oeuvre, directed by Gregory Chmara.

Les Ames mortes (adaptation of Gogol):
April 16, 1960, Théâtre de France, directed by Roger Planchon.

EUGÈNE IONESCO (1912–   )

La Cantatrice chauve:
May 15, 1950, Théâtre des Noctambules, directed by Nicolas Bataille.

La Leçon:
February 20, 1951, Théâtre de Poche, directed by Marcel Cuvelier.

Les Chaises:
April 22, 1952, Théâtre Lancry, directed by Sylvain Dhomme, sets by Jacques Noël.

Victimes du devoir:
February, 1953, Théâtre du Quartier Latin, directed by Jacques Mauclair, sets by René Allio.

La Jeune Fille à marier:
September 1, 1953, Théâtre de la Huchette, directed by Jacques Poliéri.

Amédée ou comment s'en débarrasser:
April 14, 1954, Théâtre de Babylone, directed by Jean-Marie Serreau, sets by Jacques Noël.

Jacques ou la soumission:
October, 1955, Théâtre de la Huchette, directed by Robert Postec.

L'Impromptu de l'Alma:
February 20, 1956, Studio des Champs Elysées, directed by Maurice Jacquemont, set by Paul Coupille.

Le Nouveau Locataire:
September 10, 1957, Théâtre d'Aujourd'hui, directed by Robert Postec, sets by Siné.

L'Avenir est dans les oeufs:
1958.

Appendix II

Tueur sans gages:
February 27, 1959, Théâtre Récamier, directed by José Quaglio, sets by Jacques Noël.

Rhinocéros:
January 15, 1960, Théâtre de France, directed by Jean-Louis Barrault, sets by Jacques Noël.

SAMUEL BECKETT (1906–   )

En Attendant Godot:
January 5, 1953, Théâtre de Babylone, directed by Roger Blin.

Fin de partie:
April 3, 1957, Royal Court Theatre, London; April 26, Studio des Champs Elysées, directed by Roger Blin, set by Jacques Noël.

Acte sans paroles:
April 3, 1957, Royal Court Theatre, London; April 26, 1957, Studio des Champs Elysées, directed by Roger Blin, set by Jacques Noël.

La Dernière Bande:
March 25, 1960, Théâtre Récamier, directed by Roger Blin.

SELECTED BIBLIOGRAPHY

I. PLAYWRIGHTS AND THEIR CRITICS

II. MODERN FRENCH THEATRE
IN GENERAL

III. THEORISTS AND DIRECTORS

PLAYWRIGHTS AND THEIR CRITICS

JEAN GIRAUDOUX

Théâtre complet, 16 volumes, Neuchâtel and Paris, Ides et Calendes, 1945–1951.
Les Gracques, Paris, Les Cahiers Verts XLVI, Grasset, 1958.

His Critics:

Albérès, R-M., *Esthétique et morale chez Giraudoux,* Paris, Nizet, 1957.

Høst, Gunnon, *l'Oeuvre de Jean Giraudoux,* Oslo, H. Aschehoug, 1942.

Houlet, Jacques, *le Théâtre de Jean Giraudoux,* Paris, Pierre Ardent, 1945.

Inskip, Donald, *Jean Giraudoux, The Making of a Dramatist,* London and New York, Oxford University Press, 1958.

Lesage, Laurent, "Jean Giraudoux, Surrealism, and the German Romantic Ideal," *Illinois Studies in Language and Literature,* Vol. XXXVI, No. 3, Urbana, University of Illinois Press, 1952.

Lesage, Laurent, *Jean Giraudoux, His Life and His Works,* University Park, Pennsylvania State University Press, 1959.

Magny, Claude-Edmonde, *Précieux Giraudoux,* Paris, Editions du Seuil, 1945.

May, Georges, "Jean Giraudoux: Diplomacy and Dramaturgy," *Yale French Studies* No. 5, Spring 1950.

The Tulane Drama Review, Vol. III, No. 4, Summer 1959.

JEAN COCTEAU:

Théâtre complet, 2 volumes, Paris, Grasset, 1957.

Selected Bibliography

His critics:

Dubourg, Pierre, *Dramaturgie de Jean Cocteau,* Paris, Grasset, 1954.

Fergusson, Francis, *"The Infernal Machine:* The Myth Behind the Modern City," *The Idea of a Theatre,* Princeton University Press, 1949.

Oxenhandler, Neal, *Scandal and Parade: The Theater of Jean Cocteau,* New Brunswick, Rutgers University Press, 1957.

PAUL CLAUDEL:

Théâtre, 2 volumes, Paris, Gallimard, Pléiade, 1956.

His critics:

Beaumont, Ernest, *The Theme of Beatrice in the Plays of Paul Claudel,* London, Rockhill Publications Corp., 1957.

Chiari, Joseph, *The Poetic Drama of Paul Claudel,* New York, P. J. Kennedy, 1954.

Farabet, René, *le Jeu de l'acteur dans le théâtre de Claudel,* Paris, Les Lettres Modernes, 1960.

Peyre, Henri, "The Drama of Paul Claudel," *Thought,* Fordham University Quarterly, Vol. XXVII, No. 105, 1952.

HENRY DE MONTHERLANT:

Théâtre, Paris, Gallimard, Pléiade, 1954.
Brocéliande, Paris, Gallimard, 1956.
Don Juan, Paris, Gallimard, 1958.
Le Cardinal d'Espagne, Paris, Gallimard, 1960.

His critics:

Laprade, Jacques de, *le Théâtre de Montherlant,* Paris, La Jeune Parque, 1950.

Mohrt, Michel, *Montherlant, homme libre,* Paris, Gallimard, 1943.

ARMAND SALACROU:

Théâtre, 6 volumes, Paris, Gallimard, 1947–1954.
Sens interdit, Paris, Gallimard, 1952.
Une Femme trop honnête, Paris, Gallimard, 1956.
Le Miroir, in *Femina Théâtre,* Nov. 1956, Paris, Gallimard.

His critics:

Radine, Serge, *Anouilh, Lenormand, Salacrou: Trois drama-turges à la recherche de leur vérité,* Geneva, Trois Collines, 1951.
Van den Esh, José, *Armand Salacrou, dramaturge de l'ango-isse,* Paris, Editions du Temps Présent, 1947.

JEAN ANOUILH:

Pièces noires, Paris, Calmann-Lévy, 1945.
Pièces roses, Paris, Calmann-Lévy, 1945.
Nouvelles Pièces noires, Paris, La Table Ronde, 1947.
Pièces brillantes, La Table Ronde, 1951.
L'Alouette, Paris, La Table Ronde, 1953.
Pièces grinçantes, Paris, La Table Ronde, 1956.
L'Hurluberlu, Paris, La Table Ronde, 1959.
Becket ou l'honneur de Dieu, Paris, La Table Ronde, 1959.

His critics:

Champigny, Robert, "Theatre in a Mirror: Anouilh," *Yale French Studies* No. 14, Winter 1954–1955.
Gignoux, Hubert, *Jean Anouilh,* Paris, Editions du Temps Présent, 1946.
John, S., "Obsession and Technique in the plays of Jean Anouilh," *French Studies,* Vol. XI, Oxford, 1957.
Radine, Serge, see bibl. Armand Salacrou.

Selected Bibliography

Jean-Paul Sartre:

Théâtre I, Paris, Gallimard, 1947.
Les Mains sales, Paris, Gallimard, 1948.
Le Diable et le Bon Dieu, Paris, Gallimard, 1952.
Kean, Paris, Gallimard, 1954.
Nekrassov, Paris, Gallimard, 1957.
Les Séquestrés d'Altona, Paris, Gallimard, 1959.

His critics:

Albérès, R. M., *Jean-Paul Sartre,* Paris-Brussels, Editions Universitaires, 1953.
Bentley, Eric, "From Strindberg to Jean-Paul Sartre," *The Playwright as Thinker,* New York, Meridian Books, 1955.
Fergusson, Francis, "Sartre as Playwright," *Partisan Review,* Vol. XVI, No. 4, 1949.

Albert Camus:

Le Malentendu, Caligula, Paris, Gallimard, 1944.
L'Etat de siège, Paris, Gallimard, 1948.
Les Justes, Paris, Gallimard, 1948.
Les Esprits, Paris, Gallimard, 1953.
Requiem pour une nonne, Paris, Gallimard, 1956.
Les Possédés, Paris, Gallimard, 1959.

His critics:

Brée, Germaine, *Camus,* New Brunswick, Rutgers University Press, 1959.

Michel de Ghelderode:

Théâtre, 5 volumes, Paris, Gallimard, 1950–57.

His critics:

Grossvogel, David, *The Self-Conscious Stage in Modern French Drama,* New York, Columbia University Press, 1958.

JACQUES AUDIBERTI:

Théâtre, 3 volumes, Paris, Gallimard, 1948–1956.
Le Cavalier seul, Paris, Gallimard, 1955.
La Mégère apprivoisée, Paris, Gallimard, 1957.
L'Effet Glapion, Paris, Gallimard, 1959.

GEORGES SCHEHADÉ:

Monsieur Bob'le, Paris, Gallimard, 1951.
La Soirée des proverbes, Paris, Gallimard, 1954.
Histoire de Vasco, Paris, Gallimard, 1956.

HENRI PICHETTE:

Les Epiphanies, Paris, K, 1948.
Nucléa, Paris, L'Arche, 1952.

JEAN VAUTHIER:

Théâtre, Paris, L'Arche, 1954.
Le Personnage combattant, Paris, Gallimard, 1955.
Les Prodiges, Paris, Gallimard, 1958.

JEAN GENÊT:

Les Bonnes, in *l'Atelier d'Alberto Giacometti,* Décines, L'Arbalète, 1958.
Haute Surveillance, Paris, Gallimard, 1949.
Le Balcon, Décines, L'Arbalète, 1956.
Les Nègres, Décines, Barbezat, 1960.

His critics:

Abel, Lionel, "Metatheater," *Partisan Review,* Vol. XXVII, No. 2, Spring 1960.

Selected Bibliography

Sartre, Jean-Paul, *Saint Genêt, comédien et martyr*, Paris, Gallimard, 1952.

ARTHUR ADAMOV:

Théâtre, 2 volumes, Paris, Gallimard, 1953–1955.
Paolo Paoli, Paris, Gallimard, 1957.
Les Ames mortes, Paris, Gallimard, 1959.

His critics:

Dort, Bernard, *"Paolo Paoli* ou la découverte du réel," *Les Temps Modernes* No. 142, 1957.
Lynes, Carlos, "Adamov or 'le sens littéral' in the Theatre," *Yale French Studies* No. 14, Winter 1954–1955.
Saurel, Renée, *"Tous contre tous* d'Arthur Adamov," *Les Temps Modernes* No. 91, 1953.

BORIS VIAN:

Les Bâtisseurs d'Empire, in *Dossiers du Collège de Pataphysique,* Nouvelle Série No. 6, 1958.

ARRABAL:

Théâtre, Paris, Julliard, 1958.

EUGÈNE IONESCO:

Théâtre, 2 volumes, Paris, Gallimard, 1954–58.
Rhinocéros, Paris, Gallimard, 1959.

His critics:

Lamont, Rosette, "The Metaphysical Farce: Beckett and Ionesco," *The French Review,* Vol. XXXII, No. 4, Feb. 1959.
Pronko, Leonard, "The Anti-Spiritual Victory in the Theatre

of Ionesco," *Modern Drama,* Vol. II, No. 1, May 1959, Lawrence, Kansas.

Saurel, Renée, "Ionesco ou les blandices de la culpabilité," *Les Temps Modernes* No. 103, 1954. "Saint Ionesco, l'anti-Brecht," *Les Temps Modernes* No. 158, 1959.

SAMUEL BECKETT:

En Attendant Godot, Paris, Editions de Minuit, 1952.
Fin de partie, Acte sans paroles, Editions de Minuit, 1957.
Krapp's Last Tape and Other Dramatic Pieces, New York, Grove Press, 1960.

His critics:

Champigny, Robert, "Interpretation of *En Attendant Godot,"* *PMLA,* Vol. LXXV, No. 3, 1960.

Kern, Edith, "Drama Stripped for Inaction: Beckett's *Godot,"* *Yale French Studies* No. 14, Winter 1954–55.

Lamont, Rosette, see bibl. Ionesco.

Leventhal, A. J., "Mr. Beckett's *En Attendant Godot,"* *The Dublin Magazine,* April–June, 1954.

Mayoux, Jean-Jacques, "le Théâtre de Samuel Beckett," *Etudes Anglaises,* Vol. X, No. 4, 1957, Paris.

NOTE:

For plays in English translation, see Wallace Fowlie, *Dionysus in Paris,* bibliography.

Additions to Fowlie bibliography:

Adamov, *As We Were* (*Comme nous avons été*), trans. Richard Howard, *Evergreen Review,* Vol. I, No. 4, 1957.

Anouilh, *The Fighting Cock* (*L'Hurluberlu*), adapt. Lucienne Hill, New York, Coward-McCann Inc., 1960.

Arrabal, *Automobile Graveyard* (*le Cimetière des voitures*), and *The Two Executioners* (*les Deux Bourreaux*), trans. Richard Howard, New York, Grove Press, 1960.

Ghelderode, *Seven Plays,* Mermaid Dramabook, Hill and Wang, 1960, contains: *The Women at the Tomb* (*Les Femmes au tombeau*), *Barabbas, Three Actors and their Drama* (*Trois Acteurs, un drame*), *Pantagleize, The Blind Men* (*Les Aveugles*), *Chronicles of Hell* (*Fastes d'enfer*), trans. George Hauger; *Lord Halewyn* (*Sire Halewyn*), trans. Gerard Hopkins.

Giraudoux, *The Song of Songs* (*Cantique des cantiques*), trans. John Raikes, and *Paris Impromptu* (*l'Impromptu de Paris*), trans. Rima Reck, *The Tulane Drama Review,* Vol. III, No. 4, Summer 1959.

II

MODERN FRENCH THEATRE IN GENERAL

Beigbeder, Marc, *le Théâtre en France depuis la Libération,* Paris, Bordas, 1959.

Fowlie, Wallace, *Dionysus in Paris, a Guide to French Contemporary Theater,* New York, Meridian Books, 1959.

Gassner, John, *Masters of the Drama* (third revised and enlarged edition), Dover Publications Inc., 1954.

Simon, Pierre-Henri, *Théâtre et Destin,* Paris, Armand Colin, 1959.

III

THEORISTS AND DIRECTORS

Artaud, Antonin, *le Théâtre et son double,* Paris, Gallimard, 1938. (*The Theatre and Its Double,* trans. Mary Caroline Richards, New York, Grove Press, 1958).
Lettres d'Antonin Artaud à Jean-Louis Barrault, Paris, Bordas, 1952.

Barrault, Jean-Louis, *Réflexions sur le théâtre,* Paris, Vautrain, 1949.

Baty, Gaston, *le Masque et l'encensoir, introduction à une esthétique du théâtre,* Paris, Blaud et Gay, 1926.

Baty, Gaston, and Chavance, René, *la Vie de l'art théâtral des origines à nos jours,* Paris, Plon, 1932.

Bentley, Eric, *In Search of Theater,* New York, Knopf, 1953.

Blanchart, Paul, *Gaston Baty,* Paris, Nouvelle Revue Critique, 1939. *Histoire de la mise en scène,* Paris, Presses Universitaires de France, 1948.

Boll, André, *la Mise en scène contemporaine, son évolution,* Paris, Nouvelle Revue Critique, 1944.

Chancerel, Léon, *Jean-Louis Barrault,* Paris, Presses Littéraires de France, 1953.

Cogniat, Raymond, *Cinquante ans de spectacles en France: les décorateurs de théâtre,* Paris, Librairie Théâtral, 1955. *Gaston Baty,* Paris, Presses Littéraires de France, 1953.

Copeau, Jacques, *Souvenirs du Vieux Colombier,* Paris, Nouvelles Editions Latines, 1931.

Dhomme, Sylvain, *la Mise en scène d'Antoine à Brecht,* Paris, Fernand Nathan, 1960.

Selected Bibliography

Dullin, Charles, *Souvenirs et notes de travail d'un acteur,* Paris, Odette Lieutier, 1946.

Gassner, John, *Form and Idea in Modern Theater,* New York, Dryden Press, 1956.

Gouhier, Henri, *l'Essence du théâtre,* Paris, Aubier, 1943. *Le Théâtre et l'existence,* Paris, Aubier, 1952. *L'Oeuvre théâtrale,* Paris, Flammarion, 1958.

Hort, Jean, *les Théâtres du Cartel,* Geneva, Skira, 1944.

Jouvet, Louis, *Réflexions du comédien,* Paris, Librairie Théâtrale, 1952. *Témoignages sur le théâtre,* Paris, Flammarion, 1952.

Knapp, Bettina, *Louis Jouvet, Man of the Theater,* New York, Columbia University Press, 1957.

Lenormand, Henri-René, *les Pitoëff, Souvenirs,* Paris, Odette Lieutier, 1943.

Lerminier, Georges, *Jacques Copeau,* Paris, Presses Littéraires de France, 1953.

Pitoëff, Georges, *Notre Théâtre,* Paris, Messages, 1949.

Robichez, Jacques, *le Symbolisme au théâtre: Lugné-Poe et les débuts de l'Oeuvre,* Paris, l'Arche, 1957.

Rouché, Jacques, *l'Art théâtral moderne* (revised edition), Paris, Bloud et Gay, 1924.

Sarment, Jean, *Charles Dullin,* Paris, Calmann-Lévy, 1950.

Touchard, Pierre-Aimé, *Dionysos, apologie pour le théâtre,* Paris, Editions du Seuil, 1949.

Valogne, Catherine, *Jean Vilar,* Paris, Presses Littéraires de France, 1954.

Veinstein, André, *la Mise en scène théâtrale et sa condition esthétique,* Paris, Flammarion, 1955.

Vilar, Jean, *De la Tradition théâtrale,* Paris, l'Arche, 1955.

Cahiers de la Compagnie Madeleine Renaud Jean-Louis Barrault (quarterly), Paris, Julliard, 1953-1960. See especially Nos. 1, 12, 25, 27 on Claudel, No. 2 on Giraudoux, Nos. 4 and 17 on Schehadé, No. 14 on Jean Vauthier, No. 22-23 on

Artaud and the avant-garde theatre, No. 26 on Anouilh, No. 29 on Ionesco.

Encyclopédie du Théâtre Contemporain, edited by Gilles Quéant, 2 volumes, Paris, Publications de France, 1957.

Index

Index

Diderot, Denis, 4, 8
Doat, Jan, 268
Donnay, Maurice, 11, 12
Dostoyevsky, Fyodor, 243, 248, 255, 276
Doucet, Jacques, 267
Douking, 264
Drabik, 268
Dufy, Raoul, 271
Dullin, Charles, 68, 112, 225, 247, 251–52, 255, 256, 257, 259, 265, 270, 271, 274
Dumas, *père*, Alexandre, 11, 141
Dumesnil, Jacques, 272
Dupuy, René, 276, 277
Duran, Michel, 270
Dux, Pierre, 264, 269, 271

Eliot, T. S., 124, 217, 257, 258

Fabre, Emile, 267
Faulkner, William, 167, 256, 276
Fellini, Frederico, 197, 200
Feuillère, Edwige, 50, 63
Feydeau, Georges, 14, 156n, 257
Fini, Léonor, 277, 278
Flaubert, Gustave, 63, 255
Fleg, Edmond, 13
Ford, John, 227
Fort, Paul, 6, 12
Frank, André, 228, 229
Frères Jacques, 156
Fromentin, Eugène, 97

Gaillard-Risler, Francine, 272
Gantillon, Simon, 12, 254
Garnier, Robert, 21
Gassner, John, 8, 16n, 110
Gémier, Firmin, 249–50, 251, 254
Genêt, Jean, 28, 63, *168–72*, 176, 193, 227, 228, 230, 279; *le Balcon*, 168, 169–70, 171, 176, 279; *les Bonnes*, 168, 169, 170, 171, 254, 279; *Haute Surveillance*, 168, 170, 279; *les Nègres*, 168, 170n, 171, 172, 177, 279
Ghelderode, Michel de, 155, *156–60*,

228, 259, 276–77; *les Aveugles*, 277, *la Ballade du Grand Macabre*, 158, 159, 277; *Barabbas*, 277; *Christophe Colomb*, 158, 276; *l'Ecole des bouffons*, 158, 277; *Escurial*, 276; *Fastes d'enfer*, 156, 158, 159, 276; *Hop Signor!* 158, 159, 276; *Mademoiselle Jaïre*, 158, 159, 276; *Magie rouge*, 158, 159, 277; *la Mort du Docteur Faust*, 276; *Sire Halewyn*, 159, 277; *Sortie d'acteur*, 157; *Trois Acteurs, un drame*, 157, 277
Giacometti, Alberto, 213
Gide, André, 12, 31, 48, 79, 97, 151, 223, 228, 240, 243, 249, 251, 256, 257, 258
Gielen, Joseph, 268
Girard, 267
Giraudoux, Jean, 10, *19–47*, 48, 69, 70, 85, 96, 121, 133, 151, 155, 194, 223, 224, 228, 253, 261, 263–64; *Amphitryon 38*, 24, 29, 43, 253, 263; *l'Apollon de Bellac*, 254, 264; *Cantique des cantiques*, 20, 27–28, 31, 32, 33, 254, 264; *Electre*, 20, 23, 24, 25, 29, 42, 43, 69, 224, 253, 264; *la Folle de Chaillot*, 33–34, 42, 254, 264; *la Guerre de Troie n'aura pas lieu*, 20, 22, 25, 31, 40, 43, 121, 253, 263; *l'Impromptu de Paris*, 24, 37, 38, 39, 253, 264; *Intermezzo*, 20, 23, 31, 42, 253, 257, 263; *Ondine*, 20, 42, 43, 253, 263; *Pour Lucrèce*, 24, 25, 43, 257, 264; *Siegfried*, 19–20, 29, 41, 43, 253, 263; *Sodome et Gomorrhe*, 20, 23, 31, 32, 69, 264; *Supplément au Voyage de Cook*, 20, 33, 253, 263; *Tessa*, 43, 253, 263
Gischia, Léon, 268
Gobineau, Joseph Arthur de, 101
Gogol, Nikolai, 253, 280
Goldoni, Carlo, 249

Index

Index

YALE ROMANIC STUDIES, SECOND SERIES